THE MORE YOU KNOW, THE BETTER IT GETS

The Motorcycle Safety Foundation's Guide to
MOTORCYCLING EXCELLENCE

Skills, Knowledge, and Strategies for Riding Right

Whitehorse Press
Center Conway, New Hampshire

Photography credits (alphabetical order)

American Honda Motor Co., Inc.: 164; **American Motorcyclist Association:** 42; **American Suzuki Motor Corporation:** (ii), 14, 17, 23, 154; **BMW of North America, LLC.:** Cover, 39, 76, 132, 141; **Mitch Carpentier:** Back cover illustration; **Keith Code:** 148; *Cycle World* **Magazine:** 21, 30, 167, 170; **Harley-Davidson Motor Company:** 18, 108, 137, 138; **Amy Holland,** *Friction Zone* **Magazine:** 81, 86, 102; **Jed Johnson:** 40; **Kawasaki Motors Corp., U.S.A.:** 18, 20, 137, 168, 169, 172; **Kevin Krasner:** 41, 171; **Motorcycle Safety Foundation:** (viii), 9-11, 19, 20, 24, 31-33, 36, 46, 47, 53, 59-62, 70, 89, 91, 97, 100, 103, 106, 107, 125, 153, 174, 177, 181; **© Cary Pennington Photography:** 55, 57, 63-69, 90, 104, 110, 111, 119, 121, 149, 159; **© Miriam Romais:** 12, 13, 16, 37, 48, 51, 75, 80, 87, 99, 116, 118, 120, 122, 126, 127, 131, 135, 144, 178, 179; **David Thom:** 52; **Whitehorse Press:** 28, 29, 44 49, 56, 58, 68, 71, 72-74, 77, 88, 94, 106, 112-115, 123, 128, 129, 138, 140, 143, 150, 156-158, 162, 165, 166; **Yamaha Motor Corporation, USA:** 19, 22, 31, 33, 54, 109, 111, 173

Whitehorse Press books are also available at discounts in bulk quantity for sales and promotional use. For details about special sales or for a catalog of motorcycling books and videos, write to the Publisher:

Whitehorse Press
107 East Conway Road
Center Conway, New Hampshire 03813-4012

ISBN 1-884313-47-7

10 9 8 7 6 5 4 3 2 1

Printed in China

ACKNOWLEDGMENTS
Thank you

The MSF wishes to thank the many dedicated people who work together to improve the safety of motorcyclists on the nation's streets and highways, from RiderCoaches, RiderCoach Trainers, and State Training Administrators to the National Highway Traffic Safety Administration, legislators, and roadway engineers and maintenance teams; and from riders who take motorcycling seriously to car drivers who make an extra effort to share the road safely with motorcyclists and other vulnerable roadway users. ▬▬ thanks go to MSF's funding members—BMW, ▬▬ati, Harley-Davidson, Honda, Kawasaki, KTM, Piaggio/Vespa, Suzuki, Victory, and Yamaha—who've made it possible for MSF to address motorcycling safety issues through its training curriculum, public awareness efforts, and this book.

The realization of this project was truly a team effort. Special Guest features in this book could not have been possible without the contributions from Dr. John Bodnar, Erik Buell, Keith Code, Paul Golde, Nick Ienatsch, Rich Oliver, Bruce Porter, Reg Pridmore, Kevin Schwantz, Freddie Spencer, and Paul Thede.

MSF would like to recognize Tim Buche, Dr. Ray Ochs, Ken Glaser, Don Ankrom, Dr. Sherry Williams, Elyse Barrett, Johanna Buecheler, Aaron Frank, Sheryl Van der Leun, Elisabeth Piper, and Jim O'Connor for contributing their editorial and content expertise.

MSF would also like to acknowledge Cary Pennington, Miriam Romais, Mitch Carpentier, Larry Little and *Cycle World* magazine, Primedia, the American Motorcyclist Association, *Friction Zone* magazine, Kevin Krasner, Hector Eide, David Thom, Jed Johnson, and Scorpion Sports, Inc. for providing the wonderful photographs and illustrations for this book, and especially Dan Kennedy for putting this book together.

VISION

The MSF is an internationally recognized not-for-profit foundation, supported by motorcycle manufacturers, that provides leadership to the motorcycle safety community through its expertise, tools, and partnerships.

MISSION STATEMENT

To make motorcycling safer and more enjoyable by ensuring access to lifelong quality education and training for current and prospective riders, and by advocating a safer riding environment.

KEY MESSAGES

- ▶ Get trained and licensed
- ▶ Be a lifelong learner
- ▶ Wear protective gear
- ▶ Ride Straight
- ▶ Ride within your limits

CONTACT US

Motorcycle Safety Foundation
2 Jenner Street, Suite 150
Irvine, CA 92618

General information:
 949.727.3227

Street motorcycle safety and training information:
 800.446.9227; www.msf-usa.org

Off-road motorcycle safety and training information:
 877.288.7093; www.dirtbikeschool.com

CONTENTS

This book is dedicated to everyone
who strives to be an excellent motorcyclist.

The Allure of Motorcycling

MOTORCYCLING IS FAR MORE THAN JUST A WAY TO GET FROM POINT A TO POINT B

After decades on society's fringes, motorcycling is now more popular and more socially acceptable than ever before. Motorcycles have become a fixture in music videos, mainstream magazine spreads, and movies with, more often than not, the good guy at the handlebars. Many high-profile celebrities and public figures have proclaimed their love for two-wheeled travel, and routinely participate in charity rides and other touring events.

Hundreds of thousands of people have followed these celebrities' lead, and as a result motorcycling is undergoing a renaissance. New riders are being attracted to the sport at an unprecedented rate, and riders who once abandoned motorcycling are returning in droves. And with good reason: advances in motorcycle technology have made machines easier, and more comfortable, to ride. Similar advances in riding gear and an increase in driver awareness of motorcyclists have also made the sport more enjoyable than ever. There's never been a better time to be a motorcyclist. In fact, in 2005, there were more than 9 million motorcycles in use across the United States.

Plus, the traditional benefits of motorcycling remain. Motorcycles are less expensive to own and operate than four-wheeled vehicles. They are easier to park and maneuver in crowded environments. They are an ideal choice for commuting in today's congested and busy world. In addition to these practical advantages, motorcycling engenders an invigorating sense of freedom and escape. It is simultaneously a journey and a destination; exciting

Learning to ride a motorcycle well is a challenge best met in a controlled environment with the help of MSF-certified RiderCoaches who can help you practice critical life-saving skills.

yet relaxing. Today's riders can enjoy a solo jaunt, arcing into a string of smooth corners, playing along with the rhythm of the road. Or they can seek the camaraderie that inevitably arises among two-wheeled travelers sharing the open road.

Although public perception of motorcycling has changed for the better, the realities of riding a motorcycle remain. Make no mistake: riding motorcycles well is still a challenging pursuit. Successfully piloting a motorcycle is a much more involved task than driving a car. Single-track vehicles with two

Mastering basic skills such as clutch/throttle coordination, turning, stopping, and riding in a straight line requires plenty of practice before you venture out among the hazards of the street.

wheels must be balanced when stopped or when moving slowly. A motorcycle responds quicker and more precisely to rider inputs than a car, but is also more sensitive to outside forces, like irregular road surfaces or crosswinds. A motorcycle is also less visible than a car due to its smaller size, and offers far less protection by exposing its rider to the elements and other traffic. For these reasons, motorcycling is riskier than driving. You must operate a motorcycle with more care, attention, and skill than you would an automobile. As you learn to manage the risk, you'll find that part of the joy of motorcycling is that it's not a passive activity—you're an active participant in a journey that engages all your senses.

The messages and the information presented in this book will help you understand the many dimensions of motorcycling, but there is nothing better than formal, hands-on training and lots of practice.

While we're on the subject of training, since 1973 the Motorcycle Safety Foundation® (MSF) has set internationally recognized standards of excellence in motorcycle rider education and training.

More than three million motorcyclists have graduated from MSF's Basic or Experienced *RiderCourses*. By taking a class with one or two of the more than 7,000 MSF-certified RiderCoaches, students learn not only to maneuver the motorcycle effectively, but also to acquire critical strategies for avoiding the many hazards facing street riders. Each year over a quarter of a million newly trained motorcyclists benefit by learning to manage the risks, ride within their limits, and become responsible, licensed riders.

In fact, more than 30 state licensing agencies use one of five different MSF skill tests as part of their motorcycle endorsement procedures, while more than 40 states use the MSF's *Motorcycle Operator Manual* as a study guide for applicants.

The MSF hasn't ignored those riders who find that the two-wheeled journey starts where the pavement ends: Off-road riders are realizing that formal training can be fun and effective by attending the recently developed MSF *DirtBike School*.

The MSF believes the best way to learn to operate a motorcycle is to take a course specifically designed to teach you the mental and physical skills required, and the knowledge to apply those skills appropriately. MSF recommends taking a hands-on course like the Basic *RiderCourse* if you're a beginning rider or a rider returning to motorcycling after a long absence. For those who have been riding for some time, we recommend taking one of the three available Experienced *RiderCourses*. Bettering your skills through training and practice will increase your riding enjoyment and decrease your chance of trouble.

However, until you take a course—or afterward to add to the knowledge you learn in a hands-on environment—you can read this book. Although it can't take the place of learning from a certified motorcycle safety instructor, it's filled with information to help you understand the basic mental strategies of motorcycle safety awareness and risk management.

First published in 1995, *The Motorcycle Safety Foundation's Guide to Motorcycling Excellence: Skills, Knowledge, and Strategies for Riding Right* quickly became one of the best-selling motorcycle riding skills books and the recognized standard reference for beginning riders. This second edition of *Motorcycling Excellence* is based on the latest

The RiderCoach will use the classroom portion of the Basic *RiderCourse* to help students understand basic riding strategies and risk management.

approaches to learning to ride advocated by the MSF, thanks to decades of research, field testing, input from the training community, and direct involvement in teaching people how to ride and survive.

Motorcycling Excellence doesn't assume that you know anything about how a motorcycle works or how to ride it, and so it starts with the most elementary aspects of motorcycling. Chapters 1 through 6 discuss the mental and physical preparation necessary before you even swing a leg over the seat, plus rudimentary riding skills (including mounting the motorcycle, starting the engine, and using the friction zone of the clutch to get underway), and the basics (how to locate and operate the controls, plus some care and maintenance) of the motorcycle itself.

Operating the motorcycle is only one part of the challenge of managing your risk when riding. Chapters 7 through 10 address the mental strategies motorcyclists can employ to deal with traffic and other hazards on the street, as well as riding in special situations such as when it's raining or riding with a group.

Skilled motorcyclists can improve their riding by understanding the forces that govern how a two-wheeled vehicle acts and reacts. Chapters 11 through 15 delve into more technical topics to provide a thorough understanding of traction, countersteering, and advanced turning and braking skills. To round out your education, chapter 16 covers the basics of riding off-road.

Throughout the book, you'll find sidebars written by world champion racers and other motorcycling experts. While some of their tips and perspectives apply to advanced riding and racing skills, it helps to understand the whole array of "tools" available to motorcyclists—you may face a challenging situation on the street many years from now where one of their tips proves valuable.

Remember, the learning never stops. Be a lifelong learner by continually improving your mental strategies and riding skills.

If you're reading this book, you're already intrigued by two-wheeled transportation. And you're not alone—motorcycles continue to fascinate people from every walk (or "ride") of life. Welcome to the ever-evolving, exciting world of motorcycling!

CHAPTER 1

Preliminary Considerations

STARTING OUT RIGHT AS A MOTORCYCLIST MEANS ASSESSING YOUR DESIRES AND ABILITIES, AND COMMITTING TO SAFETY

MEETING THE CHALLENGE

Like any vehicle that is in motion, a motorcycle involves risk, but this risk can be managed with a finely tuned skill set, proper physical preparation, and sharpened mental processes. To help build the skills necessary to meet this challenge, it is helpful first to understand a bit about the characteristics of motorcycling.

A motorcycle rider is physically vulnerable. While 20 percent of passenger vehicle crashes result in injury or death, according to the National Highway Traffic Safety Administration (NHTSA), an astounding 80 percent of motorcycle crashes result in injury or death. Many injuries and deaths in automobile accidents are often avoided by drivers who wear seat belts, pay attention, drive unimpaired, and observe traffic rules. Likewise, many motorcycle deaths are prevented when motorcyclists complete training, wear protective gear, and ride sober. The likelihood of injury can also be greatly reduced when the rider (and passenger) are outfitted with proper protective gear, including a helmet designed to meet Department of Transportation (DOT) standards, proper eye protection, abrasion-resistant jacket and pants, full-fingered gloves, and appropriate over-the-ankle footwear.

But even with proper gear and intentions, a rider's judgment and attitude are the most critical factors in avoiding an incident. In most single-vehicle crashes, rider error is the dominant factor. Many collisions (and the resulting injuries) could have been completely avoided had the rider applied a

Besides being just plain fun, motorcycles (when piloted by skilled riders) are easier to maneuver and park than cars in crowded urban environments, making two-wheelers an ideal choice for commuting in today's congested world.

good mental strategy, or known the proper technique of swerving or braking. These are learned behaviors—skills that come only through practice and renewal.

Another consideration is the relative lack of visibility of a motorcycle. In a common type of car-motorcycle accident, in which an automobile turns in front of an oncoming motorcycle, drivers almost invariably say that they "just didn't see" the oncoming motorcycle. Or, if they did see the bike, they tend to misjudge its speed or distance. The more visible a motorcyclist is, the less likely he or she will be involved in this type of crash.

These factors tell a story—but not the whole story. Rider education and training go a long way toward helping riders manage the hazards of motorcycling—consider that riders who were self-taught, or learned from family or friends are roughly twice as likely to be involved in crashes. Also, more than 40 percent of those involved in crashes lacked a motorcycle endorsement on their driver's license.

Education is important. Quality rider education goes beyond simply acquiring skills. It aims to improve your preparedness and give you the experience necessary to quickly assess unexpected situations as well as the skills to execute the correct actions that will get you out of those situations intact. Reading this book, as well as considering the skills, exercises, and hypothetical situations presented within, is another step toward that end.

MANAGING RISK

Almost every action a human being undertakes involves a certain level of risk. Walking to the store, mowing the lawn, or eating a cheeseburger are all routine actions that could result in unpleasant, even dangerous, consequences. Living a happy and successful life means managing such risks at an acceptable level. The same logic applies to motorcycling—riding a motorcycle safely and successfully means properly assessing the risks involved, acknowledging and riding within your own skill level, and then managing your actions to reduce those risks as much as possible.

There is always the risk of an undesirable or harmful event occurring when you ride. And the probability of such an event changes every moment—sometimes with frightening rapidity. Managing this risk becomes an engaging game of perception and response—the sooner you perceive a risk, and the sooner you begin mentally processing that risk, the better prepared you are to

Motorcycling offers an invigorating sense of freedom and escape, as well as the camaraderie shared among all those who choose two wheels over four.

confront the situation. End result: the risk is lessened. When a rider becomes complacent to a situation, or when hazards go undetected, that risk is elevated—and danger may soon follow.

You often hear the following from riders who have crashed "I was just riding along, then boom! I was down on the ground!" There is no such thing as a "JRA" (just riding along) crash. All crashes are a result of specific factors: some foreseeable, others not; some avoidable, others not. As a responsible rider, it's up to you to begin anticipating these risks and to learn to respond properly.

When riding you are constantly receiving input, and then analyzing it to establish the present level of risk. The human mind is an amazing tool when properly trained. It easily (and often, unconsciously) predicts and prioritizes hazards, compares the best and worst possible outcomes, then spits out a list of possible reactions. When riding a motorcycle, you are not a passive participant—you are an active agent, and your actions and decisions determine the amount of risk at any given moment. You are not rolling aimlessly toward oblivion—your fate lies squarely in you own mind and hands. This one idea, actively assessing risk, is perhaps the single most important determinant of safe riding. Too many novice riders hand their fate wholesale over to other road users, and place their safety in the hands of the other drivers—sometimes with disastrous results.

On a motorcycle, there is too much at stake to trust the judgments and abilities of the other drivers on the road. At intersections, never assume that an oncoming car will wait for you to pass before turning. Don't expect that a merging minivan will yield, allowing you the right of way. To ride safely—and to ensure that the situation always shapes up in your favor—you have to take total responsibility for your actions by creating time and space to respond. You must be prepared to respond properly so that every outcome is the one you desire, regardless of what anyone else on the road does. This abiding sense of personal responsibility, mental attention and physical preparation, and skill-building knowledge and practice, are the essential elements for meeting the challenge of motorcycling, managing risk, and riding safely.

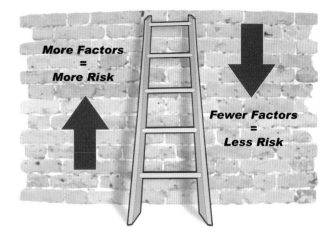

In the "ladder of risk," each rung of the ladder represents a factor. More factors result in more risk; fewer factors result in less risk. Good riders keep the number and significance of factors in check.

PREPARE TO RIDE

In addition to senses and skills, prepping your bike is another important aspect of safe riding. Make sure it is in proper working order, with no worn or broken parts or other maintenance needs that could compromise your control or safety. Also, select the right protective gear, make sure it fits well, and check that it is in good condition.

And, of course, make sure that you learn to ride correctly. A salesperson shouting "one down, four up, and don't hurt yourself!" over his shoulder isn't a proper introduction to the art and science of riding a motorcycle. You want to be sure that you have a solid foundation upon which to build your motorcycling skills. Various Motorcycle Safety Foundation courses, especially the *DirtBike School* (expressly designed for folks who have never even sat on a motorcycle) and the Basic *RiderCourse* are an excellent introduction to the skills and mental attitudes necessary to begin a successful motorcycling career. Last, but no less important, make sure that you conform to your state motor vehicle agency's motorcycle licensing requirement, so you have the proper motorcycle endorsement on your driver's license. Studies have shown that getting this endorsement, and completing the proper coursework, will reduce the likelihood of being involved in a serious motorcycle accident.

**Proper preparation and finely tuned mental and physical abilities are necessary in order to focus intently on the serious task of piloting a motorcycle.
A smart pilot rides within his or her limits, and pays constant attention to the ever-changing set of challenges involved in riding.**

Experienced motorcyclists know that a key to riding safely is always to ride your own ride. Peer pressure—or any pressure to exceed your abilities and ride faster or more aggressively than you are comfortable riding—doesn't only come from other motorcyclists. This sort of pressure can just as easily come from the SUV crowding your taillight, or the kids in the sports car cruising along beside you. A confident rider stays above petty games, and stays focused on the task at hand—always having sufficient time and space to respond smoothly and appropriately. A smart rider stays engaged in, and attentive to, the ever-changing set of challenges that compose his or her own unique ride.

The immediate and intimate relationship between the rider, the bike, and the environment is part of what makes motorcycling such a uniquely satisfying pursuit. To reach the state of mental oneness that comes with such intense focus on a single dynamic activity is one of the great gifts of the motorcycling experience. Proper preparation and finely tuned mental and physical abilities are necessary to reach that state. A lack of focus, a know-it-all or "it-will-never-happen-to-me" attitude, or susceptibility to peer pressure, are your mortal enemies on the road. Accept responsibility for your actions, resist the urge to be a passive road user, and you are well on your way to becoming a safe, successful, satisfied motorcyclist.

MOTORCYCLING EXCELLENCE MEANS:

► Motorcycling adds significantly to the quality of your life.

► You are committed to safety in meeting the challenges of the road.

► You recognize the need to be more perceptive and skillful than the average motorist.

► You have an awareness of your personal risk acceptance and know you can choose your personal risk levels; you understand your personal abilities and your motorcycle's capabilities, and make decisions to stay within personal limits.

► You choose a motorcycle based on your needs and skill level.

ASSESSING YOUR ABILITIES

Operating a motorcycle well is an acquired skill, and your abilities will continue to grow and expand with practice over time. To ride safely, it's important that you understand your abilities and become familiar with your limits—and be careful always to operate well within these limits, lest your actions outpace your abilities!

▶ YOUR FIRST MOTORCYCLE
BY NICK IENATSCH

SELECTING A BIKE

Whether shopping for shoes, wandering the aisles of the local supermarket, or just ordering a cup of coffee, the number of choices in modern life can be overwhelming. Therefore, making a big decision, like choosing a new motorcycle, can be particularly daunting. Answering some key questions can simplify your decision and help you make the right one. For example, what sort of rider do you hope to be? What sort of riding do you hope to do? Do you want to tilt the horizon on a twisty road, or lazily lope along an empty desert highway? Make your commute to work more fun and efficient, or pack up for a month-long trip to Alaska? Or would you like to leave the road entirely and explore the dirt trails in the nearby foothills? All of the above? Something else? Luckily, no matter what sort of motorcycling experience you wish to pursue, there is an appropriate size and type of motorcycle for you.

Just as today's car buyers can opt for sedans, minivans, sports cars, or sport-utility vehicles, the basic motorcycle form has morphed into a wide variety of niches: standards, cruisers, sportbikes, touring machines, scooters, dirt bikes, and even category-crossing hyphenates like sport-tourers, adventure-tourers, or dual-purpose machines. Each niche has a distinct purpose and benefits that make it uniquely suited for a particular style of use. And, thanks to rapidly improving technology and materials, motorcycles are more versatile than ever, and very capable of multi-tasking—making many styles of motorcycle appropriate for more than one type of riding. Finding the right bike is a matter of accurately assessing your intentions, then matching those to the best-suited motorcycle available.

THE THRILL OF THE CHOICE
Standard

The most basic, and most versatile category of street-based motorcycle is the so-called "standard" motorcycle. Referred to by some manufacturers as "traditional" or "naked" bikes, the "standard" is the type of machine that most laypersons picture when they envision a motorcycle. A standard is characterized by its upright handlebars and intermediate, comfortable riding position. They typically are without fairings (aerodynamic front bodywork that incorporates a windshield) or other bodywork, and are as close as you can get to a do-it-all machine. Because of the no-frills nature of a standard and the lack of fancy options and accessories, standards are some of the most affordable street bikes on the market. Also, due to the lack of expensive bodywork that may be damaged in the event of a static tip-over, standards are less expensive to insure.

Beyond economics, a standard is also a great bike on which to learn to ride. Their upright riding position and relatively small size and light weight make standards easy to maneuver. Standards offer comfortable ergonomics for almost every size of rider and split the difference between the sport-

The standard, general-purpose motorcycle is ideal for getting your start in motorcycling.

Cruisers are the factory-built descendants of the classic custom motorcycle.

bike crouch and the cruiser lay-back. They are also easy to maintain, as the lack of a fairing makes engine access simple.

Standards excel in versatility. They handle commuting, recreational riding, and even light sport riding and touring with equal aplomb. You can grow with a standard, too—a wide variety of aftermarket accessories (windshields, luggage, etc.) allows you to easily modify a standard motorcycle to make it more appropriate for either sport riding or touring, should your riding preferences change over time.

Cruiser

For more than 15 years, "cruisers" have been the best-selling street motorcycles in America. Cruisers have an unmistakable classic style wrapped around modern technology. These bikes are distinguished from others by their wide, pulled-back handlebars and a rather relaxed, feet-forward riding position. With lower seat heights than any other category, the bikes themselves are long and low, with broad saddles, kicked-out front suspension forks, and plenty of glittering chrome. Cruisers are well-suited for either trolling from stoplight to stoplight, or lazily loping along a deserted country road. The relaxed riding position of cruisers allows them to

serve many of their happy owners as reliable bikes for commuting to and from work. Many owners add saddlebags and a windshield to enhance the touring abilities of their favorite machines.

Sportbike

On the opposite end of the motorcycle spectrum from cruisers are sportbikes—these are the street-legal alternative to the all-out performance machines seen on the racetracks. Sportbikes are draped in sleek, aerodynamic bodywork and put the rider in a forward-canted riding position in order to achieve the optimum front-to-back weight distribution and aid spirited riding on twisty roads. Sportbikes are built with optimum performance, power, and handling in mind using cutting-edge engine, braking, and suspension components and exotic lighweight materials. For this reason, they often appeal to the technology-minded rider. The aggressive riding position of sportbikes means these models might not be the first choice for covering long distances, but these bikes are not designed with easy-chair comfort as a top priority. The high performance offered by larger-capacity sportbikes can be overwhelming, especially for inexperienced riders. But for riders with a good base level of experience and a taste for excitement, a sportbike is an adrenaline-producing vehicle.

Sportbikes capture the spirit of their all-out competition cousins.

Touring motorcycles are designed to provide the highest levels of comfort and carrying capacity.

Tourers

Riders who gauge a good ride in terms of miles per day are typically drawn to touring motorcycles—the Winnebagos of the two-wheeled world. Designed to be ridden comfortably over long distances for hours at a time, touring bikes offer a host of convenience features, including large fairings for protection from wind and a full complement of luggage, including a trunk and saddlebags for transporting gear. Luxury touring motorcycles take the concept one step further, providing an unparalleled level of convenience for both the rider and the passenger, with features such as driver and passenger backrests, cruise control, stereos, intercoms, and plush, automatically adjustable suspensions. Some models even feature a healthy dose of sporting performance that belies their conservative appearance.

Sport-Tourers

An increasing number of motorcyclists use a sport-touring motorcycle to combine the long-distance capabilities and carrying capacity of the touring motorcycle with the more athletic personality of a sportbike. Just as the hyphenated name suggests, a sport-tourer is a mixture of the sportbike and touring styles, combining long range, comfortable cockpits (usually appropriate for rider and passenger) and light luggage capacity (often via easily removable saddlebags) on a more nimble, sportbike-type chassis. A sport-tourer is an excellent choice for day trips or recreational riding. The riding position is typically more upright than an all-out sportbike, so these machines are comfortable both on an interstate and deep into the twisty bits. Also, the lighter weight and smaller physical size of these machines compared to full-fledged tourers make them much easier to handle (especially at low speeds) than true touring machines.

Sport-touring motorcycles are a cross between a grand-touring rig and a sportbike.

Dual-Purpose

For many enthusiasts, a perfect ride involves getting a fair distance off of the beaten path—sometimes quite literally, by exploring trails, fire roads, and other unpaved surfaces that provide entry into the lesser-seen areas of our countryside. If this is the direction you want to go, dual-purpose motorcycles are for you. The dual-purpose concept begins with the basic design of a true off-road bike, including small, narrow frames for easy maneuverability, and long-travel suspensions for a smooth ride on unpaved surfaces. Then, they graft on just enough features, such as full lighting and less-aggressively knobbed tires, to make them appropriate, and legal, for street travel. Dual-purpose models are great play machines, perfect for getting from trail to trail on public roadways without the hassle of trailering an off-road bike. They are also surprisingly capable city commuters, thanks to a high, upright riding position, great maneuverability, and soft suspension that swallows even the biggest alley potholes. However, their narrow, firm saddles, lack of wind protection, and smaller fuel tanks can make these bikes less convenient over long distances.

Adventure-touring bikes offer some off-road capability along with the fuel range and carrying capacity of a street-oriented touring motorcycle.

Adventure-Tourers

Riders who are willing to forgo a bit of off-road capability for significantly more on-road rideability might consider the so-called "adventure-tourers." They are built around the same basic concept as a dual-purpose, but boast a larger engine, greater fuel range, and more road-oriented tires and suspension. Some models even come with a standard windshield or luggage rack to bolster their long-distance capability. An adventure-tourer can be a very satisfying road bike and still maintain at least enough off-road ability to make traversing dirt and gravel roads a reasonable possibility.

Dual-purpose motorcycles are street-legal, yet can be ridden on dirt trails.

Modern scooters feature step-through frames, automatic transmissions, nimble handling, and excellent fuel economy.

Scooters

If you want to experience the joys of two-wheeled travel in a somewhat simpler manner, you may want to consider a scooter. Compared to traditional motorcycles, scooters have a few important differences: step-through frames, smaller wheels, and an engine positioned below and behind the rider. Lower, slower, and easier to handle than a motorcycle—and usually fitted with an automatic transmission—scooters are an excellent alternative to motorcycles. Also, because of their small size and excellent fuel economy, scooters are great local commuters. Most scooters have small engine displacement and are appropriate only for in-town use, though recently some manufacturers have introduced scooters with engines powerful enough to maintain interstate highway speeds, making them appropriate for more traditional motorcycle uses. Some enthusiasts even happily tour cross-country on these large-displacement scooters.

Dirt Bikes

Dirt bikes (also called trail bikes, off-road bikes, or off-highway motorcycles) are the passport to a world beyond the concrete grid of the city. Featuring distinctive "knobby" tires designed for gripping soft surfaces, and long-travel suspensions that can soak up bumps, ruts, and other obstacles typically found along the trails, these bikes thrive on everything from tight trails in the woods to wide-open sandy desert terrain. These motorcycles are not intended for use on public roads, however, as they're not equipped with street-legal lighting or tires.

This category is unique in that there are smaller-displacement models (and appropriate MSF training courses) available for riders as young as six years of age, making off-roading an ideal family activity. The skills and responsibilities learned by children under the watchful eye of their parents can help children learn to approach other recreational activities with a safety-first attitude. On the other end of the dirt bike spectrum resides full-on motocross racing bikes that duplicate the look and performance of the bikes that the Supercross stars race.

Dirt bikes are not equipped for operation on the street, but for riding off-road, they are light and extremely maneuverable.

MAKING THE DECISION

It's complicated, isn't it? For a new rider who has never experienced two-wheeled travel before, choosing the size and type of motorcycle to ride can be a daunting process. But as you do your research, you'll find that it's hard to make a bad choice—modern motorcycles are well-built, the technology is advanced, and the machinery is better than ever. Some bikes are certainly better than others in certain situations, but modern motorcycles are competent enough to do a passable job at just about any task. You can tour long distances on a dual-purpose. You can negotiate a twisty road on a cruiser. Besides, courtesy of the huge motorcycle aftermarket, there are many options and accessories available to help you customize any motorcycle to suit your needs—make sportbikes more comfortable, make cruisers even flashier, and make standards do just about anything. If all else fails, you can always trade up.

No matter what type of motorcycle you choose, make sure that you get one that fits you well and makes you feel confident in the saddle. Keep in mind that it's better to start on a smaller machine, and as your skills and experience grow, you can buy a larger, more powerful model.

Once you find your first bike, there are a few things you will need to work out before you even think of that first ride. The best place to start is by completing a Motorcycle Safety Foundation *Rider-Course* to familiarize yourself with the safe operation of a motorcycle. You can even take the course *before* choosing a bike, to help you better understand the dynamics of motorcycling and to determine if motorcycling is right for you. Then make sure that you get the proper motorcycle-operator endorsement added to your driver's license, that you obtain the proper insurance coverage for you and your machine, and that you outfit yourself with appropriate safety apparel. Get very familiar with your bike's owner's manual, too. And, of course, read the rest of this book, which is designed specifically to transform you from tentative first-timer to an informed, safe, confident motorcycle operator. Enjoy the ride!

A PERSONAL OBSERVATION: YOUR FIRST "MOTORCYCLES"

I'm a big fan of learning lessons with minimum pain—and a small-displacement dirt bike can be a great teacher. Getting to the edge of traction, and beyond, is a whole lot less painful at 15 mph in the mud than at 45 mph on pavement—trust me on that. No matter what you get—cruiser, sportbike or standard—add a dirt bike to your shopping list and bring home a full complement of dirt-riding gear, too. With the dirt bike, you'll soon learn to monitor and gauge traction by balancing brake pressure and throttle settings against lean angle. You will learn that aggressive, abrupt inputs hurt. I don't know one professional roadracer who doesn't practice his art on a dirt bike, learning to flirt with the edge of traction without risking too much. So my advice: don't buy one bike, buy two—whatever street bike you love, plus a little dirt bike on which to learn (relatively) pain-free lessons. And one more thought: One or even two bikes simply isn't enough—I say four is a good start! ■

Nick Ienatsch writes for Cycle World *magazine, works at the Freddie Spencer High Performance Riding School, and has written a book entitled* Sport Riding Techniques.

FAMILIARIZE YOURSELF WITH THE CONTROLS AND FUNCTIONS OF THE MOTORCYCLE BEFORE YOU ATTEMPT TO RIDE.

Getting underway on a motorcycle is considerably more complicated than climbing on and twisting the throttle. In fact, it's considerably more challenging than driving a car. Because of this, it's important to familiarize yourself completely with the controls and functions of the motorcycle before you attempt to ride. This chapter will show you the location of the motorcycle controls and introduce the procedures necessary to make the motorcycle go and stop. This chapter won't teach you how to ride—nothing but lots of practice can do that—but it will give you a familiarity with the machine and its controls so that you can go out and practice on your own. An MSF *RiderCourse* is an ideal environment in which to start learning the operating skills.

MOTORCYCLE CONTROLS

The first step toward riding a motorcycle is learning how to operate the controls that you use to ride a motorcycle. Besides the handlebars, there are five other primary controls, operated with either the hands or feet, that make a motorcycle go and stop.

Throttle Located on the right handgrip, it controls engine speed. Use your right hand to roll the throttle "on" (top of the grip rolls toward the rider) and "off" (top of the grip rolls away from the rider). If released completely while rolled on, the throttle will spring back to the idle position.

Clutch Lever Located in front of the left handgrip, it connects power from the engine to the rear wheel. Use your left hand to squeeze the clutch

When turning, look through the turn in the direction you want to go. Turn your head, and keep your eyes up.

lever toward the handgrip to disengage power; release the lever *slowly* away from the handlebar to again engage power to the rear wheel.

Gear Shift Lever Located in front of the left footrest, it shifts the transmission from one gear to the next. Lift the lever with your left foot to upshift one gear at a time; press the lever to downshift one gear at a time. The lever operates as a ratchet mechanism: after each shift, the lever returns to its "home" position. The typical gear shift pattern, from the bottom to top, is 1-Neutral-2-3-4-5-(6). Your bike may have a sixth gear.

Good posture—back straight, head and eyes up—will make you comfortable on your bike and improve your riding.

Front Brake Lever Located in front of the right handgrip, it operates the front wheel's brake. Use your right hand to squeeze the lever toward the handgrip to apply the brake.

Rear Brake Pedal Located in front of the right footrest, it operates the rear wheel brake. Press down with your right foot to apply the brake.

OTHER CONTROLS AND EQUIPMENT

In addition to the primary controls, there is an array of other controls that make motorcycles different from cars. They include:

Fuel Supply Valve Usually located on the left side underneath the gas tank, it controls the flow of fuel to the engine. Fuel supply valves differ, but often include ON, OFF, RESERVE, or PRIME positions. Not all modern bikes have manual fuel supply valves.

Ignition Switch May be located in or near the instrument pod in front of the handlebars, or in some cases on the left side below the seat. Common key positions are ON, OFF, PARK, and LOCK.

Choke May be located near the left handgrip, below the instrument panel, or below the left side of the gas tank. Put the choke ON for cold starts, then OFF once the engine has warmed up. Some fuel-injected bikes don't have a choke.

Engine Cut-Off Switch Located near the right handgrip, it shuts off the engine immediately. Use your right thumb to move it to the RUN or OFF positions.

Electric Start Button Located near the right handgrip, use your right thumb to press the button to start the engine. (Be sure to hold in the clutch lever as you do so.)

Additional controls and equipment include the high/low beam headlight switch, turn signal switch(es), the horn button, the speedometer and tachometer, and indicator lights for neutral, high beam, turn signals, and oil pressure. In some cases the bike may also have a kick starter. The Motorcycle Controls chart in this chapter will help you locate all the various controls.

MOUNTING THE MOTORCYCLE

Start by mounting the bike from the (rider's) left side. This is especially important when the motorcycle is parked on its side stand and therefore leaning to the left. Mounting a bike from the right side could upset the balance of the bike on the side stand and bring it crashing down on top of you. When mounting the bike, hold the handlebars with both hands and squeeze the front brake to keep the motorcycle from rolling forward. Swing your right leg over the seat, and once you are straddling the bike and holding it upright, use your foot to retract the side stand (or, push the bike forward off the center stand and be ready to support its weight). Adjust the mirrors so that you have a good view of the roadway behind you.

STARTING THE ENGINE

FINE-C is a useful term to help you remember the various steps of the pre-start checklist. You should run through this checklist before every single ride.

Fuel Turn the fuel supply valve (sometimes called the petcock) to the ON position. Note that many newer motorcycles use an electronic or automatic fuel supply valve, which does not need to be turned on and off manually.

Ignition Insert the key and turn the ignition switch to the ON position.

Neutral Shift the transmission to neutral. Check the neutral light (green light indicates neutral) and roll the motorcycle forward or back a few inches with the clutch released to double-check that the motorcycle is not in gear.

Engine Cut-Off Switch Make sure the engine cut-off switch is set to the RUN position.

Choke and Clutch There are two "Cs"—choke and clutch. Set the choke, if necessary, according to the engine temperature (ON for cold starts). Squeezing the clutch lever when you start the engine (to disengage the driveline) is a good idea as an added safety precaution. Some newer motorcycles incorporate a cut-off switch into the clutch mechanism that requires the clutch lever to be squeezed in before the motorcycle can be started.

To start the engine on an electric-start motorcycle, simply push the starter button. When the engine is cold, leave the throttle closed; if the engine is warm, the throttle may need to be opened (rolled on) slightly. To start a kickstart-equipped motorcycle, lean the motorcycle slightly to the left, flip out the kickstart lever, place the ball of your foot on the lever, and sharply kick the lever downward. Repeat as necessary until the motorcycle starts. Fold in the kickstarter and you will be ready to ride.

THE FRICTION ZONE

Rule number one of getting underway on your motorcycle—the friction zone is your friend. Find the friction zone, get to know the friction zone, spend some quality time in the friction zone, and stalling the motorcycle will seldom be a problem. The friction zone is the area of clutch lever travel that starts where the clutch just begins to transmit power from the engine to the rear wheel and ends just before the clutch is fully engaged. The friction zone is the result of partial engagement of the clutch. While partially engaged, the clutch slips slightly, allowing you to precisely control the amount of power that is transmitted from the engine to the rear wheel.

Finding the friction zone and learning to use it well takes practice. With the engine running and transmission in neutral, squeeze the clutch lever and shift the motorcycle into first gear by pressing down on the gear shift lever. With both feet planted firmly on the ground, *slowly* ease out the clutch lever until you hear the engine begin to slow and feel the bike creep forward. You have now entered the friction zone. Squeeze the clutch lever in, roll back and practice again until you can consistently and predictably locate the friction zone every time you release the clutch.

FRICTION ZONE

The friction zone is that area of clutch-lever travel where the clutch just starts to transmit power to the rear wheel, as shown by the red triangle.

Be aware that the engine may stall if you do not apply some throttle or if you release the clutch too far. If you feel the engine beginning to stall, just squeeze the clutch lever in again. Using too much throttle can cause the bike to jump forward. It may help to add some throttle as you get more adept at controlling the clutch lever. Proper use of the friction zone, and properly modulating the throttle and the clutch to smoothly engage the engine without stalling or jumping forward, are the skills necessary to ride a motorcycle smoothly away from a stop.

RIDING POSTURE

Maintaining good posture in the saddle is an important component of good riding. Not only will paying attention to your posture help you stay comfortable over long distances, it will also enhance your control of the motorcycle by helping your body stay relaxed.

Sit on the motorcycle in an upright position with your back straight, your head up, and your eyes focused on the roadway ahead. Ride with your knees and elbows turned inward. They should be comfortably bent (not locked) so you can quickly move or respond to changes in riding conditions. Keep both feet on the footrests at all times so you can quickly position them to operate the rear brake pedal or shift lever. Grip both handgrips firmly with your wrists turned slightly downward and knuckles pointed up. Make a conscious effort to keep your body limber and relaxed. Tensed muscles will cause you to fatigue quickly, and will lessen your ability to respond promptly to any obstacles that might appear in your path. A relaxed rider is a ready rider. The better your skills are, the more relaxed you'll be.

TURNING POSTURE

COUNTERWEIGHTING POSTURE

(Top) A wrist-down position on the throttle hand is recommended. It will help avoid overrevving the engine and will make it easier to reach for the front brake lever when it comes time to slow down.

(Bottom left) In a standard turn, lean with the motorcycle for smoothness and stability.

(Bottom right) In a slow, tight turn, such as turning around in a parking lot, it helps to counterweight by leaning in the opposite direction of the motorcycle and direction of the turn. Put pressure on the outside footrest.

STOPPING

Your motorcycle is equipped with both front *and* rear brakes. To achieve optimum braking performance, both the front and rear brakes must be used in unison. However, because of the way that a motorcycle's weight distribution changes (shifts forward) under deceleration, the front brake provides a majority of the motorcycle's stopping power—up to 70 percent or more! Consequently, it is essential to familiarize yourself with the operation of your motorcycle's front brake, to learn to trust the front brake, and to use the front brake (in conjunction with the rear) every single time you stop.

To bring a motorcycle to a complete stop, you'll need to use both hands and both feet together. Squeeze the front brake lever and press down on the rear brake pedal at the same time, varying the amount of force depending on how quickly you need to stop. At the same time you apply the brakes, squeeze in the clutch lever and downshift toward first gear. If you wish to use engine braking to further slow down, gently ease out the clutch between downshifts.

Even though the full braking force of each wheel may not be required for normal, planned stops, it is important to get into the habit of using both brakes at all times so you will respond reflexively should a panic situation arise. Remember to pay attention to what your hands are doing in a braking situation: roll off the throttle when slowing, to prevent over-revving the engine; to prevent lugging or stalling when slowing, remember to squeeze the clutch lever.

CHANGING DIRECTION

Once you're familiar with the friction zone and have mastered the mechanics of forward motion, the next skill to learn is turning the motorcycle. To understand the art of changing direction on a single-track vehicle, break down the turn into four basic steps: slow, look, press, and roll.

Slow Take care of slowing and braking *before* you enter a turn. Reduce speed before the turn as needed by rolling off the throttle and applying both brakes smoothly and evenly; downshift the motorcycle if necessary.

Look Turn your head and look through the turn. Use your eyes to help with directional control—the motorcycle tends to follow your eyes and go where you're looking. Turn your head, not just your eyes, nor just your shoulders. Keep your eyes up and moving, level with the horizon. Doing all of this together will help you move smoothly through the turn.

Press To turn, the motorcycle must lean. To initiate a lean, press forward on the handgrip corresponding to the direction of the turn. In other words: press left, lean left, go left; press right, lean right, go right. This is called countersteering, and though it is not intuitive, this is the way that all single-track vehicles, like motorcycles, change direction. Refer to Chapter 13 for a detailed explanation of the countersteering process.

Of course, higher speeds and/or tighter turns require a greater degree of lean. In normal turns, the rider (and passenger) should lean with the motorcycle into the direction of the turn. In slow, tight turns, lean the motorcycle only and keep your body straight and upright. In very tight turns (a U-turn in a parking lot, for instance), you might actually need to lean your upper body slightly toward the outside of the turn. This technique is called counterweighting, and is explained in Chapter 15.

Roll Roll on the throttle gently through the turn, maintaining a steady speed or slightly accelerating. Gently rolling on the throttle through the corner will settle the suspension and help to stabilize the bike through the corner. Avoid rapid deceleration in the corner, because it can load up the front suspension and/or overwhelm front tire traction. Also avoid rapid acceleration, which can cause the rear tire to lose traction or cause you to run wide in the turn. These concepts are explained in Chapters 11 and 12.

SHIFTING GEARS

Most motorcycles are equipped with manual transmissions, which, just like manual transmissions in automobiles, allow you to change gears to match engine speed with road speed. This keeps the engine operating in the heart of its powerband, which is where the engine is most responsive. Most motorcycles have either five or six gears: the lower gears are used at lower speeds; higher speeds call for higher gears.

As you go faster, you will need to shift your motorcycle into a higher gear. Shift up into a higher gear well before the engine rpm reaches redline, which is the maximum recommended engine speed as shown on the tachometer (if equipped). As a rule, shift up soon enough to avoid over-revving the engine, but not so soon as to cause the engine to lug.

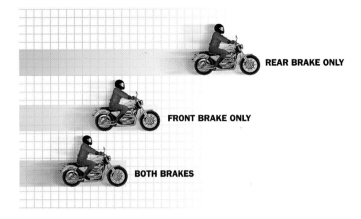

REAR BRAKE ONLY

FRONT BRAKE ONLY

BOTH BRAKES

Always use both brakes together. This will help you stop in the shortest distance when you need to.

Use a three-step process to smoothly upshift into a higher gear. First, simultaneously roll off the throttle and squeeze in the clutch lever. Once the throttle is closed and the clutch is completely disengaged, the second step is to lift the shift lever firmly until it stops, engaging the higher gear. Step three is to smoothly ease out the clutch lever to restore power to the rear wheel, simultaneously rolling on the throttle. Don't forget to drop your foot away from the shift lever, allowing the shift lever to reset to its "home" position.

Downshifting is done either in conjunction with slowing the motorcycle or when you want to quickly raise the rpm and make more power available for acceleration (when passing another vehicle, for example). Downshifting is slightly more involved than upshifting, because you have to work carefully to closely match engine speed to road speed. If you haven't slowed sufficiently, it is easy to over-rev the engine when you shift into the next lower gear. Also, selecting a lower gear and releasing the clutch too quickly (or not rolling on the throttle enough) can have an effect similar to stomping on the rear brake, and could lock the rear wheel and cause it to lose traction. Extra practice at low speeds will help you master downshifting smoothly and consistently.

As with upshifting, downshifting is a three-step process that involves modulating the clutch and throttle to precisely match engine speed with road speed. Begin the downshifting process by rolling off the throttle and squeezing the clutch lever simultaneously. Once the clutch is disengaged and

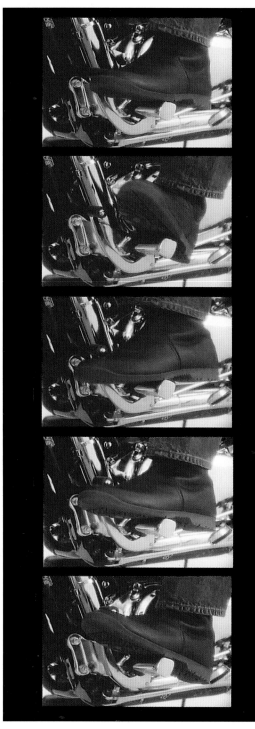

6
5
4
3
2
N
1

The relative position of the gears is shown in this numeric diagram. In the Neutral position, the engine is not engaged with the rear wheel. To reach first gear, shift down one position below Neutral. To reach all other gears, shift up through Neutral to second, then successively to third, and so on.

the throttle is closed, shift the motorcycle into a lower gear by pressing down on the gear shift lever. Once the shift is completed, ease out the clutch lever slowly and roll on the throttle. Rolling on the throttle while easing out the clutch lever helps the engine speed to come up quickly and will make the downshift smoother. Again, remember to release your foot and allow the shift lever to reset for the next shift. As mentioned before, shifting to a lower gear can cause an effect similar to applying the brakes—this effect is called engine braking. To use engine braking to your benefit when decelerating, shift down one gear at a time and ease the clutch lever through the friction zone. Keep the clutch in the friction zone until engine speed stabilizes, then ease the lever out all the way until ready for the next shift.

In most cases, you will want to shift one gear at a time. It is useful to note, however, that it is possible to shift through more than one gear when the clutch is squeezed. After squeezing in the clutch and rolling off the throttle, simply press down repeatedly on the gear shift lever without releasing the clutch until the bike is in first gear. The technique can be helpful, for instance, if you want to avoid the drama of engine braking when coming to a stop.

SHUTTING DOWN

Shifting and stopping a motorcycle can be somewhat complicated tasks, requiring several steps and the careful coordination of multiple controls. This isn't the case with shutting off the motorcycle—the easiest of the basic skills presented in this chapter.

After coming to a complete stop, and with your legs firmly supporting the motorcycle, reach up

To upshift smoothly, use a three-step process. First, simultaneously roll off the throttle and squeeze in the clutch. Second, move the toe of your left foot under the gear shift lever and lift the lever firmly until it stops, thus engaging the higher gear. Third, smoothly ease out the clutch as you roll on the throttle. Remember to return your left foot to a position above or near the gear shift lever, ready to upshift or downshift as necessary.

with your thumb and move the engine cut-off switch to the OFF position. Make this your habit, so you can easily and instantly find the engine cut-off in an actual emergency. Turn off the ignition switch and, if your motorcycle is so equipped, turn the fuel valve to the OFF position.

DISMOUNTING

Select a firm, flat surface on which to park. Check to be sure the motorcycle is in first gear (parking the bike in gear lessens the chance of it rolling while parked). Squeeze the front brake lever and lower the side stand. Lean the motorcycle onto the side stand and swing your right leg over the seat— all while squeezing the front brake lever. Turn the handlebars toward the side stand (to enhance stability) and engage the fork lock.

Consider this chapter a primer on the basic skills necessary to operate a motorcycle. Use this chapter as a guide, not as the last word. Remember, every motorcycle is different and, more important, riding situations are much more complex out on the road than in the pages of any book. In addition to coordinating the basic skills presented here, you must assess roadway conditions and the behaviors of other roadway users, gather information, and make plans for responding to those conditions. Because of this complexity, you must mentally prepare yourself to confront these challenges before you ride on the road.

In summary, it's best to become proficient in the fundamentals first and foremost. Whether you're a new or experienced rider, learning or renewing the fundamentals is part of every MSF *RiderCourse*.

MOTORCYCLING EXCELLENCE MEANS:

▶ You are completely familiar with the features of your motorcycle and refer to the owner's manual frequently.

▶ You understand the value of knowing and practicing the fundamentals of basic riding skills, and frequently practice important skills in a safe area.

▶ You refresh your skills and techniques by completing training events at least once a year and as often as every six months.

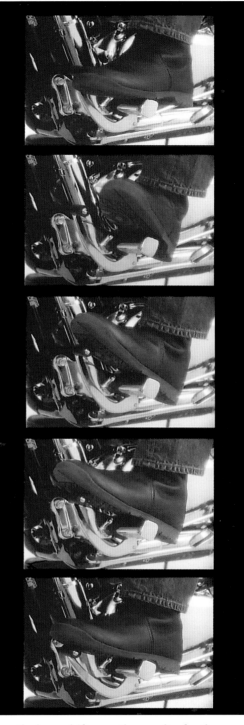

Smooth downshifts are the result of a three-step process as well. First, roll off the throttle and squeeze in the clutch. Second, shift the motorcycle into a lower gear by pressing down on the gear shift lever with your left foot. Third, ease out the clutch slowly as you roll on the throttle to match the engine speed with your road speed.

►MOTORCYCLE CONTROLS

If you've never ridden before, a motorcycle's controls might seem only slightly less intimidating than the control panel of a fighter jet, with many unfamiliar switches, levers, and warning lights. That unfamiliarity soon evaporates, though, when you realize that motorcycle controls are arranged in a very logical and intuitive manner. Because of the unique demands of riding a motorcycle, all the controls on the machine are arranged to be at your fingertips (or toetips) and easily accessible without looking away from the road. The information presented here explains what controls are necessary to ride the motorcycle, where those controls are located, and how they are operated.

PRIMARY CONTROLS

Primary controls, including the handlebars, are operated directly with hands and feet, and are the controls that make the motorcycle go, turn, and stop. Besides the handlebars, here are five primary controls:

1. Throttle The right handgrip, which controls engine speed. Roll "on" toward the rider to accelerate; roll "off" away from the rider to decelerate. The throttle is spring-actuated and automatically snaps back to idle position if released.

2. Clutch Lever Located in front of the left handgrip and operated with the fingers of the left hand, the clutch lever controls the clutch, the component of the motorcycle that transfers power from the engine to the rear wheel. "Squeeze in" the lever to disengage the clutch, and "ease out" the lever to engage the clutch and initiate forward movement.

3. Gear Shift Found on the left side of the motorcycle, in front of the left footrest, and operated with the left foot. Lift the lever upward with the toe to shift up to a higher gear; press the lever downward to shift down to a lower gear. The

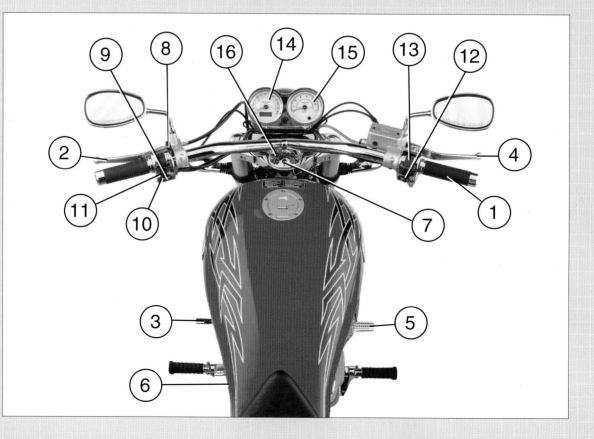

lever operates as a ratchet mechanism, so after each shift the lever returns to its "home" position. Most modern motorcycles have either five or six gears, with neutral located midway (a "half-lift" or "half-press") between gears one and two.

4. Front Brake Lever Located in front of the right handgrip and operated with the fingers of the right hand. "Squeeze" it inward to apply the front brake.

5. Rear Brake Pedal Found in front of the right footrest and operated with the right foot. "Press" it downward to apply the rear brake.

SECONDARY CONTROLS AND OTHER EQUIPMENT

Secondary controls and other equipment are located within easy reach or view of the rider, and they either control the machine's secondary functions or allow the rider to monitor the condition or operation of the machine.

6. Fuel Supply Valve Controls fuel supply to the engine, usually located under the fuel tank and operated with the left hand. Manually operated valves have three or four positions: ON, OFF, RESERVE, and sometimes PRIME. The RESERVE position taps into an extra portion of fuel that allows you to ride a short distance to a filling station after the main fuel supply has been used up. Not all motorcycles have a fuel supply valve—many, especially modern, fuel-injected motorcycles, feature automatic valves that are not accessible to the rider.

7. Ignition Switch Typically located near the instrument cluster, the ignition switch usually offers three key positions: ON, OFF, and LOCK. The LOCK position engages a steering mechanism lock that prevents the handlebars from being turned after the key has been removed. Some motorcycle models offer additional key positions; for instance a PARK position that locks the steering mechanism but also sends power to the tail light for visibility when parked at night, or an ACCESSORY position that delivers power to certain functions without requiring that the engine be running.

On the left handlebar are several important controls: horn button, turn signal switch, headlight beam selector, choke, and clutch lever.

On the right handlebar are located the throttle, engine cut-off switch, and starter button.

Note the floorboard and the "heel-and-toe" design of this shift lever. Instead of lifting the front of the lever with your toe to upshift, you can press on the rear of the lever with your heel.

This is the pilot's view of a KTM 950 Adventure, an example of orderliness.

8. Choke Control Usually located either on or near the handlebars or on or near the engine, the choke enriches the fuel mix to the engine to assist with starting when the engine is cold. The choke must be turned off when the engine reaches a proper operating temperature. Some fuel-injected motorcycles will have a fast-idle control instead of a choke control to assist with quick warm-up.

9. Horn Button Again, near the left handgrip and operated with the left thumb.

10. Turn Signal Switch Located near the left handgrip and operated with the left thumb. Most must be manually cancelled after the turn or lane change is completed, though some turn off automatically.

11. Headlight Beam Often located atop the left-side switch housing near the left handgrip, and operated with the left thumb. This switch allows the rider to easily toggle between the low and high headlight beam.

12. Engine Cut-Off Switch Located near the right handgrip and actuated with the right thumb, the engine cut-off switch allows you to easily and quickly shut off the engine without removing your hand from the grip. This may be helpful in an emergency situation.

13. Starter Button Located adjacent to the right handgrip and operated with the right thumb. After the key has been turned to the on position, depressing the starter button is what starts the engine.

14. Speedometer Located on the motorcycle's instrument panel, the speedometer displays the motorcycle's road speed and typically incorporates both an odometer and a resettable trip odometer.

15. Tachometer Also located on the motorcycle's instrument panel, the tachometer indicates engine speed in terms of revolutions per minute (rpm). A "red line" is typically drawn onto the tachometer face, indicating maximum safe engine speed, which if exceeded could cause engine damage.

Digital instruments are finding more use on motorcycles. This example by Yamaha presents several pieces of information in a compact space.

16. Indicator Lights Designed to alert the rider to various operating conditions, these can include the following: neutral, high beam, turn signals, oil pressure, side stand down, low fuel, and others.

17. Side and Center Stands These support the motorcycle when it is parked. Not all motorcycles are equipped with both. Many modern motorcycles are equipped with an ignition cut-out that prevents the motorcycle from being ridden away while the side stand is down.

It is important to realize that not all of the above-mentioned controls and features are present on all motorcycles. Many late-model motorcycles, for instance, are not equipped with a fuel supply valve, and many cruisers don't come with tachometers. Refer to your owner's manual for a detailed description of the specifics of these controls as they pertain to your particular motorcycle. ∎

ON THE BRAKES

Modern motorcycles use standardized braking controls, consisting of a lever operated by the right hand to apply the front brake and a pedal worked by the right foot to apply the rear brake. These simple controls are easy to operate and when used together have been proven effective at stopping a motorcycle in the shortest distance possible. Given that a motorcycle has two separate brake controls (rather than a single pedal like a car), smooth and effective braking technique, especially achieving proper distribution of braking force between the front and rear wheels in emergency stops and other instances of maximum braking, remains elusive to some riders.

Improper braking technique also remains a significant contributing factor in many motorcycle crashes. According to research collected for the "Motorcycle Brake Testing" report issued jointly by the U.S. Department of Transportation and the National Highway Traffic Safety Administration in February 2002, 13 percent of all motorcycle fatalities between 1990 and 1999 were related directly to braking maneuvers, and nearly one quarter of all motorcycle fatalities (22 percent) were related to a combination of braking and steering maneuvers.

In light of data like these, motorcycle manufacturers have for some time been developing technologies to make proper use of brakes easier. Two of the most noteworthy efforts in this direction have been the development of integrated- or linked-braking systems (LBS) and anti-lock brake systems (ABS). Such systems are becoming more and more common.

Linked brakes connect the front and rear brake on the motorcycle, applying braking pressure to both the front and rear brakes when either the front lever or rear pedal is applied. An integrated braking system is a variation of the linked system: partial front braking is applied when the rear brake is activated (two pistons of a four-piston caliper will engage, for example). An anti-lock braking system uses sophisticated electronic sensors to automatically release brake pressure prior to the wheel locking up, helping the rider to avoid skids in straight-line panic situations.

Unlike cars, which use one brake pedal to control brakes on all four wheels, motorcycles typically use a front brake lever to control the front brake, and a rear brake pedal to control the rear brake. Linked brakes and integrated brakes are the exception. (Top) In a typical integrated brake system, the rear brake pedal applies braking pressure to both the front and rear brake, which helps counteract riders' underbraking of the front that is often evident in panic situations. (Bottom) Anti-lock Braking Systems (ABS), common in modern cars, are becoming more available on motorcycles as well. An anti-lock braking system uses sophisticated electronic sensors to automatically release brake pressure prior to the wheel locking up, helping the rider to avoid skids in straight-line panic situations.

Anti-lock braking systems rely on precise speed information from each wheel. The serrated ring on this wheel delivers speed information to the ABS controller, so it can detect skids.

These three systems seem to have some obvious advantages—but do they make a difference either in terms of reducing braking distance or preventing braking-related accidents? The aforementioned U.S. DOT/NHTSA study set out to answer exactly this question. First the research panel evaluated the braking performance of five different types of motorcycles (sport, cruiser, touring, dual-purpose and scooter) with regard to application of front brake, rear brake, and both brakes together. One of these (the touring bike) was equipped with ABS, while another (the sport bike) was equipped with LBS. Braking performance was evaluated at a variety of speeds (from 30 to 80 mph) and on a variety of surfaces: wet and dry asphalt, concrete, brick, and others.

DOT/NHSTA testing demonstrated the conditions in which each system has an edge. Not surprisingly, when only the rear brake was applied on all the test bikes, the bike equipped with the linked braking system consistently recorded the shortest stopping distances (remember, application of the rear brake on a linked bike also initiates partial front brake application). And when braking in a straight line on wet or slippery surfaces, the ABS bike posted the shortest stops, and also boosted rider confidence because of its ability to prevent wheel lock-up.

When all was said and done, however, there was no clear-cut advantage that was applicable to every riding situation. More importantly, there was no replacement for a sound understanding and proper application of braking technique; of how the bike responds to braking inputs, traction management, and maintaining directional stability in maximum-braking situations—in short, all the basic braking techniques presented earlier in this book. Linked brakes, ABS, and other technological advancements are fine aids, but should not be considered a replacement for sound knowledge, understanding, and judgment when it comes to stopping safely. So be familiar with your owner's manual. Fully understand how your motorcycle's brakes operate, and practice quick stops frequently in a safe area or in an MSF *RiderCourse*, where a trained, MSF-certified RiderCoach can help fine-tune your braking skills. ∎

▶ BASIC SCOOTER SKILLS

IF YOU THINK THAT A SCOOTER IS NOT A MOTORCYCLE, THINK AGAIN.

Scooters are indeed considered motorcycles. They're just a different style, and have their own characteristics.

Besides being smaller, one of the most obvious differences is that scooters don't have traditional motorcycle frames. Where you would normally see a fuel tank, there is nothing but air. This makes it easy to mount a scooter. You can still swing your leg over the seat, but most riders prefer to simply step through, then sit on the seat. Whatever method you use, just make sure you squeeze the front brake so the machine doesn't roll out from under you.

Since there's no gas tank for scooter riders to put their knees against, they should be tucked in comfortably within the limits of the fairing (bodywork in the front) and floorboard. Riding a scooter can be quite a different experience than riding a motorcycle. Scooters are commonly equipped with an automatic clutch that engages the transmission gears at a pre-set engine speed above normal idle. When moving slowly, the clutch becomes disengaged and no power is transmitted to the rear wheel. This also creates a lag between rolling on the throttle and when power actually gets to the rear wheel.

"Revving" the engine activates the automatic clutch. So always be sure the scooter is restrained by the brakes or (when parked on its center stand) that the parking brake lock is set. A spinning rear wheel that suddenly contacts the ground could cause a spill. When ready to go, ease off the brakes slowly and roll on the throttle to move forward.

Once underway, there is no need to shift, since scooters have automatic transmissions. Stopping a scooter can be much the same as braking a regular motorcycle. Some models have both brakes operated by hand, with the left side activating the rear brake. Other scooters have a traditional rear brake activated by the right foot.

Whatever the configuration, scooter riders should learn and practice maximum braking techniques. Since weight shifts forward under braking, make sure your riding posture includes keeping your left foot forward on the floorboard to help brace yourself under hard braking.

The amount of force necessary to steer a scooter differs from that of a full-sized motorcycle as well. (See Chapter 13, Countersteering). Generally, a scooter responds more quickly to a press on the handgrip because it has smaller diameter wheels, a shorter wheelbase, a lower center of gravity, and a steeper steering angle. Therefore, only a relatively light press on the handgrip is required.

Understanding the distinct nature of scooters will help make your ride a more pleasant experience. Enroll in the MSF *ScooterSchool*, which is offered at many training sites around the country. And just as can be said about riding a regular motorcycle, the more you know, the better it gets. ■

A scooter generally responds more quickly to steering input because of smaller-diameter wheels, shorter wheelbase, lower center of gravity, and steeper steering angle.

CHAPTER 3

WHAT'S THE MOST IMPORTANT PREREQUISITE OF SAFE MOTORCYCLING? GOOD TIRES? STRONG BRAKES?

Good tires? Strong brakes? A powerful, responsive engine that allows you to quickly get out of harm's way? While all of these are important and potentially life-saving features, the most important component when it comes to staying safe is the complex software-pile between your ears—your brain.

Just as a good rider won't ride on bald tires or ride with old oil, your brain needs proper care and maintenance to remain in top shape. Like other elements of safe riding, readying your mind is a combination of preparation and applied practice. Get into the habit of making a "Ride Plan" each time you get on the motorcycle. Plan your ride before you even start the bike. Consider carefully the conditions and situations that you might encounter, and how you will deal with them. Free your mind from distractions that might occupy your thoughts on the road. Stress, anger, grief, and other emotions can diminish your concentration—allowing dangerous situations to arise while, or because, you weren't paying attention.

Knowledge and familiarity—know the machine you are riding, the roads you are traveling, and especially know your experience and abilities as a rider. These are huge determinants of your safety. The more information you can add to your mental library—from this book, from the MSF Basic *Rider-Course* or a more advanced riding course, from any other resources, printed, online or otherwise—the better prepared you will be for challenges that might arise on the road. A mind focused on safety can keep the body safe.

Mental preparation is an essential part of managing risk when riding. Plan your route before you set off, and think ahead to how you will deal with the hazards you're likely to encounter.

It is equally important to remove or minimize any factors that might impair or otherwise inhibit your ability to safely operate a motorcycle. Alcohol and other drugs will wreak havoc on your thinking and coordination, and should absolutely be avoided anytime you are near your motorcycle (refer to Chapter 4 for more information on alcohol, drugs, and their deleterious effects on safe riding). Physical needs, like hunger, the need to use restroom facilities, and fatigue, can also be significant distracters.

Drowsiness is increasing as a factor in fatal crashes. According to the NHTSA, drowsiness is a

CHECK IN, DON'T CHECK OUT

Have you ever caught yourself on the road wondering what you were doing for the past couple of minutes? It happens to many of us when we are thinking about something other than where we are and what we're doing . . . and that's when crashes can happen! In fact, 68 percent of all crashes occur during the first 12 minutes of a trip, and 57 percent happen during a trip of less than five miles when the rider has other things on his or her mind.

Mental preparation is an essential part of managing risk when riding. Take a few minutes to check your motorcycle and gear before you ride. Even when nothing needs to be adjusted or fixed, the time you spend will help to focus your attention on a safe ride ahead.

It's also a good idea to plan your ride before you set off. Based on your intended route, what hazards might you most likely encounter? Where will you have to deal with intersecting traffic? What lanes will you want to be in to follow your intended route? Where will you park at your destination? While traffic conditions may cause you to adjust your plan once you're under way, the act of creating a ride plan reinforces your mental focus so that you can effectively manage any risk. ■

factor in two percent of fatal crashes, though some groups suggest that the problem is much more significant than that. One group of international transportation safety experts suggests that as many as 1.2 million accidents each year (20 percent of the total number) have fatigue as a contributing factor. In some specific locations the numbers are much worse—for instance, 40 percent of fatal crashes on New York State Thruway in recent years have been attributed to drowsy, fatigued drivers, according to traffic experts. Fatigue is difficult to identify statistically as a contributing factor because it is not easy to identify at a crash site. There is no measurement, like there is for blood-alcohol content (BAC), to indicate how well-rested a deceased driver was. As a result, fatigue is often not noted by police in accident reports.

One thing is certain—people are more likely to be driving while tired now than ever before. Over the course of the last century, Americans have shortened their nightly sleep time by an average of 20 percent. Furthermore, according to a recent poll by the National Sleep Foundation,

51 percent of motorists reported having driven while drowsy, and 17 percent said they have dozed off while driving.

These stats, coupled with a host of other mitigating factors—more drivers on the road; more people working two jobs and making longer commutes; multi-tasking; an aging society more susceptible to the effects of fatigue; an increased use of medications that can cause drowsiness; a higher incidence of sleep disorders—mean that fatigue is having a larger effect on road safety and is making itself more prevalent.

An entire cottage industry has evolved to create a technological solution to alert car and truck drivers to fatigue. Roof-mounted sensors to detect a driver's head falling over, a device worn on the temples that registers eye blinks, even a talking computer that asks drivers questions and monitors responses for clarity and speed, then shoots a jet of cold water if the driver seems drowsy, have all been tested. (Don't laugh—the last was developed by IBM.)

These are not solutions—they just alert drivers before they doze off, and do nothing to address the root cause of fatigue. Fatigue—and its effect on you as a safe motorcyclist—is something over which you have complete control. There is no replacement for being well-rested before you take to the road. Make sure you get a good night's sleep before you set off on a long ride, and if you are out on a multi-day trip, make sure you rest sufficiently between each day on the road. While you are out on the road, take frequent rest stops—once per tank of gas, if not every hour—and make sure that you stop, get off the bike, and walk around a bit at each stop. Realize that motorcycling itself is a more tiring activity than driving a car, since riding is more demanding on your body and mind. Limit the time you ride to a reasonable amount—for most riders, six hours a day is plenty. And, by all means, if you feel yourself nodding off while you are on the road, pull off as soon as possible and get the rest you need before you continue riding.

MOTORCYCLING EXCELLENCE MEANS:

▶ You understand the importance of having good mental strategies as well as excellent riding skills.

▶ You know there is a risk-reducing advantage in having a healthy and positive attitude about safe riding practices.

▶ You take time to mentally prepare for each ride.

► AN ALERT MIND IN A HEALTHY BODY

Don't let the ease of using the throttle fool you—motorcycling is a physically demanding activity. Guiding a 600-pound cruiser through traffic or a 450-pound sportbike through a twisting set of corners requires a surprising amount of strength—even holding yourself up against a 60 mph headwind requires muscle strength. Riding a motorcycle puts you in the natural environment, exposing you to the sun, wind, and rain. Fighting off these elements, while remaining mentally alert, demands energy, and hazards such as dehydration, heat stroke, and hypothermia are real threats to motorcyclists. Dr. John Bodnar, medical director for the American Motorcyclist Association's Pro Racing Medical Advisory Board, shares some guidelines here for dealing with health concerns that motorcyclists might encounter on the open road.

DEHYDRATION

Dehydration is a serious concern for every motorcyclist, not just those in warm climates—you can become dehydrated in cold weather too. The key to staying well-hydrated on a motorcycle, Dr. Bodnar says, is to plan ahead. Hydrate before you ride (starting as long as 48 hours before a planned trip) and continue drinking for the duration of the activity. Try to drink a quart of fluid for every hour if riding in extreme heat or under physically demanding conditions; half that amount is sufficient for normal situations.

Perspiration isn't your only enemy, evaporation will also dry you out—which is another reason, besides injury protection, to keep your skin covered while riding. In addition to losing moisture to wind, exposed skin is subject to sunburn and other types of heat stress.

Dehydration symptoms include lightheadedness, nausea, and blurred vision. The only remedy is to rehydrate. Dr. Bodnar suggests that plain water is best for rehydration. Some sports drinks are formulated with salt solutions that can help them be absorbed into the body more quickly, but he notes that most have sugar mixed in so you are taking on calories as well. Water is more than adequate for rehydration purposes.

HEAT EXHAUSTION AND HEAT STROKE

Heat exhaustion is an advanced stage of dehydration. A person suffering from heat exhaustion perspires profusely, depleting water reserves, and rapidly uses up other energy stores to stave off the effects of heat. Heat exhaustion will cause body temperature to rise to a low-grade fever. Symptoms are similar to dehydration (dizziness, nausea, feeling faint), only more extreme. A person suffering from

A healthy body promotes a well-functioning mind. Plan ahead to stay hydrated to counteract your exposure to heat and wind while motorcycling.

Guard against hypothermia by dressing in appropriate cold-weather apparel and taking frequent breaks.

Staying covered is your best defense against hypothermia. When riding in cold conditions, make sure that every bit of your body is covered with windproof, waterproof, breathable gear. Electrically heated clothing can also be an ally against hypothermia. An electric vest can help maintain your core temperature, and electric glove liners (or heated grips on the motorcycle) will keep cold hands from dragging that core temperature down.

Plan for a break every hour or so in cold conditions to stretch and keep blood circulating. Symptoms of hypothermia include sleepiness and an extreme chill that turns into general numbness of the body. If this happens, pull off the road immediately and go to a place where you can get a warm shower—warm water is the best way to replenish body heat quickly. Frostbite—actual frozen body parts—is a different subject, and recovering warmth to frost-damaged extremities should be done only at the hospital.

FATIGUE

Fatigue is a serious risk for anyone traveling by motorcycle. Conventional "pick-me-ups"—caffeine or over-the-counter pills—are ineffective against fatigue. The only thing that fights off real fatigue is rest, and preferably sleep. Pull over at a rest stop for a short nap if possible, or stop riding for the day so you can get some sleep. Riding when you're exhausted is taking your life, and the life of others, in your hands—do whatever you can to get some rest before continuing to ride.

GENERAL CONDITIONING

A decent base level of physical conditioning is a good first step in protecting yourself from all of the above-listed health hazards. It's not a bad idea to do some stretching exercises to prepare your muscles for a long ride. Before participating in any physical activity, including motorcycling, you should consult your physician. A simple physical fitness program, jogging, walking, or some other low-impact physical activity a few times a week can make riding a much more pleasant and safe experience. It helps to have a strong and limber back, neck, arms, and legs to maximize riding endurance and minimize stress and strain on your body.

CHEMICAL IMPAIRMENT

Chapter 4 explains how alcohol and other drugs can seriously impair your ability to ride safely. ■

heat exhaustion needs to be cooled off as quickly as possible to prevent heat stroke. If you have access to a cold bath or swimming pool, put the victim in the water to immediately cool them off.

Heat exhaustion can be remedied with rehydration and other basic first aid measures—heat stroke, on the other hand, is much more dangerous and requires hospitalization to provide for the victim's safety. Heat stroke causes the loss of all auto-regulatory functions. The body shuts down, losing the ability to perspire or otherwise shed excess heat. A person suffering heat stroke will appear dry, but red and hot to the touch. Body temperature can rise as high as 105 degrees and the victim can become delirious, suffer seizures, or lapse into a coma as the body overheats. Heat stroke can be fatal, and the victim needs to be transported to a medical facility as quickly as possible.

HYPOTHERMIA

Extreme cold can be as dangerous to a motorcyclist as heat. The most common enemy in cold conditions is hypothermia—a dangerously low body temperature caused by prolonged exposure to cold. Hypothermia is especially worrisome to motorcyclists because a rider typically sits very still for an extended period, exposed to both cold air and the severe wind chill produced at high speeds.

RESPONSIBLE MOTORCYCLISTS KNOW THAT BIKES AND BOOZE DON'T MIX.

For many American motorcyclists, riding is a recreational activity. As such, it sometimes gets mixed up with another popular American pastime—imbibing alcohol. Stopping points during road rides often serve some type of alcohol. Given the peer pressure to join in the fun, separating drinking from riding can be difficult. Nonetheless, responsible motorcyclists know that bikes and booze don't mix. Be a leader. Separate alcohol from riding, and encourage others to do the same.

We've already established that riding a motorcycle is a demanding and complex task, one that requires focus and attention. Your ability to think clearly and respond quickly is directly related to your safety and performance on the road. It is a well-documented fact that alcohol and other drugs, even in small quantities, are the enemy of clear thinking, sound judgment, and quick, precise reactions.

SOBERING FACTS

Another well-documented fact: alcohol is a major contributing factor in motorcycle crashes, especially fatal motorcycle crashes. Data suggests that almost 50 percent of riders killed in motorcycle accidents had been drinking. One recent study of motorcycle accidents in the state of California found that of 140 motorcycle fatalities in a one-year period, 69 involved riding under influence of alcohol or other drugs. The second most common contributing factor, excessive speed, was a factor in 44 accidents. When experts considered injuries

Drinking alcohol or taking drugs impairs not only your physical abilities to see, respond, and control a motorcycle, but severely impacts your judgment as well. Riding a motorcycle is challenging enough without introducing alcohol or other drugs into the equation.

along with deaths, they found that more than 850 motorcycle crashes in California that year showed alcohol as a primary contributing factor.

Don't confuse these alcohol-related crashes with random incidents. Another study conducted by the University of Washington found that intoxicated motorcyclists were at fault in accidents 50 percent more often than non-intoxicated motorcyclists.

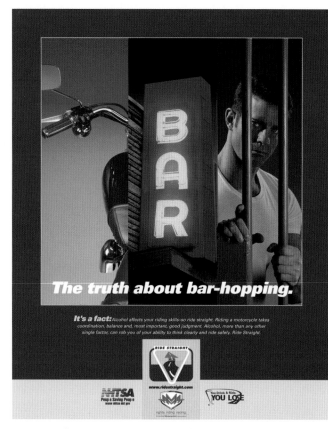

It's a fact: Alcohol affects your riding skills–so ride straight. Riding a motorcycle takes coordination, balance and, most important, good judgment. Alcohol, more than any other single factor, can rob you of your ability to think clearly and ride safely. Ride Straight.

In 2003, the American Motorcyclist Association (AMA) and the National Highway Traffic Safety Administration (NHTSA) formed a partnership to address the serious problem of impaired riding. And it is a problem: in 2001, 31 percent of the fatally injured motorcycle riders were impaired with a blood alcohol content (BAC) of 0.08 or higher. One result of the partnership was AMA's hard-hitting Ride Straight Campaign, which incorporates segments of NHTSA's "Friends Don't Let Friends Ride Drunk" campaign.

We congratulate AMA for taking a leadership position on this issue.

These sobering statistics aren't unique to motorcyclists: the percentage of motorcyclists who choose to ride under the influence roughly mirrors the percentage of automobile drivers who do the same. The difference is that motorcyclists are significantly more vulnerable than automobile drivers in the event of a crash. Furthermore, intoxicated riders are less likely—one-third less likely, in fact—than sober riders to wear a helmet. It all comes back to values and proper judgment. Safe riding requires that you place a high value on reducing risk—and nothing clouds personal values or erodes good judgment more reliably, or predictably, than alcohol.

HOW ALCOHOL AFFECTS RIDING

Just exactly how does drinking alcohol affect your ability to safely operate a motorcycle? To answer this question, the editors of *Motorcycle Cruiser* magazine devised a controlled experiment a few years ago to gauge the effect of drinking on a person's ability to control a motorcycle. The results of this study were very illuminating, and should be enough to give anyone reason to refuse drinking before riding a motorcycle.

The premise of the experiment was simple: editors gathered riders of various drinking and riding backgrounds, then got them intoxicated and watched them ride. Four men and one woman volunteered for the experiment, plus a sixth control rider who remained sober throughout the trial. Riding the same bike in a controlled environment on an MSF training range, these riders were judged on time and performance through a simple skills course. Riders started by riding the course sober, to establish baseline performance figures. After this was done, they started drinking and riding through the course to gauge how their skills were affected as they became intoxicated. The results were revealing. Alcohol—even as little as a single drink—had a severely deleterious effect on the rider's ability to safely operate a motorcycle.

Round one began with each rider downing a double shot (2.5 ounces) of vodka. After 15 minutes, each subject was administered a breath alcohol test to determine blood-alcohol concentration (BAC). First-round BAC results for the five subjects ranged from 0.023 to 0.043 percent.

A BAC of 0.08 is the legal limit of intoxication for adult drivers in the United States. Though none of the participants was considered legally drunk after the first drink (the highest BAC of the five was 0.043, just slightly more than half of 0.08), they were all intoxicated to some extent. When the subjects returned to the riding range, the results of this intoxication on their ability to operate a motorcycle were somewhat surprising. Almost all of them rode more smoothly—and, in some cases, even faster—than when sober. How could this be? Was the old myth about driving better after a drink maybe true?

Of course not. To understand why this isn't the case, first understand the affects of alcohol in what is called the "first stage" of intoxication. Stage one intoxication is marked by the familiar relaxing effects of booze—because alcohol is a depressant, inhibitions begin to melt away, and a person becomes less cautious and more likely to increase risk-taking behavior. After drinking, people sometimes believe that they become more confident—but this perceived effect is a false confidence, and is really just a lack of caution. This is where trouble can start—false confidence can be problematic, because it can lead to situations where a person might not have the skills necessary to remain safe.

Studies have shown that, in the first stage of intoxication, subjects may do well at single-task tests (counting light blinks, for example, and pressing a button when a prescribed number of blinks is reached). Add a second task or any additional stimulus (pressing the button when a different-colored light flashes in the periphery), though, and intoxicated subjects quickly become confused. This inability to multi-task can have terrible consequences when riding, as riding requires you to monitor an array of inputs and actions at the same time.

For instance, all participants from the *Cruiser* staff rode smoother and faster in the pure riding portions of the course—all they needed to pay attention to was moving forward. But when it came time to respond to commands or monitor anything beyond the simple forward motion of the motorcycle, alcohol's intoxicating effects came to the fore. Once the riders completed a pass of the skills course, they were asked to ride in a straight line across the training ground. The speedometers of the motorcycles were taped over, and the riders were asked to maintain what they perceived to be a 20 mph speed. They were then clocked with radar to see how far their perception was off.

At the end of the timed speed run, they were given a hand signal telling them to swerve either right or left. Then they had 15 feet to swerve and complete a panic-stop before "colliding" with a virtual "back of a bus"—a bus-sized rectangle painted onto the pavement. This last task was meaningful—plowing into the back of a slower-moving vehicle would not be pleasant.

The tasks had two stages—concentrate on riding forward at 20 mph, then respond to a hand signal, by swerving and braking to a halt without rear-ending the bus. Remember, everyone's BAC was between 0.023 and 0.043—well within the legal

EFFECT OF BAC ON PERFORMANCE

Round	Average BAC	Average Time to Complete Course
Base	0.000	49.92
1	0.033	50.28
2	0.039	51.16
3	0.077	53.76
4	0.114	59.05
5	0.130	68.43

Don't be fooled—one can of beer, one mixed drink, and one glass of wine all contain the same alcohol content, which the body processes at a rate of approximately one drink per hour.

limit in all 50 states. Every single rider rode below 20 mph in the radar trial, and three of the five smashed into the back of the virtual bus.

The second trial took place one hour later, after riders had been served another mixed drink and their breath analyzed. During this trial, the male subjects' BAC remained steady—all were in the 0.03 range—while the female subject's BAC shot up from 0.043 to 0.063. On the course, everyone's riding times and responses remained roughly the same, except for the sober control rider, whose times and skills improved significantly.

By the time the third trial came up, any orderly tracking of doses and effects were lost—the subjects, having long ago thrown caution to the wind, had begun surreptitiously dosing themselves. Breath alcohol results varied from 0.03 to 0.12, and most riders were now entering the second stage of intoxication, the effects of which include: mild euphoria; increased false confidence; sociability; talkativeness; diminution of attention, judgment, and control; and sensory motor impairment. On the course, riders were less cautious, and more careless.

Trial four BAC levels ran from 0.09 to 0.132, and everyone was well on their way to the third stage of intoxication, marked by: loss of previous euphoria (replaced with emotional instability); seriously impaired perception, memory, and comprehension; decreased sensory response and increased reaction time; sensory-motor incoordination; impaired balance; reduced visual acuity, night vision, peripheral vision, and glare recovery. In short—they were wasted. Stalled bikes, missed stops, and major deviations from the course were the rule. This round was also marked by the first crash (remember, this was a controlled, low-speed setting), and also the first appearance of vomit.

Though the test continued for a few more rounds, the point had been made crystal clear—alcohol, even in slight amounts, wreaks havoc on a person's ability to safely operate a motorcycle. Alcohol affects human abilities on every level, and the more a person drinks, the worse performance and behavior get. Even more troubling, the *Cruiser* study also shattered a bunch of dearly held myths about intoxication and its effects. One of the biggest surprises to the *Cruiser* bunch was the effect of time, and its ability (or, rather, inability) to help a person sober up. For instance, the female subject (who was way out in front of the pack early on in the BAC race) stopped drinking about halfway through the experiment. By the time the sixth round rolled around, her BAC had returned to 0.066 (well within the range for legal operation of a motor vehicle) from a previous high reading of 0.123. Despite the fact that she was less than half as intoxicated as she was a few rounds earlier, she was riding more poorly than ever before, more slowly and with more errors.

Studies have shown that even when a person's BAC returns to 0.00, abilities can still be negatively affected—as the *Cruiser* staff witnessed on the range that day. One reason may be that even when

Society has developed low tolerance for those who drink and drive, and today every state imposes severe penalties on those who do. If you're lucky enough to get caught instead of crashing, you can look forward to heavy fines, possible revocation of your license, and in some cases, jail time.

the alcohol is gone, exhaustion and confusion remain. It might take a good night's sleep to restore the body and brain to peak performance. Earlier we wrote that coffee, cold water, exercise, eating, and other conventional "cures" for drunkenness had no effect, and that time was the only remedy. Sometimes, as this experiment proves, not even time is on your side. The only clear way to avoid trouble is to never drink when riding a bike.

THE SURVEY SAYS

Other recent drinking studies have further laid to waste popular myths about drinking and riding. Take, for instance, the preposterous belief that a motorcycle rider has a better chance of avoiding injury if he or she is drunk, because the body will remain more relaxed in the event of a crash. In a study of more than one million auto accidents, the American Association for Automotive Medicine (AAAM) found that intoxicated drivers were actually more likely to suffer serious injury. "In any given crash, alcohol increases the vulnerability to injury," AAAM researchers concluded.

More specific to motorcyclists, a University of Washington study of motorcycle accidents involving head injuries found that "the protective effect of helmet use was lost on the intoxicated group, who sustained head injuries twice as frequently." In this study, the mortality following the critical head injury was twice as high among intoxicated patients (80 percent vs. 43 percent). And this study was restricted to helmeted riders; remember the statistic quoted earlier, noting that intoxicated riders are one-third less likely to wear a helmet compared to sober riders. Helmet or not, the well-known "Hurt Report," a University of Southern California study investigating 900 motorcycle accidents in the Los Angeles, California area, concluded that drunk riders were more likely to die from injuries. According to the findings of this study, four percent of non-drinking riders were killed in the event of a crash, as opposed to 21 percent of those who had been drinking. Statistically, this is very significant—drinking riders who crashed were about 5.6 times more likely to die as non-drinking riders involved in accidents. Sobering statistics indeed.

ABCs OF BAC

Three primary factors determine a person's BAC: the amount of alcohol consumed, the number of hours a person has been drinking, and that person's individual body weight. In addition to these factors, BAC can be further influenced by physical condition and gender.

Rate of consumption is important when determining BAC; the particular type of alcohol consumed is less important. One "drink" contains half an ounce of alcohol. A 12-ounce beer, a 5-ounce glass of wine, and a shot of hard liquor all contain the same amount of alcohol—an essential, and frequently misunderstood, point. Hard liquor does not get you more intoxicated than beer. A beer buzz is not more mellow, or any less impairing, than that produced by wine or hard liquor. Intoxicated is intoxicated, no matter what you've been drinking.

As a general guideline, your body will burn off the alcohol at a rate of one drink per hour. To figure out a close approximation of how much alcohol is in your body after drinking, take the number of drinks consumed and subtract the number of hours since you began drinking to figure how much alcohol is left in your bloodstream.

Remember, this is just a rough guide. BAC represents the percentage of alcohol in relation to blood, so a larger person, who has more blood, will not accumulate as high a BAC for each drink consumed compared to a smaller person. Similarly, women, who generally have a higher fat-to-muscle ratio, will generally become intoxicated more quickly and metabolize the alcohol more slowly than men. The ability to remove alcohol from the bloodstream is utterly unaffected by so-called "cures" like coffee, cold water, exercise, and eating. These have no effect. Time is your only ally when sobering up. ■

LAST CALL

Drinking and riding can have terrible personal costs—there's no need to overstate the consequences of dying on the highway, and the horrible aftermath of what something so senseless as a drinking and riding death will have on a deceased rider's family and friends. But even if you choose to drink and ride and are lucky enough not to crash, being arrested and convicted of drinking and riding has severe consequences. Today, all 50 states impose severe penalties on drinking riders. And, unlike in the past, many of these penalties are mandatory—meaning that judges *must* impose them.

If you are convicted of riding while intoxicated, you could be subject to any of the following:

License suspension Forty states have administrative license revocation laws that allow arresting officers to take away the license of riders who fail or refuse to take a breath test *at the time of the offense*, meaning that you lose your license immediately, well before any criminal trial. In the remaining ten states, it is almost certain that you will lose your license for some period of time following conviction for driving under the influence (DUI).

License revocation can last anywhere from 15 days to a year. In addition to inconvenience, the loss of license can also affect your ability to get or hold onto certain jobs. A DUI conviction showing on your police record can make you ineligible for some jobs, and will hurt your chances of getting others.

Incarceration Mandatory in 20 states, jail terms for DUI conviction can range anywhere from one to five days. For the record, you're now an ex-con.

Fines These can run anywhere from $150 to $10,000, depending on the terms of your conviction.

Other costs In addition to penalty fines, a DUI arrest will cause you to incur a host of other costs, including court costs and lawyer's fees, lost wages (if not a lost job), towing, storage, and other fees. Additionally, a DUI conviction will cause your insurance rates to skyrocket—if not make you completely ineligible for insurance from most companies.

Community service Many states also now mandate some form of community service as part of restitution, usually around 50 hours. And get ready to go back to school for a stint of mandatory alcohol education classes, also common in many states.

It all makes the prospect of relaxing with a drink and a ride sound something less than relaxing, doesn't it?

OTHER DRUGS

Though most of this chapter relates to alcohol, the effects of other drugs (illegal or over-the-counter) can be every bit as deleterious to safe riding as a swig of booze. Because it is more difficult to accurately assess the influence of these other drugs in motorcycle crashes (there is presently no field-ready equivalent of the breath alcohol detector for marijuana or cocaine users, for example), there is significantly less statistical data available regarding drugs and motorcycle crashes. Despite this statistical shortcoming, it is well known that drugs have a degenerative effect on the reflexes and other faculties necessary to safely operate a motorcycle. It is equally well known that the combined effect of alcohol and any other drug (over-the-counter or otherwise) can be far more dangerous than either taken by itself.

Do not operate heavy machinery after drinking.

MSF www.msf-usa.org • 800.446.9227

The Motorcycle Safety Foundation's "When you ride, think—don't drink" campaign addresses the serious problem of impaired riding.

Depending on the categorization, specific drugs have specific effects on a person's ability to safely operate a motorcycle or other motor vehicle. Here is a rough breakdown of common drugs and the sorts of negative effects you might expect these to produce.

Depressants   These include sedatives, barbiturates, and tranquilizers (Quaalude, Librium, PCP, angel dust, and others). Depressants tend to cause confusion, lack of coordination, drunken appearance, slurred speech, and a quick temper. These drugs impair every vital riding skill.

Stimulants   These include cocaine, speed, crystal meth, amphetamines, and Benzedrine. Stimulants may make a person seem more self-confident or alert, but this is often followed by depression and extreme fatigue when the drug wears off. Stimulants encourage risk-taking and impair judgment of the riding environment, road-surface awareness, perception of other vehicles, turning-speed selection, and defensive-riding ability.

Marijuana   This drug alters a person's time/space perception and fragments thought. Reaction time increases and short-term memory is impaired. This leads directly to impairment in road-surface awareness, scanning, perception of other vehicles, night vision, turning-speed selection, braking, defensive-riding abilities, and evasive maneuvering.

Heroin   Drowsiness, daydreaming and general stupor are some side effects of heroin. Like depressants, heroin impairs every skill vital to safe riding.

Over-the-counter and/or prescription drugs
In addition to illegal drugs, many common over-the-counter and prescription drugs can grossly affect your ability to safely operate a motorcycle. Many over-the-counter allergy medications, for instance, contain stimulants or sedatives and can produce the same effects described above. More potent prescription medications can be even more dangerous—some anti-depressants have side effects that include dizziness, drowsiness, and fatigue; common ulcer/heartburn/indigestion medications can cause confusion, dizziness, drowsiness, and hallucinations—all of which could greatly

MSF's Riding Straight Module, complete with interactive Fatal Vision® Simulator Goggles, is an informative and fun-filled event-in-a-box. The hands-on demonstration allows participants to experience how alcohol interferes with the skills needed to safely operate a motorcycle—without having to deal with a hangover or a crash.

complicate the matter of safely operating a motorcycle. If you are taking any type of over-the-counter or prescription medications, make sure that you are aware of any possible side effects and make appropriate adjustments when planning to ride.

MINIMIZING RISKS

This much is clear—drinking, drugs, and motorcycles never mix. Any time the activity of imbibing alcohol or taking drugs intersects with the activity of riding motorcycles the stakes are raised, and the participants are put at a significantly higher risk of running into trouble on the road. The key to staying safe is to do everything possible to minimize risks. When it comes to riding motorcycles, the only smart solution is not to drink at all.

If you're riding, don't drink; if you're drinking, don't ride. If you're headed out to the bar, leave the bike home and arrange for a designated driver to take you home in a car. If you end up on a ride that stops at a tavern, choose soda over the "sauce." If the temptation is too great, find an alternate activity to occupy your time. The stakes surrounding drinking and riding are just too high.

There are a variety of measures that you can take to protect yourself from the consequences of drinking and riding, but even when you do the right thing there is no guarantee that others will follow your lead.

PROTECTING YOUR FRIENDS

When you are in a group situation with other riders who have made bad choices and are considering riding drunk, it's up to you as the wiser party to step in and make sure that they don't get in a situation where they might cause harm to themselves or others. Seldom do people want to intervene—it's uncomfortable, embarrassing, and often causes conflict. But the alternatives can be much worse.

You have several options when it comes to protecting friends and other riders from the effects of riding drunk. Here are just a few of the many possible solutions:

Arrange a safe ride Provide an alternate way for them to get home, preventing them from riding their motorcycle.

Re-direct their drinking Try to direct the drinker to other activities that would discourage drinking, or at least slow the pace.

Keep them there Do anything you can to keep them from leaving. Start a game. Serve them food or coffee to pass the time. Start a conversation addressing concerns over his or her safety in the event of a crash. Explain your concerns about the possibility of their getting arrested or wrecking their bike.

Isolate the motorcycle If you can't control the ride, at least control the bike. Take the keys away. Do anything you can think of to separate the motorcycle from your buddy and keep him from riding it.

Enlist others It can be difficult to stand up to a drunk and possibly belligerent rider alone, but the more people you have on your side, the easier it is for you to be firm and the more difficult it is for a drunk rider to resist your reasoning.

Whatever you do, make sure that you choose appropriate methods and do everything within your means to keep a friend who has been drinking from riding his or her motorcycle. Though it will no doubt make you uncomfortable in the moment, and you will most likely receive plenty of resistance from the intoxicated party, everyone will feel much better about the situation the next day. And you'll never catch yourself saying "If only I had . . . "

And for yourself, the responsible, conscientious motorcyclist that you are—don't drink and ride. It's as simple as that.

MOTORCYCLING EXCELLENCE MEANS:

▶ You refuse to mix alcohol and riding.

▶ You do your part to encourage others to separate riding and alcohol.

▶ You stay informed about the effects of drugs, both prescription and non-prescription, on riding capabilities.

CHAPTER 5

Protective Riding Gear

TAKE EVERY REASONABLE PRECAUTION TO PROTECT YOURSELF FROM INJURY AND HARM.

A hockey star wouldn't set skate to the rink without his pads, just like a firefighter wouldn't dare enter a blaze without a full battery of flame- and smoke-resistant gear. Similarly, you shouldn't think of hitting the road unless fully dressed in proper motorcycle riding gear—just in case you end up "hitting" the road in the literal sense. If this happens, you want to make sure that you've taken every reasonable precaution to protect yourself from injury and harm.

The right gear will go a long way toward making your riding experience more comfortable, allowing you to more easily regulate your temperature (whether it's warm or cold), and also reduce fatigue. Proper riding gear (for rider and passenger) should include, at a minimum, over-the-ankle boots, long pants, a riding jacket, full-fingered gloves, eye protection, and—above all—a helmet manufactured to meet U.S. DOT standards.

Protective riding gear is particularly important for motorcyclists because of their increased vulnerability compared to those who choose other forms of transportation. Unlike automobile drivers, who are surrounded by a steel cage, motorcyclists are completely exposed to the elements: hot and cold weather, rain, bugs, stones, or other road debris, all of which can negatively affect your comfort and safety on the road. Proper riding gear minimizes this discomfort and danger, and can also save your life in the event of a crash or fall.

Managing your risk includes wearing proper protective gear in case of a crash. At a minimum, you will want to wear a helmet, eye protection, riding jacket, long pants, full-fingered gloves, and over-the-ankle boots.

USE YOUR HEAD

It's impossible to overstate the importance of wearing a helmet each and every time you ride your motorcycle. A bare head is no match for blacktop at even five miles per hour, to say nothing about highway speeds. In addition to protection, full-face helmets go a long way toward making your riding experience more pleasant, keeping airborne debris from hitting your face, keeping windblast out of your eyes, and cutting down on wind noise, all of which will help you to ride longer and with less fatigue.

There are no downsides to wearing a helmet, and helmet technology and design have made helmets lighter, more aerodynamic, better ventilated, and more comfortable than ever. Yesterday's myths and criticisms of helmets have been proven false. Helmets work to keep you safe, and there is no rational excuse for not taking advantage of the comfort, conspicuity, and protection these provide.

While some states have mandatory helmet laws, in other states helmet use remains a matter of personal choice. Wearing a helmet, whether required by law or not, is a reflection of your attitude toward riding motorcycles. And that attitude is plainly visible to other riders and non-riders alike.

About Helmets

A modern motorcycle helmet is a technological marvel, every bit as innovative as a modern motorcycle. Though helmet construction seems simple on the surface, engineers and scientists have spent nearly as much energy studying helmet design and effectiveness over the past two decades as their counterparts have spent studying steering geometry and fuel injection systems.

Think of a helmet as an "energy management system," a device whose main job is to manage the energy of an impact. A motorcycle helmet is composed of four component systems: a hard outer shell, an impact-absorbing liner, comfort padding, and a retention system.

Starting at the outside, a helmet's shell is constructed of a rigid material, usually some form of fiber-reinforced composite like fiberglass or injection-molded plastic. This is the first level of protection.

Immediately inside the shell is the second level of protection—the impact-absorbing liner, usually made from an expanded polystyrene material (commonly abbreviated as EPS). When your head contacts another object in the event of a collision, the helmet stops, but your head and brain want to keep moving. It is the impact-absorbing liner that absorbs this motion, by compressing or otherwise deforming.

Both the helmet shell and liner are designed specifically to spread the forces of an impact throughout the helmet's structure. The more impact energy that is deflected or absorbed by the helmet's materials, the less that is transmitted to your head. Helmets are intended to self-destruct on impact, crushing, cracking, delaminating or otherwise breaking apart to spare your head that force.

A helmet that shows visible damage on impact is not evidence of a low-quality product—it's evidence of a product that has done its job right. And because a helmet is designed to break on significant impact, it should always be discarded after an impact or inspected by the manufacturer for damage. Even if damage is invisible to the naked eye, it could be that the shell is delaminated or damaged, or the impact-absorbing liner has been crushed and compromised.

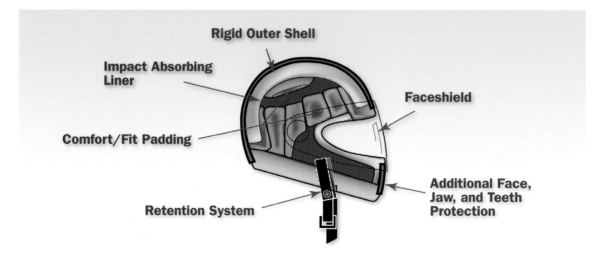

Rigid Outer Shell

Impact Absorbing Liner

Faceshield

Comfort/Fit Padding

Retention System

Additional Face, Jaw, and Teeth Protection

BASIC HELMET CONSTRUCTION

Even if it looks great, it likely has less protective value and should be replaced.

Comfort padding is the plush layer immediately adjacent to your head. This is typically composed of soft foam with a cloth covering. In addition to keeping everything comfortable, this layer is also what keeps the helmet fitting snugly to your head. On some helmets, this comfort lining can be removed for cleaning.

Keeping everything on your head is the retention system (chinstrap). This system is composed of two straps that attach to both sides of the helmet's shell and come together beneath your chin, usually connecting with a pair of D-rings or, on some helmets, a quick-fasten/release buckle. Every time you slip on your helmet, fasten the chinstrap snugly and securely. Riding without the helmet securely fastened might allow the helmet to fly off if you crash.

Choosing The Right Helmet

Choosing the right helmet is more complicated than picking your favorite color. When choosing a helmet, visit a well-stocked dealership with a large selection of helmets. There you can try on many different sizes and styles and compare various features before choosing the helmet model that best suits your needs. In addition to choosing the helmet that offers you the most protection, you've also got to give thought to shell shape and comfort, ventilation, and price.

Every head is shaped differently, and every type of helmet shell has a slightly different shape, so trying a helmet before you buy is essential. Fitting a helmet properly is important—a properly fitted helmet, for example, won't irritate your head (too small) or slip and move on your head when fastened (too big), thus offering less protection. Fit is important for both comfort and safety.

Modern motorcycle helmets come in three basic styles: full-face helmets, three-quarter (open-face) helmets, and partial coverage (half) helmets. A full-face helmet offers the highest level of protection, providing coverage for all of your head including your chin and jaw. A movable face shield protects your face from wind and debris and can be easily opened with one hand to provide access and additional ventilation. A three-quarter helmet is constructed from the same basic components but doesn't offer the face and chin protection of a full-

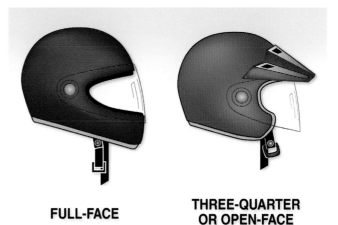

FULL-FACE   **THREE-QUARTER OR OPEN-FACE**

A full-face helmet (left) provides the most protection and includes a face shield for eye protection. In addition to open-face helmets (right), there are half-helmets, and flip-up helmets in which the entire chin bar flips up.

Jackets designed specifically for use by motorcyclists include features such as protective padding in the elbows, shoulders and back, zippered openings for ventilation in hot weather, collars that don't flap in the breeze, and reflective highlights that improve conspicuity.

HEAD SIZE

Head size is usually referred to in one of three ways: as a measurement in inches, in centimeters, or what is commonly called "hat size." To find your head size measurement, measure your head at its largest circumference—usually just above the eyebrows in front, over your ears and around the back. To ensure that your number is as correct as possible, it's helpful to measure several times and average the number. To convert the number from inches to centimeters to hat size, use this table. ∎

Size	Inches	cm	Hat Size
XX-SMALL	20 1/8–20 1/2	51–52	6 3/8–6 1/2
X-SMALL	20 7/8–21 1/4	53–54	6 5/8–6 3/4
SMALL	21 5/8–22	55–56	6 7/8–7
MEDIUM	22 3/8–22 7/8	57–58	7 1/8–7 1/4
LARGE	23 1/4–23 5/8	59–60	7 3/8–7 1/2
X-LARGE	24–24 3/8	61–62	7 5/8–7 3/4
XX-LARGE	24 7/8–25 1/4	63–64	7 7/8–8

David Thom, of the Collision and Injury Dynamics Laboratory, prepares a helmet for impact attenuation testing on the monorail test machine.

face helmet. Half helmets are similar to three-quarter versions but expose more of the lower jaw, sides, and back of your head.

Some riders find half and three-quarter helmets more comfortable and less restrictive, but it is important to note that these helmets offer less protection than full-face versions. Studies suggest that the better your face is protected, the less likely your chances of brain and face injury in the event of a crash.

If you do choose to ride with a half or three-quarter helmet rather than a full-face model, consider adding a face shield or wearing a pair of securely fitting goggles. Ordinary glasses or sunglasses are not sufficient eye protection for motorcyclists, as they can easily shatter, move, or fly off. Goggles attach securely on the outside of the helmet with a strap and seal eyes off from the elements, protecting from debris and wind.

Standards and Ratings

It's difficult to buy an ineffective motorcycle helmet nowadays, providing that you make sure of one thing—that the helmet shows a DOT or Snell certification sticker somewhere inside or outside the helmet. This sticker signifies that the helmet meets or exceeds all relevant safety test standards of the U.S. Department of Transportation (DOT) and/or the Snell Memorial Foundation, a private helmet testing group. Several manufacturers are now importing European helmets qualified to either the British Standards Institute or European Community standards in addition to DOT. These are also excellent choices.

Both DOT and Snell implement similar testing protocols. Helmets are assessed for: 1) impact management, or how well the helmet performs in collisions; 2) retention, or the strength of the chinstraps under stress; and 3) extent of protection, meaning the area of the head covered by the helmet. In addition to these four primary criteria, a helmet's penetration resistance (its ability to withstand a blow from a sharp object) and its effect on peripheral vision is studied. Approved helmets for the street must provide a minimum side vision of 105 degrees to each side (most people's usable peripheral vision is only about 90 degrees to each side). Any helmet you wear should be checked for its fit on your head. Do this by putting it on and fastening the strap. Then reach behind your head and try to roll the helmet forward over your face. If it can cover your eyes or the helmet comes off do not wear that helmet. Pick another brand, size, or style that stays on.

Since 1980, all helmets for on-highway use have been required to meet the DOT standard. When choosing a helmet, make sure that it has this certification. Don't buy a fake helmet; if someone tries to sell you a helmet without the DOT certification, do not buy it. Be especially aware of so-called "novelty" helmets, usually beanie-type helmets sometimes sold on the street at motorcycle rallies; some may even have a fake DOT sticker. Cheap, thin, lightweight, and virtually ineffective at protecting you in the event of a crash, these helmets exist mainly to escape citations from police officers in states where there is a mandatory helmet law. There is no sense in using a novelty helmet. If you're going to go to the trouble to strap a helmet to your head, wouldn't you want to at least make sure that it would actually protect you in the event of a fall? A fake helmet is just like a fake fire extinguisher—it looks OK until you really need it.

Bottom line: it's not hard to buy a good motorcycle helmet. As long as you are dealing with a reliable retailer and the helmet is marked with the genuine DOT or Snell certifications, you can be assured that you are going to get a quality helmet. Whether the helmet costs $100 or $700, as long as both are equipped with the DOT sticker, both have passed minimum standards and will provide at least the same minimum amount of protection. More expensive helmets often offer more features—things like better ventilation and visor systems, more sophisticated paint schemes, and are often lighter weight due to more advanced materials (for instance, Kevlar®- or Aramid®-reinforced) that allow the manufacturers to use thinner construction and still maintain sufficient strength and impact resistance.

Taking Care of Your Helmet

A modern helmet is a high-tech piece of equipment, and as such, should be treated with care. Most manufacturers will supply detailed instructions for caring for your particular helmet—follow these to the letter. Use only the mildest soap recommended for cleaning your helmet (inside and out). Avoid any petroleum-based solvents or

Clean the bugs and dirt from your helmet and face shield using a soft cloth and mild soap.

cleaning fluids, especially on polycarbonate helmets—exposure to these cleaning agents can break down the materials that compose the helmet's shell, compromising its protective value. Avoid setting your helmet on a bike's seat; a slight movement of the bike could send that nice piece of protective gear toppling to the ground, chipping its finish or scratching the face shield.

Keep your face shield clean and free of debris to maintain clear vision. To clean the shield, use a soft cloth with mild soap and water or a cleaner specially formulated for use on clear plastics. If the shield develops scratches, either replace it or polish the scratches out with plastic polish. Scratches in the shield can be especially dangerous in bright sun or at night, when they will distort incoming light.

Take care not to store your helmet near gasoline, cleaning solvents, heat sources or other elements that could damage the helmet. Helmet materials can react chemically to these elements, and the damage will often be invisible. Likewise, take extreme care before stripping, painting, or applying decals to your helmet. Many thermoplastic or polycarbonate helmets will react negatively to aftermarket paints or decals. The label inside the helmet will tell you what is acceptable and not for use on your particular helmet.

If you plan to use a radio or other communication device when you ride, take this into consideration before you purchase a helmet. Look for a model that doesn't require drilling speaker holes in your helmet's liner. (Before you purchase any communication system or speakers, check your state's laws regarded their use in helmets, as some states prohibit these.)

Replacing a Helmet

Remember, helmets are designed to be damaged in order to absorb the impact of a crash, and as such, after even a single impact it will lose some of its effectiveness. Even if the helmet shows no visible evidence of damage, it should still be retired. Many times cracks in the shell will be microscopic and compression of the EPS liner can be difficult to detect. Some helmet manufacturers will inspect your crashed helmet and tell you if they think it is still safe to use. If you can, take advantage of this service. If not, replace it and destroy the damaged one.

Impacts aside, age can also have a negative effect on a helmet's ability to protect. Repeated use can compress the comfort/fit liner. Ultraviolet rays can break down the outer shell. But an even better reason to replace your helmet regularly (every few years) is that helmet technology continues to advance. Regularly upgrading your helmet will keep you outfitted with the best possible protective gear. Helmets several years from now will no doubt be stronger, lighter, cooler, more comfortable (and probably cheaper) than ever before.

If you are uncertain of the age of your helmet, check for permanent labeling inside or on the chin strap cover—federal law requires that all helmets have the month and year of production stamped on them. Also be aware of the manufacture date before you buy closeout or sale-priced helmets.

The classic choice for protective gear—and still the best—is leather, when used in motorcycle-specific apparel.

OTHER RIDING GEAR

When it comes to proper protective gear for riding motorcycles, helmets and eye protection are just the beginning of the story. In addition to a quality helmet, you should always wear—at the minimum—a riding jacket, full-fingered gloves, long pants, and over-the-ankle boots (all motorcycle specific, preferably). Motorcycle riding apparel has made huge advances over the past few years, and is now every bit as high-tech and functional as motorcycles themselves. Using a variety of innovative materials, space-age ventilation and armor systems, and other patented and proprietary features, protective riding gear is now safer, more comfortable, and even more affordable than ever before. There's no excuse not to be properly outfitted for the ride.

Footwear

Over-the-ankle boots provide the highest level of protection for the feet, ankles, and shins, and also are least likely to come off in a crash. Sturdy boots will protect your feet from stones and other road debris kicked up from the highway, can stave off burns from hot exhaust pipes, and will help you operate the shift lever and brake pedal more effectively. Rubber soles provide good grip on the pavement when you're stopped and will help keep your feet on the footrests while riding. Boots come in street riding and competition (racing) styles. Street riding (or touring) boots usually include some padding over the toe, ankle, heel and shin areas, and are engineered for comfort and style off-the-bike as much as for protection during a crash. Racing boots are designed for maximum protection, and usually feature hard armor (often replaceable) over the toe and other critical areas. They are usually quite rigid for support, and as such, can be uncomfortable when walking around off the bike.

Gloves

A good pair of motorcycle-specific gloves performs a variety of functions: providing protection from sun, wind, and cold; helping to maintain a secure hold on the handgrips; and of course, in the event of a crash, minimizing cuts, bruises, and other damage to your hands. Anyone who has ever broken a

Gloves (left) designed for motorcyclists feature a natural curved shape that enhances comfort and padding in critical areas to minimize abrasion injuries in case of a crash. Riding boots (right) should cover your ankles and have non-slip soles. Many motorcycle boots on the market today are waterproof as well.

finger or skinned a palm can tell you exactly how essential a good pair of gloves is to any rider.

Gloves are available in a variety of styles, ranging from lightly padded models to all-out racing types with hard-plastic armor covering all possible contact points. Obviously, a fully-armored racing glove is going to provide the highest level of protection, but something like this might be uncomfortable for day-in, day-out use. Lightly padded gloves provide more freedom of motion while only sacrificing a minimum of protection. Choose the type that is most suitable for your intended use.

No matter what type of glove you choose, make sure that you try before you buy to ensure that you get a proper fit to your hand. A glove that is too bulky will make it difficult to operate the motorcycle's sensitive controls. Gloves that are too tight will restrict circulation and cause your hands to lose feeling or become overly sensitive to temperature. A good-fitting glove should be snug without restricting circulation or movement.

Make sure your gloves have a secure strap system to keep them on in the event of a crash—preferably a Velcro® or other type of strap around the wrist to keep them from sliding off over your hands. Gloves with a gauntlet will provide more protection for your wrists, and will also be slightly warmer in cool temperatures. In addition, gloves are available in different weights for different seasons (lighter for summer, heavier for winter), making it easy to find the right glove for any type of riding.

Clothing

If you haven't shopped for motorcycle-specific clothing recently, you'll be surprised at the technology and sophistication of modern motorcycle riding gear. It has become every bit as high-tech as anything made for mountaineering, downhill skiing, or any other athletic pursuit. Like gloves and footwear, motorcycle clothing is all about comfort, protection, and conspicuity. Your goal when shopping for appropriate motorcycle gear should be those three factors, in that order.

Just as there are different types of motorcycles geared toward different sorts of riding (sportbikes, cruisers, touring machines, etc.), there are different types of motorcycle clothing geared toward different sorts of riding—often with special cuts so they fit better in a specific riding position, and with features of special value to those sorts of riders. If you are a sportbike rider, it's likely that you'll be most happy with a jacket designed for sportbike riding; likewise for touring apparel, which is most likely to satisfy the needs of touring riders.

Once you've determined what style of jacket and pants to look at, it's time to explore features. First consider what material to select—leather or textiles. Each has its own advantages, depending on intended usage. In general, leather offers better abrasion resistance and breathability, while textile garments are going to be more weatherproof and better in cold temperatures, and are often less expensive than leather.

REFLECTIVE MATERIALS

You'll find many garments and riding accessories that use reflective or "retroreflective" materials to increase night visibility. Retroreflective is a little different than regular reflective; what makes retroreflective materials work so well are tiny crystals that are formed into a thin film and laminated to a garment or other product. The crystals are shaped to reflect light back in the direction from which it came, unlike the way an ordinary mirror reflects light. The result is a brilliant reflection of light back toward its source, making it seem to "light up" to a driver approaching. Many road signs are now being made with retroreflective lettering. Next time you see one, notice how bright it looks, even from a distance of several hundred yards. ■

Adding retroreflective materials to your helmet or other apparel can greatly improve your visibility to other road users. Be proactive in making yourself seen by others while riding.

More important even than material, though, is the fit of the protective garment. It's the fit of the piece of gear that will determine both comfort and protection. Fit varies from person to person and application to application, making it essential that you try before you buy. Make sure that your riding apparel fits snugly, more so than any fashion apparel that you might be accustomed to wearing. Riding clothes should fit tighter and be more form-fitting. This is especially important with armored riding gear—the gear has to fit properly so that the armor isn't shifting around. It has to be positioned correctly to do its job.

Not only must the gear fit well, but it also must fit in the riding position. For example, the fit of a sport jacket is tailored for a sportbike riding position. This is critical, because if the front of a jacket is too long, when you lean over on the bike it will push the shoulders up. If the back is too short, it will pull up and expose your back. Therefore, on sport jackets the front is cut shorter than the back, which feels all wrong walking around the showroom but makes perfect sense when you sit on the bike.

You might feel overwhelmed by all the features offered with modern riding apparel. Hard armor, soft armor, venting details, laminated-composite protection panels, aerodynamic aids—the myriad options, and distinctions between those options, can turn choosing clothing into a conundrum. Our advice? Don't make too big a deal over this stuff. The average rider doesn't need to know that the sleeves are rotated 15 degrees, that it's 660-denier, or that the armor absorbs 430-joules-per-second of force. As long as it feels good and offers protection when you're wearing it, that's usually enough.

Other Riding Gear Considerations

Dressing properly is important no matter what the weather may be. Remember that even in warm weather, constant exposure to wind when riding could cause hypothermia. Hypothermia can cause you to lose your ability to concentrate and react to changing traffic conditions. Motorcyclists are especially susceptible to rapid chilling, which leads to a loss of reflexes. The biggest danger of hypothermia is the deterioration of the ability to think clearly. Proper riding gear, such as a windproof jacket and insulated layers of clothing, is essential to prevent this.

On a cold day (40 degrees Fahrenheit, 4 degrees Celsius), a motorcyclist riding at highway speeds of 60 mph (96 kph) experiences a temperature equivalent to 25 degrees Fahrenheit (minus 4 degrees Celsius), or just below freezing. Riders not dressed properly for the chill could suffer the effects of hypothermia.

Clothes that are just right when you leave in the morning might be too hot after you've been riding for a few hours. To prevent this, dress in layers so that you can remove and replace clothing as needed. When preparing to ride in cold weather, several layers of clothing are necessary, usually starting with thermal underwear. Extra layers of pants, shirts, and jackets should be layered loosely to aid body heat in forming warm insulating pockets. Topping your clothing with a windproof outer layer will prevent the cold wind from reaching your body.

Insulated riding suits offer another alternative in cold weather. These lightweight suits provide the warmth needed to prevent hypothermia. Another option available to motorcyclists is an electrically warmed vest or suit.

Even in hot temperatures, you should always wear at least a jacket to reduce the chance of becoming dehydrated. Wind rushing over exposed skin quickens dehydration, and a jacket will protect your skin from the drying wind. On hot, sunny days it is best to wear light-colored clothes. Lighter colors reflect the sun's rays rather than absorbing them—this can make a difference of up to 10 degrees Fahrenheit or more on hot days.

Choose brightly colored clothing whenever possible, to help make yourself more visible. If you wear dark clothing, consider a reflective vest over your jacket. It is also a good idea to affix reflectorized tape to garments you wear regularly when riding. Many modern jackets incorporate retroreflective material into their construction.

If you ride often in a wet climate, a rain suit can be a boon. A dry motorcyclist is a more comfortable and alert motorcyclist. Rain suits can commonly be purchased in one- or two-piece designs in many materials—the most common being polyvinyl chloride or nylon. These are usually designed to slip easily over your other protective gear, and feature high collars, flaps over all zippers, and elastic at the wrists, ankles, and waist to seal out water. For added protection from the wet, consider also glove and boot covers.

One additional consideration for the well-prepared rider is hearing protection. Whenever you ride, even if you have a quiet motorcycle and a full-face helmet, your ears are exposed to wind noise. Long-term exposure to wind noise can cause irreversible hearing damage. Properly worn hearing protection can reduce wind (and engine) noise and make your ride more enjoyable, while allowing you

Some riders wear additional body armor for maximum protection in case of a crash.

to hear important sounds like car horns and sirens. You can choose from a variety of styles, from disposable foam plugs to reuseable custom-molded devices. Make sure you are in compliance with state laws when using any hearing protection.

You've prepared your mind for the ride, and now you've outfitted your body with the proper attire—you are armored and ready, thanks to the protection that riding gear can provide.

MOTORCYCLING EXCELLENCE MEANS:

▶ You wear proper personal protective gear on each ride.

▶ You choose a helmet and clothing that are designed for comfort and protection.

▶ You choose a quality helmet and replace it periodically or after a severe blow.

▶ You choose riding gear that helps make you more conspicuous in traffic, both day and night.

▶ KEVIN SCHWANTZ ON SAFETY GEAR

Though intended mostly for street riders, the Kevin Schwantz Suzuki School advanced riding classes are taught exclusively on the racetrack. School owner (and 1993 Grand Prix World Champion) Kevin Schwantz says that in polling students at his school he sometimes notices an interesting inconsistency in their attitudes toward what is proper safety gear on the racetrack compared to on the street.

"It's funny," Schwantz says. "Most of them think that the racetrack is where something bad is going to happen, so of course they are very serious about the gear they wear on the track. But when you ask them about riding on the street, their attitude toward safety gear is sometimes much more casual. They seem to think that the street, because the speeds are usually lower, is a safer place, so they're less likely to gear up. Of course, the absolute opposite is true!"

What Schwantz means is that the racetrack is a controlled environment, with fewer obstacles and unknown hazards compared to the always-changing street scene. In actuality, a motorcycle rider is more likely to meet trouble in the street environment compared to the racetrack. Because of this, it is just as important, if not more important, to protect yourself for street riding as well as riders do on the track.

Schwantz's school, for example, mandates full-coverage, motorcycle-specific gear for your upper and lower body (leather or reinforced textile), racing boots, protective gloves, and a quality DOT-compliant motorcycle helmet. Schwantz says student attitudes toward helmets especially surprise him—sometimes students will tell him that they have a very expensive helmet for the track, and a less expensive one for riding on the street. "You know the old saying," Schwantz says. "How much is your head worth? There's probably not more than $500 worth of wisdom in my head, but, I'd still like to protect it."

The bottom line, Schwantz says, is that it's much better to be over-equipped than under-equipped, and gear that is considered mandatory on the track is every bit as important and valuable for street riders. It's a lesson that he works hard to instill in every one of his students, and one that you, as a serious, safety-conscious street rider, would do well to consider. ■

World champion road racer Kevin Schwantz has seen the protective value of proper riding gear in action on the track and urges students of his riding school to buy the best gear they can afford.

► FASHION VICTIMS

THE DIFFERENCE BETWEEN "MALL LEATHER" AND MOTORCYCLE-SPECIFIC RIDING GEAR

If you've gone shopping for motorcycle-specific riding apparel, there's a good chance that you've been shocked by what appear to be exceptionally high prices. This is easy to understand—after all, to the untrained eye, a $100 fashion leather jacket and a $400 piece of protective motorcycle gear look pretty similar hanging on the rack. The difference, of course, is in the details—and the differences between mall leather and motorcycle leather can save a great deal of suffering if a rider actually has to put that gear to good use in a crash.

To help you understand this distinction, Paul Golde, Product Development Manager of Fairchild Sports, the company that distributes some of the best-known brands of protective apparel, took a few moments to explain the differences between the two types of product.

"Beginning with the material, fashion leather is usually made from lower-quality, split-grain leather, often lambskin that is only 0.6 to 0.7 mm thick. A quality motorcycle jacket, on the other hand, will be made from premium top-grain cowhide leather measuring anywhere from 1.0 to 1.5 mm thick, for maximum abrasion resistance. The thinner leather, especially lambskin, is not up to the rigors of a crash on asphalt. Not only is the quality of the material better on the motorcycle jacket, the construction techniques are more advanced as well. Fashion jackets usually feature raw seams that are butted together and single stitched, usually with a cheap cotton or plastic thread. Protective jackets, pants and gloves use sophisticated, rolled, lipped and double-stitched seams held together with multi-ply nylon (or sometimes Kevlar®) thread, all to help the jacket hold together better in the event of impact.

"Quality motorcycle gear offers other options that significantly increase the protection quotient. These options often include soft or hard CE-approved armor ('CE-approved' indicates that the garment complies with a European apparel standard somewhat analogous to the DOT standard for helmets) to protect vulnerable bones, and a motorcycle-specific cut with a dropped back and rotated arms to ensure that the wrists and lower back stay protected even when the rider is hunched forward in a riding position. Don't forget your lower extremities: motorcycle-specific pants, boots and gloves all are designed to stay on your body in a crash and protect you from 'gravel rash,' but like a helmet, once they have done their job, replace all damaged apparel."

Those are just the protective advantages—motorcycle-specific riding wear offers a variety of comfort options that are virtually unavailable on the garments from the local Leather Loft; features like easily removable, non-bulky liners for cold weather, enhanced cargo capacity, and high-tech ventilation systems. Despite these numerous advantages, many consumers are still unwilling to make the jump from fashion victim to well-protected rider. The average consumer wants his purpose-designed motorcycle jacket to fit and look like a fashion garment, but remember, what feels good at a nightclub doesn't necessarily feel good at 65 mph—or in a crash. ■

(Top) Fashionable, but neither protective nor conspicuous enough for motorcycling.

(Middle) Good protection.

(Bottom) Good protection plus enhanced conspicuity.

► HOW TO PROPERLY FIT A HELMET

BY BRUCE PORTER

Motorcycle helmets are anything but "one-size-fits-all," and finding a helmet that fits properly is essential both to ensure that the helmet is comfortable to wear and that it protects as advertised. An ill-fitting helmet can shift on your head during an impact, and because of this can compromise the level of protection it offers. Although knowing your "head size" (see sidebar, page 52) is a good place to begin, it is important to try the helmet before you buy. Because interior shapes vary between brands, a specific size helmet from one brand might fit you better than the identical size from another brand.

A helmet marked in your head size is a good place to start. Holding the helmet by the chinstraps, with the front of the helmet facing you and the top of the helmet facing down, spread the helmet gently by the straps and slip it over your head. If the helmet slides down on your head with little or no resistance, you have your first indication that it may be too large. Obviously, if it will not slide down over the head at all, it is too small. A helmet should fit snugly and may even feel a bit too tight until it's all the way down over the head. It should sit squarely on your head and the cheek pads should touch your cheeks without pressing uncomfortably. There should be no gap between your temples and the brow pads. For full-face helmets, look in a mirror to confirm that your eyes are about midway between the top and bottom edge of the eye port.

Next, securely fasten the chin strap. With the strap fastened, your skin should move slightly as the helmet is moved from side to side. The helmet padding should not slide easily over the skin, but should pull the skin in the direction of rotation. You should feel as if a slight, even pressure is being exerted all over your head by the helmet. Remember that a helmet will loosen up slightly as the comfort liner compresses through use. With this in mind, a new helmet should be as tight as you can comfortably wear.

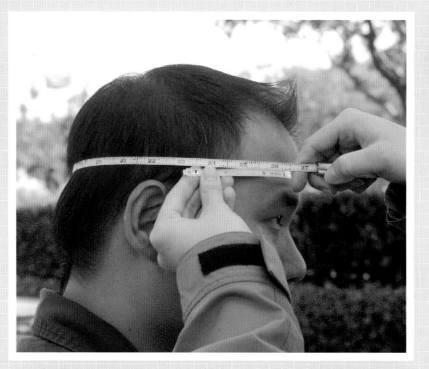

Getting a helmet that fits your head size and shape is important. A helmet that is too large may not stay on your head during the force of a motorcycle crash.

Now, grab the helmet in your hands, one hand on either side, and try to rotate the helmet from side to side. Note any movement of the skin while doing this, as well as the amount of resistance to movement while you hold your head steady. Next, move the helmet up and down, again noting skin movement and resistance. If there was little or no skin movement in either the vertical or horizontal tests, and/or the helmet moved very easily, the helmet is too large. A properly fitted helmet will cause the skin to move as the helmet moves—and the wearer will feel as if evenly distributed pressure is being exerted around the head.

With the chin strap securely fastened, grab the back of the helmet (by the bottom edge) and try to roll the helmet forward off of your head. If it comes off, or comes close to coming off, it is either too large or incompatible with your head shape, so try another size or model. A helmet that is too large will move around and up and down on your head. This could allow the helmet to move and potentially block your vision, and can be annoying because it can be noisy and let wind in. Plus, in the event of an accident, it could come off!

After testing for retention and wearing it for a while, remove the helmet and look for any evidence of pressure points. Red spots or soreness can indicate pressure points that can be very uncomfortable and can cause headaches during long rides. If the helmet you are trying produces pressure points, try on the next larger size or try a different brand. Some models come with a variety of cheek pads to help you customize the fit (assuming the helmet fits the top of your head well). Human heads are not all the same shape, and neither are helmets.

You are going to be wearing your helmet every time you ride, so it is exceedingly important that you choose one that fits your head perfectly to provide maximum comfort. Visit a well-stocked dealer with a wide variety of helmets in many different styles and sizes, from different brands, to give you a better chance of finding one that fits properly. In addition, dealer staff is often trained in proper

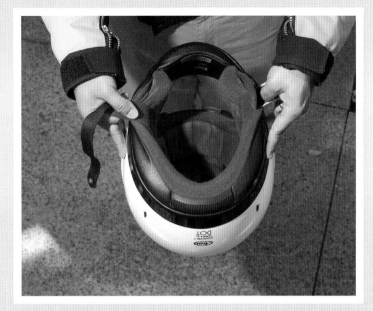

To put on your helmet, first take hold of the chin straps and gently spread the sides of the helmet.

Next, while spreading the helmet with the straps, place the helmet on your head. Some helmets go on more easily with a rolling motion, starting near your forehead and continuing backward and downward.

Pull the chin strap through the two D-rings . . .

. . . then around the outer D-ring and back through the inner one.

helmet fitting, and will be able to give you valuable suggestions in this direction. Allow plenty of time to select and purchase your helmet to ensure that you get the right one. A helmet is an important investment, no matter how much you spend. ■

Bruce Porter, Director of Marketing and Professional Motorsports Promotion for Arai Helmets Americas, Ltd., has 21 years of experience in the industry. He's involved in Arai's professional motorcycle racing program in North America, and conducts safety seminars for distributors and retailers.

With the chin strap tightened, rotate the helmet from side to side. If the helmet fits properly, your skin will move with it.

Try to roll the helmet forward. Excessive movement means it's too large.

REGULAR MAINTENANCE AND PREVENTIVE CARE WILL GO A LONG WAY TOWARD A TROUBLE-FREE RIDE.

There is something almost magical about the act of riding a motorcycle, and the way that the gyroscopic effect of the wheels turning cheats gravity and allows you to glide along upright on two skinny tires without falling. In some ways, riding a motorcycle is an act of faith—faith in the physics that keep you upright through the curves and over the hills, and faith in your machine to keep you moving without a breakdown or other troubles that could bring your ride to a halt.

A big part of riding safely is having confidence in your machine to get you where you are going without incident. To possess this confidence you have to trust your bike unconditionally. Approaching a downhill curve, you have to know that your brakes will slow you to a proper entry speed. Before you roll on the throttle to pass a slow-moving minivan, you need to be confident that your final drive—chain, belt, or shaft—won't fail. Making sure that your motorcycle is in tip-top operating condition, that everything is functioning properly, not worn out or near failure, forms the foundation for this trust. Remember, a minor technical failure is usually nothing more than an inconvenience for an automobile driver, but the consequences can be much more serious for a motorcycle rider.

Because the consequences can be more severe, proper care and maintenance of your motorcycle warrants more frequent attention. Attending to every aspect of your motorcycle's well-being, and making sure that all of its components and systems are maintained in proper working order, will go a

Check your bike over before every ride to help ensure a trouble-free journey. The owner's manual will outline the pre-ride inspection procedures.

long way toward allowing you to ride more confidently. The reliability of modern-day machines has made getting stranded on the roadside mostly a thing of the past, but even the best-cared-for motorcycle can develop problems. Usually, however, you can discover a potential problem developing, and have plenty of time to fix the minor trouble before it causes a major crisis on the highway.

T = Tires & Wheels

C = Controls

L = Lights & Electrics

O = Oil & Other Fluids

C = Chassis & Chain

S = Stands (Side or Center)

Use T-CLOCS to remind yourself what parts of the bike to check before each ride.

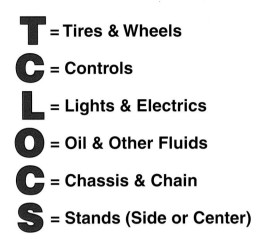

Proper tire pressure will promote good handling and long tire life.

Check tires for punctures as well as small cracks along the sidewalls.

Regular maintenance and preventive care will go a long way toward a trouble-free ride. Check your bike for problems before every ride. Even a simple check of your machine's general condition and fluid levels can be enough to reveal problems on the rise and help you catch and correct issues that could become trouble down the road. To help you through a quick and easy pre-ride inspection of critical components and systems, we recommend using the acronym T-CLOCS, which refers to: Tires and Wheels; Controls; Lights and Electrics; Oil and Other Fluids; Chassis and Chain; and Stands (side or center).

TIRES AND WHEELS

T stands for tires and wheels, perhaps the most important components of a motorcycle with regard to safe riding. Don't underestimate the importance of having good tires. The small contact patches provided by the front and rear tires are the motorcycle's only source of traction. Even the slightest compromise of quality or condition of your tires can be enough to overwhelm this contact patch and bring a good ride to an abrupt end.

Check the air pressure in your tires regularly, and adjust it according to the manufacturer's recommendations. Maintaining proper air pressure is important for tire life and tire performance. Incorrect pressure can lead to uneven tire wear. Low pressure can cause excessive heat buildup or instability—especially at high speeds or when carrying heavy loads—and can affect available traction. If, under normal loads and operation, a tire needs air added every time you ride, you should assume there is a small puncture, slow leak, or other problem that can cause a failure. Address the problem immediately.

Regularly inspect the tire tread depth to ensure that adequate tread remains. Most modern tires have small wear bars molded into the tread grooves. When these wear bars are exposed, the tread should be considered worn out and the tire should be replaced. Although it may look like a sufficient amount of tread remains, it won't be enough to maintain traction in wet conditions, and worn tires are thinner and easier to puncture.

Flat tires can and do occur. Of course, there is no sure way to predict when you might run over a nail (though anecdotal evidence seems to suggest that

this is most likely to happen in the first 10 miles after installing a new tire!). Nonetheless, you may be able to spot other signs of an impending tire failure or blowout. Before each ride, take a moment and glance over the tires' tread for any evidence of wear, cuts, embedded objects, bulges, or weathering.

While you are inspecting the tires, put the motorcycle on its center stand (or otherwise raise the wheels securely using a shop stand or jack so that they can spin freely) and check the wheels as well. Most modern motorcycles are equipped with cast-spoke wheels. Make sure that these wheels are free of cracks or dents, especially at points where the spokes join the rim and along the bead (outer edge) portion of the rim. If your bike uses spoked wheels, periodically check to make sure the spokes remain tight. Regardless of the type of wheel, be sure the rim is straight and round.

As long as the wheels are up and off of the ground, check the wheel bearings for wear by grasping the tire at the top and bottom then pushing and pulling on it. There should be no free play or audible noise from the hub or axle. Inspect the bearing seals for cracks or discoloration.

Now is a good time to inspect the brakes as well. Make sure that the calipers are mounted securely to

(Top) Use a tread depth gauge to make sure your tires have adequate tread left. If the tread is down to the wear bars, it's time for a new tire.

(Bottom) Check brake pads for wear and make sure the brake disks are problem-free.

Check the operation of the brake lever (top), and clutch lever (bottom). Make sure the levers aren't bent and are fully operational. Take a moment to inspect the brake and clutch hoses or cables for cracks, cuts, or leaks.

the forks in the front and the swingarm in the rear. Spin the wheels to confirm that the rotors pass freely through the calipers without dragging, which might indicate a worn or stuck piston, a warped rotor, or other problems with the braking system. Check the brake pads or brake shoes for wear.

The above checks are especially important on fully loaded motorcycles or motorcycles that frequently carry passengers—the extra weight puts a greater load on wheel bearings, spokes, rims, tires, and brakes. Extra attention to maintenance should be considered essential when carrying such loads.

CONTROLS

C stands for controls: the levers, the throttle, and all the cables and hoses associated with the motorcycle controls. The controls are the means through which you communicate with your motorcycle, and it is important to maintain these systems in order to ensure that your motorcycle responds quickly and correctly to your inputs.

Start your inspection with the levers. Make sure that these are tight in the mounts but still pivot freely, and make sure that the levers are not cracked or bent. A bent lever might restrict the available travel of that lever, possibly preventing complete engagement of the clutch or brakes. Also inspect the cable ends, looking for signs of fraying. Look carefully at cable routing and make sure there are no kinks. Control cables usually fray before breaking completely, and catching a frayed cable ahead of time can keep you from being stranded on the side of the road. A rough or gritty feel at the lever can be a warning sign that the cable it is attached to is beginning to fray. Also look at the cable ends, which occasionally come off unexpectedly. If you are touring long distances, it might be a good idea to carry spare cables in case one should break. Spare cables are cheap compared to the expense of being stranded.

Pay special attention to the throttle cable routing, to make sure that it doesn't pull when the handlebars are turned. The throttle should rotate freely on the handlebars and snap closed when it is released. Most modern motorcycles are equipped with two throttle cables—a second cable pulls the throttle closed, and both of these cables need to be working. If you notice the throttle sticking open, try to close it manually. If closing the throttle manually works, you will need to service that second cable so that the throttle automatically snaps closed when the grip is released. If the throttle should stick while you are riding, you'll have to use the clutch and brakes to control your speed as you safely maneuver out of traffic to where you can stop and shut down the engine using the engine cut-off switch.

Most disc brakes are hydraulically actuated, and use hoses instead of cables. Make sure to inspect these regularly for cracks, cuts, leaks, bulges, chafing, or other deterioration. When you are checking out the brake levers and hoses, it's also a good time to check the function of the brake light switches—make sure that when the front brake lever is squeezed in or the rear brake pedal is pressed down that the brake light illuminates.

LIGHTS AND ELECTRICS

L is for lights and electrics. Electrical components are relatively sensitive to vibration and weather, which makes it important to inspect these systems regularly. Electrical failures can be particularly difficult to diagnose or deal with along the side of the road, making this maintenance even more essential.

Your headlight should work properly and be aimed correctly on both low and high beam settings. Same for your brake and taillight—make sure that the brake light illuminates with both the front brake lever and rear brake pedal. Regularly check the function of your other electrical switches—including turn signals, horn, and engine cut-off switch—to make sure that these are functioning properly as well. Regularly inspect all electrical wiring for cracks, fraying, mounting, and chafing of the insulation. Keep an eye out for disconnected or broken wires and repair them when necessary.

Your bike will not run without electrical current, so keep the battery fully charged and properly serviced. If you ride infrequently, or store your motorcycle for an extended periods, you may want to invest in a trickle charger to keep the battery in fully charged condition.

Many new motorcycles are equipped with sealed, maintenance-free batteries. If yours is not, and still uses a serviceable battery, make sure to check it frequently and keep the electrolyte level topped off. Regardless of the battery type, keep the terminals clean and tight and make sure the battery leads and grounds likewise remain clean and tight.

OILS AND OTHER FLUIDS

O refers to oil and other fluids. Always keep the engine oil filled to the proper level and change it at regular intervals according to the manufacturer's recommendations as detailed in your motorcycle owner's manual. Changing the engine oil is probably the most important service that you can perform on your motorcycle for engine longevity. After a few thousand miles of use, the molecules in

motor oil break down and the oil loses its ability to properly lubricate the engine parts. This is important because in a motorcycle engine, the engine oil also lubricates the transmission and clutch. The added stress of lashing gears and the additional heat created by the clutch puts additional strain on the oil molecules, making regular oil changes that much more critical.

Engine failures occur in times of especially high stress—over-revving, overloading, or when vital lubricants run too low or are too old and worn out to function properly. Fortunately, engine failure almost never occurs unannounced—this usually is preceded by such long-term symptoms as poor

Make sure the brake light works when you press down on the rear brake pedal or squeeze the front brake lever. Letting the drivers behind you know that you're braking is often just as important as the action of braking itself!

Liquid-cooled bikes feature radiators, and it's wise to check to make sure that the radiator fluid is at the proper level.

The oil in most street bikes lubricates the engine as well as the transmission, so it's doubly important to make sure the oil level is correct. On newer bikes, it's easily done through the sight glass, which typically features high and low marks.

Checking the fluids includes the hydraulic systems for the brakes and clutch, if your bike is so-equipped. A sight glass on the master cylinder makes it easy to check the hydraulic fluid levels.

starting, sluggish throttle response, and unusual noises. In addition to engine oil levels, also check all engine surfaces and gaskets to catch any oil leaks. And don't forget to check the levels of brake fluid and any other hydraulic fluids as well.

If your motorcycle is liquid cooled, inspect the coolant level at the reservoir or recovery tank. Be sure to check the radiator and hoses for cracks or other signs of leaks or potential failures. Don't neglect your fuel system. Replace your fuel filter regularly before it becomes clogged with dirt. If your bike has a fuel valve (petcock) it should turn from ON to RESERVE to OFF/PRIME (if so equipped) smoothly. A leaky petcock will allow fuel to flow into the carburetors and possibly overfill or "flood" them. If the O-rings inside the petcock are particularly degraded, some bikes may even leak if it is left in the OFF position.

CHASSIS AND CHAIN

The second C in T-CLOCS refers to chassis and chain. Inspect the frame (especially around the gussets and accessory mounts) to look for cracks or other signs of trouble. Raise the front wheel off the ground and move the handlebar side to side, checking to make sure that the forks move freely and easily without any evidence of side play or any knocking noises. Raise the rear wheel and inspect for signs of play in the swingarm by pushing and pulling on the rear wheel. Once both ends are back on the ground, check the suspension for smooth movement. Pay special attention to fork and shock seals to make sure that no hydraulic fluid is leaking out.

The vast majority of motorcycles use chain drive, and motorcycle drive chains require frequent attention in order to provide long life and optimum service. It is essential to keep the chain at proper tension and alignment, so be sure to refer to your owner's manual for instructions on how to adjust this system properly and how often to perform the inspection. Depending on riding conditions, you may need to lubricate the drive chain often as well. Lubricating the chain is best done at the end of a ride while the chain is still hot—the heat will help the lube penetrate the links better. When applying the lube, direct the stream between the plates and rollers, not down the center or against the sideplates.

Check the steering by turning the handlebar all the way to the right and left. Check the front suspension at the same time by pushing down on the handlebars to compress the front forks.

A badly worn chain is much more likely to break or derail than one that is properly maintained, and a broken chain can do serious damage to the engine cases or swingarm, not to mention potentially locking the rear wheel and possibly causing a crash. Proper chain maintenance is of paramount importance. You'll want to inspect the sprockets for wear as well. Look for hooked or broken teeth, and make sure that the rear sprocket remains securely attached to the rear hub.

Replace your chain when you can pull it away from the rear sprocket and expose more than half a tooth; if it is rusted, pitted, or cracked; if it has numerous kinked "tight spots"; or if the rear axle adjusters have reached their farthest limits. If you are unsure of your chain's condition, see your dealer's service technicians for advice.

Motorcycles that use belt or shaft final drives are usually lower-maintenance than chain-drive units,

but these are by no means maintenance-free. Just as you would with a chain, regularly inspect the belt to look for cracking, fraying, missing teeth, or other evidence of impending failure. On shaft-drive bikes watch for leaks at all seals or contact points, and make sure that the fluid levels remain at factory specifications.

STANDS

S is for stands, including the side stand and the center stand. (Not all motorcycles are equipped with center stands.) Make sure that the side and center stand both retract fully out of the way when riding. Hanging stands can easily catch the pavement

Keep the chain at the proper tension and alignment (refer to your owner's manual), and lubricate it often.

when leaning into a corner and cause a crash. To prevent this situation, many modern motorcycles are equipped with an engine cut-off that prevents the engine from running if the stand is down while the transmission is in gear.

OTHER MAINTENANCE CONSIDERATIONS

T-CLOCS checks are most effective when performed on a clean bike. Dirt, grease, and road grime can easily conceal potential problems. Regular cleaning not only keeps your motorcycle looking new, it also extends its life by protecting it from dirt, debris, and other corrosive agents that cause wear.

No matter how clean you keep your motorcycle, or how attentive you are to preventive maintenance, you can't stop certain consumable parts from wearing out. Catching and replacing worn parts *before* they break (and potentially cause further damage by breaking other parts along with them) will go a long way to keeping your bike safe and solid for years of good riding.

Make sure to follow the manufacturer's recommended maintenance schedule to keep your motorcycle running at peak performance and reduce the chance of mechanical failure. Keep a detailed maintenance log as well—this will not only help you keep track of what maintenance was performed and when, but it can add value to your bike, should you choose to sell it, by proving that it was properly maintained.

No matter how well you keep on top of maintenance, sometimes incidents occur that can cause your bike to sustain damage. In the event of a minor incident such as dropping your bike in the garage, for example, make sure to immediately and thoroughly inspect it for damage before putting it on the road again. Pay especially close attention to any moving parts, such as controls and steering and suspension components. Check for any binding in these systems that could indicate bent components. Although minor misalignments of parts like the handlebars or footrests might be tolerated for a short emergency ride home, any damage that interferes with the free movement of controls is an invitation for catastrophe, and should be repaired properly before the bike is ridden.

In the event of a right-side tip over, pay special attention to the throttle assembly. Underneath the right handgrip is a plastic tube on which the throttle rotates. This tube will often split or splinter in the event of a crash, which can cause the throttle to stick. It can also shift within the control assembly and bind. Simply loosening the control assembly screws and relocating the throttle tube will often fix this problem.

Your motorcycle's owner's manual or warranty booklet is an essential and valuable tool—it will have a maintenance schedule, it might suggest which inspections and maintenance tasks can be performed by a mechanically inclined owner, and it may even have detailed instructions for performing certain routine maintenance procedures.

Many motorcycle repairs and routine maintenance are simple and can be easily performed by the owner. However, other repairs require the expertise of a trained technician with access to special equipment. Know your limits as a mechanic—if you are unsure of your ability to perform particular task, take your motorcycle to an authorized dealer. An incorrectly repaired mechanical problem can be every bit as dangerous as a worn or stressed part. Don't compromise your safety just to save a few bucks or a few minutes.

How well you ride is directly proportional to how well your motorcycle performs—and how well your motorcycle performs is a function of how well it is maintained. Ensuring quality care for your bike is a huge advantage for safe and confident motorcycling.

The motorcycle owner's manual (your "MOM") is a valuable resource for key information such as proper tire pressures, suspension adjustments, and routine maintenance requirements.

MOTORCYCLING EXCELLENCE MEANS:

▶ You inspect your motorcycle before each ride.

▶ You inspect and maintain your motorcycle in a way that keeps it operating like it was new.

▶ You maintain your motorcycle according to the owner's manual and heed indications that corrective maintenance may be needed.

▶ You choose a competent mechanic for repairs and maintenance that you are not capable of performing.

▶ SUSPENSION TECH

BY PAUL THEDE

Modern motorcycles offer more suspension adjustability than a high-end Barcalounger®—and when set up properly, they can be just as comfortable to ride. But any time there is a high degree of adjustability, there is a higher likelihood for maladjustment or other mistakes. With this in mind, it's good to have a decent understanding of what adjustments are possible with motorcycles, and what difference these adjustments make to the motorcycle's ride quality and handling, before you start twiddling the knobs.

Modern motorcycles are remarkably capable out of the box, and for this reason, many riders leave their machines at the factory settings and never look back. But unlike an automobile, a motorcycle is very sensitive to changes in riding surface, riding style or load. For this reason, if you frequently ride with passengers, or alternate between highway commutes and twisty back roads, it can be very helpful to understand how simple adjustments to your suspension components can make your motorcycle more comfortable and more controllable.

Suspension tuning can be a threatening prospect, what with its obscure language (static sag, compression damping, rebound damping) and multiple variables that all affect one another. Luckily, once you wrap your head around a few very basic concepts, the details are easy to grasp. The first step to adjusting the suspension on your motorcycle should be reading the owner's manual—this will help you determine what sort of suspension your bike is equipped with, what particular adjustments it allows, and how those adjustments are performed. In addition to the information contained in your owner's manual, here's a quick primer on the basic terms and ideas of suspension tuning, should you decide that you're ready to tweak the dials.

All motorcycles use a suspension system that consists of some sort of spring (usually coiled steel, sometimes compressed air) paired with some sort of damper (not "dampener"), usually fluid, to modulate the action of that spring. The most basic suspension setting is spring preload. Adjusting the spring preload changes the amount of "static sag,"

Different bikes offer different levels of suspension adjustment. Typically, adjusters at the top of each of the front forks allow changes in preload and rebound compression.

or the amount that the suspension compresses from fully extended with the rider onboard the motorcycle. Spring preload on the rear shock is usually adjusted using a special tool that works on the adjusting collar. Some collars can be turned with a blunt chisel but you should use caution or you can damage them. The front fork preload is usually adjusted by turning a knob or nut at the top of the fork.

Changing static sag affects the handling and stability of the bike and has some effect on bottoming out as well. It does not, however, take the place of correct spring rates. Motorcycles are much more sensitive to rider weight than cars because the rider is a much higher percentage of the total weight. If you find that after the static sag is set, the bike "tops-out" when the rider gets off the bike, the spring rate is probably too soft. On the opposite end, if the bike settles more than 15 mm the spring is probably too stiff.

Once preload and static sag are adjusted to your weight and preferred riding style, adjustments to the bike's suspension damping circuits can be made. There are two types of damping at work on motorcycle suspensions: compression damping and rebound damping. Compression damping resists forces from incoming bumps and loads by controlling upward wheel motion. Rebound damping is the opposite, and controls the rate at which the suspension extends after compressing from a bump.

Damping doesn't affect the spring rate or shock preload—it only controls the rate at which the spring is allowed to compress or extend, usually by controlling through a valve the rate that the suspension fluid can travel from one portion of the shock reservoir to another.

If your motorcycle allows damping adjustments (not all do), these adjusters will usually be found in the following locations: on the rear shock, the rebound adjuster is usually located near the bottom of the shock on the shock shaft, while the compression adjuster will be found adjacent to the reservoir; fork rebound adjusters are usually located at the top of the fork, while front compression adjusters are almost always found on the bottom of the fork leg.

Compression damping is a tradeoff between road feel and bottoming resistance and harshness.

The rear suspension often consists of a single shock absorber that includes a heavy coiled spring and remote fluid reservoir. Compression damping is adjusted by turning the knob on the reservoir.

With more damping, there is more road feel and better bottoming resistance, but it will be more harsh. Rebound damping is a tradeoff between traction, plushness, and a feeling of control. Traction and control will suffer at either extreme (too slow or too quick) but for most riders the feeling of control falls off while traction is still improving. The less the rebound damping, the plusher the suspension will usually feel.

Again, your owner's manual is your friend when it comes to dialing in your suspension. Start at the manufacturer's recommendations and

(Left) On this motorcycle the rebound compression is changed by using a large blade screwdriver on a slotted adjuster at the top of each front fork.

(Above) Modern motorcycles make it easier than ever to make suspension adjustments. Preload on the rear shock of this Suzuki can be adjusted with a simple turn of a knob.

make adjustments from there. Most, but not all adjusters are considered to be at "zero" when they are shut off (fully clockwise). Start small—often just one or two clicks in either direction can make a noticeable difference. Some adjusters, most notably shock compression adjusters, will hardly make a noticeable difference from one extreme to the other. Minimize variables by changing only one setting at a time, and keep track of your changes so you don't lose your place. Finally, don't be afraid to fiddle. Though there is plenty of adjustment available, there's seldom enough to make the bike dangerous or unrideable, and you can always put it back to the original settings.

As a final note, the adjusters do not take the place of internal valving and external springing.

Just because the bike has external adjustment doesn't mean the best ride is within the range of adjustment. The manufacturer has many compromises to make when selecting a suspension setup. If you really want the best ride for your application, consider internal valving changes. When it comes to the ultimate in handling, keep in mind that the other critical pieces of the puzzle are chassis geometry and alignment. ∎

Paul Thede, owner and chief engineer of Race Tech, is a mechanical engineer with 41 years of experience riding and racing motorcycles. Paul is a published author and teacher, and has become a "professor" of sorts amongst suspension technicians around the world.

SEARCH, EVALUATE, EXECUTE.
RIDING MOTORCYCLES IS ANYTHING BUT A PASSIVE ACTIVITY.

Staying safe on the street demands that you be an active participant, paying attention and responding to your surroundings, making decisions based on your observations, then acting to see those decisions through with proper and well-timed actions. Motorcycles, being smaller and less visible than automobiles, operate at a comparative disadvantage to four-wheeled vehicles in the traffic mix. To counteract this vehicular inequity, you have to ride defensively and act with confidence. You need to remain in full control of your motorcycle at all times, and remain constantly aware of your immediate riding environment. This means monitoring many factors to stay one step ahead of potential hazards and problems.

Roadways can be chaotic places, especially as lifestyle changes—like the rise of two-career families, with more-demanding jobs and longer commutes—continue to crowd our streets and highways with more stressed-out, distracted, inattentive and fatigued drivers. According to a study released in 2003 by The Road Information Program (TRIP), a non-profit, Washington D.C.-based transportation group, travel on the nation's 45,000 miles of interstate highway has increased 37 percent between 1991 and 2001. Congestion and traffic density is such that two of every five miles of urban interstate suffer significant traffic delays on a daily basis. And TRIP predicts that these numbers are only going to get worse: the group suggests that traffic on interstates will increase 42 percent

Riding on the street calls for proactively making yourself visible, gathering visual information, positioning your motorcycle within the traffic flow, reading and evaluating traffic patterns, and making predictions as to how potential hazards will affect you and other motorists.

over next two decades, while truck traffic will grow 54 percent. Data like this suggests that in large urban areas there are lots of targets that demand your attention. Sensory overload (and the resulting confusion and lack of focus) is always a danger.

Of course, there are effective steps that you can take to combat this confusion. There are many techniques you can use to remain aware of your riding environment and anticipate what is going to happen on the road ahead. Start by working to improve your riding skills to the point where they become second nature, leaving your mind free to concentrate on monitoring your surroundings. Then take active steps to make yourself more visible to other motorists, to position yourself properly in the traffic flow, and to accurately evaluate and respond to potential hazards.

Making yourself visible, gathering visual information, positioning your motorcycle within the traffic flow, reading and evaluating traffic patterns and making predictions—these are your street strategies, the mental touchstones that you will rely on to make the right decisions when riding on the street. This chapter will help you understand and refine these strategies so you can begin to implement them every time you ride.

VISIBILITY

Research continues to suggest that being visible to others is an important component of any safe-riding strategy. "I never saw the motorcycle," is an oft-heard refrain in the moments following a car-bike

Being seen by other drivers is a vitally important part of your street-riding strategy. Along with the headlight, bright-colored clothing and a light-colored helmet will help you stand out.

collision. Because motorcycles are smaller than automobiles, they can be more difficult to see and it can be more difficult to judge their speed. Don't underestimate the fact that many motorists simply aren't looking for motorcycles. For these reasons, it's in your best interest as a safe motorcyclist to do everything possible to make yourself visible and leave plenty of space to respond to the other roadway users.

Being Seen

Being seen means not only making yourself and your motorcycle visible (with bright clothing and reflective surfaces, for example), but also riding your motorcycle in a manner that clearly communicates your presence and intentions. There are several strategies you can use to accomplish this.

Dress in a way that makes you conspicuous. Choose bright-colored clothing and a light-colored helmet so you stand out to other drivers. Consider also using reflective material on your clothing, helmet, and even on your motorcycle to make yourself even more conspicuous, especially in low-light situations.

Many states require by law that you ride with your motorcycle's headlight illuminated, even during daylight hours. Even if it's not required by law, you should always ride with your bike's headlight switched on—this is one of the easiest, and most effective, ways to stand out in the eyes of oncoming traffic. (Since 1979, new motorcycles sold in the United States have headlights that switch on anytime the ignition is on.) For enhanced visibility during daytime hours consider adding a headlight modulator that pulses your headlight beam, if legal in your state.

Although we might not typically think of it this way, being visible is one of the key ways that motorcyclists communicate with other roadway users—communication that becomes especially important when you are moving through traffic. Enhance this communication with other drivers by using a good lane position and always signaling your intentions. Use your turn signals when changing lanes, and whenever it's safe, consider using hand signals to further clarify your intentions. Don't forget to cancel your signals after you've completed your maneuver—a false signal is misleading and can be as dangerous as no signal at all.

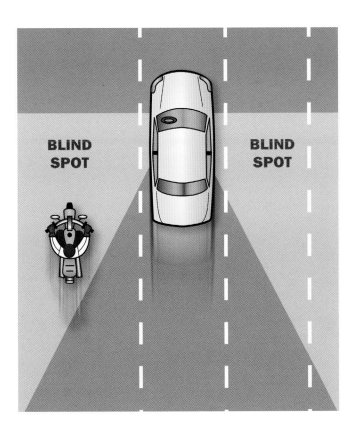

BLIND SPOT

BLIND SPOT

(Above and right) An important aspect of making yourself seen is never to linger in another driver's blind spot. If he doesn't see you he is more likely to change lanes, thinking you're not there.

Signaling is not enough—double-check with a glance. Pair your mirror checks with a glance over your shoulder at your blind spot area before changing lanes.

Turn signals are effective because a flashing light attracts more attention than a steady one. Remember this rule and use it during stopping maneuvers to make yourself more visible from behind. Flash your brake light before braking (except in emergency braking situations) to make yourself more conspicuous to traffic following you.

Your horn can also be a useful tool, especially in potentially dangerous situations. Use it when necessary to gain attention, but don't rely on your horn alone to prevent a dangerous situation—many motorcycle horns cannot be heard over traffic noise or surround-sound car stereos.

While all of the techniques discussed are effective for enhancing your safety, being conspicuous should not be relied on alone to provide for your safety on the open road. Even if you're dressed in a high-vis yellow, reflector-pasted riding suit and signal your intentions religiously, you still shouldn't assume that others see you or will respond to your actions. Your best protection is still to ride defensively, to study the traffic and anticipate potentially dangerous outcomes, and prepare to take measures to avoid these. Be responsible, take your safety into your own hands, and act accordingly to ensure the outcome you desire in every interaction with traffic.

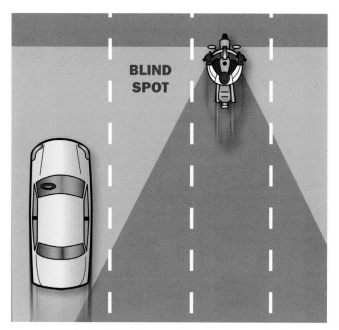

Be aware of what's going on all around you while riding—including within your own blind spots. Take precautions to make sure other drivers aren't in the way before you change direction or position.

SEEing

In addition to "being seen," actively "seeing" potential hazards is equally important. Though we use the word "seeing," a variety of other active verbs that start with the letter "S" would just as easily suffice in this situation, including "searching" or "scanning." The key word here is "active"—seeing is the act of looking for things that could possibly affect you when traveling on your bike. Gathering information through your eyes, aggressively and actively scanning the immediate environment for potential hazards, is a necessary habit for safe motorcycling.

Proper seeing goes beyond noticing what is immediately in front of you, and includes everything to the side of you and even what is happening behind you. Scan 360 degrees around you. The key to successful scanning is to always keep your eyes moving. Don't let your eyes pause or fixate on any one object for more than a split second. Roving eyes notice more, which will help you to be aware of anything that might affect you in the next few seconds.

Your goal should be to scan about 12 seconds ahead of you. This means looking ahead to an area that it will take you 12 seconds to reach.

Scanning into the distance gives you time to prepare for situations before these materialize in your immediate path of travel (the area four seconds ahead of you). Situations within four seconds need to be responded to immediately. Accounting for situations before they appear in your immediate path of travel will give you a better chance of responding appropriately and maintaining control over your motorcycle.

Other roadway users—drivers of cars and trucks, and even pedestrians—should receive the majority of your attention, as they are most likely to influence your travel. But in addition to other vehicles, also give thought to the environment that you will be passing through, including objects on the roadside and on the roadway itself. Be aware of potential problem spots—trees can shelter damp or icy spots on the road; shadows can conceal debris or other hazards; potholes or loose shoulders can spread gravel on the roadway, especially in corners. Remain aware of the movement of the traffic around you, including that which is behind you. Use your mirrors to check behind you, but don't depend on them entirely—turn your head to check blind spots that your mirrors miss, especially before changing lanes, turning or slowing down.

Maintain an added measure of awareness at intersections, where other vehicles could potentially cross your path. Other spots that warrant extra attention include side streets, driveways, and parking lots where other vehicles enter the traffic flow. Also pay special attention to children and animals on the side of the road—both are unpredictable and can act suddenly.

Remember to keep your eyes moving and gathering information. The best way to ensure your safety is to take responsibility for knowing what is going on ahead of and around you.

GATHERING GOOD VISUAL INFORMATION

Ninety percent of your impressions of the traffic scene come through visual inputs. Because of this, your eyes should be considered your first and best line of defense.

To use your eyes as effectively as possible, it is helpful to understand exactly how your sight process operates. Think of your vision as separated into two distinct fields: central and peripheral. Central

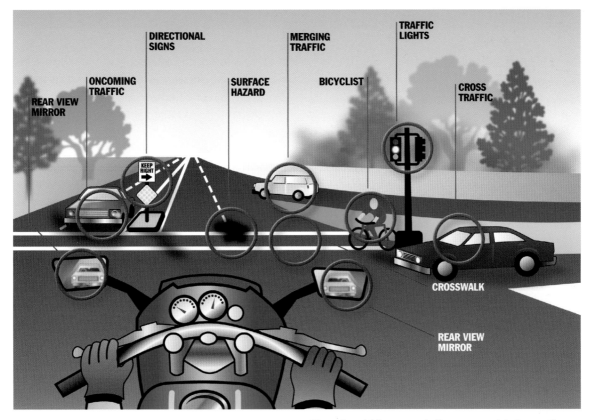

REAR VIEW MIRROR

ONCOMING TRAFFIC

DIRECTIONAL SIGNS

SURFACE HAZARD

MERGING TRAFFIC

BICYCLIST

TRAFFIC LIGHTS

CROSS TRAFFIC

KEEP RIGHT

CROSSWALK

REAR VIEW MIRROR

You should be especially aware at intersections, where other vehicles can cross your path of travel. There are many things to scan for, including traffic devices, road surfaces, and the traffic and pedestrians around you.

vision is what you use to see something clearly. Your central vision consists of a cone of sight measuring just three degrees in width, in the center portion of your line of sight. This is what you use to read the words on this page, and is also used to focus on specific elements of traffic, to estimate distance or view other specific details in traffic.

Peripheral vision refers to everything that is visible beyond the core three degrees of sight. You are unable to focus directly on things that appear in your peripheral vision, but peripheral vision is sensitive to light and movement. Peripheral vision helps you to detect items approaching you from anywhere other than directly in front of you, and in emergency situations will draw your attention to objects of importance that you aren't presently looking directly at. It is important to keep your eyes moving. Although your total field of vision is 180 degrees or more, your eyes effectively use only a small portion of your visual field.

Visual Cues and Eye Movement

As your eyes check out the scene in front of you, there are many factors to observe. The challenge you face as a safe motorcyclist is to filter this scene

and make sure that your eyes pick up on all-important data without being distracted by, or otherwise fixating on, any unimportant factors. A tendency toward such distractions and unnecessary fixations is one of the primary dangers faced by riders with less refined visual habits.

Proper scanning should involve a systematic movement of the eye over the visual scene. Keep your eyes moving, but with purpose. Vision researchers at Ohio State University have developed an eye-movement recording system to determine where motorists look when driving. These researchers found that novice drivers tended to have overactive search patterns and to fixate on unimportant or irrelevant clues. Experienced drivers, they found, evolved a more systematic in-and-out search pattern, where they split their attention between the immediate lane position and intermittent glances to spots further ahead. This is a more effective and safer eye movement pattern.

Developing Good Eye Habits

Experienced motorcycle riders develop habits that allow them to use central and peripheral vision in a complementary manner. Your goal as a safe street rider should be to develop an eye movement pattern that pairs far-ahead glances in the projected path of travel with peripheral vision to identify factors that could affect you.

Knowing this is all well and good, but how exactly do you go about developing these habits? Here are the three core concepts critical to developing good eye habits:

▶ Concentrate your vision on your intended path of travel. Don't let your eyes focus for too long or otherwise become distracted by unimportant objects.

▶ Make a concerted effort to keep your eyes up to keep your field of vision open far ahead of you.

▶ Force your eyes to move frequently so that you receive a wide field of visual information and remain alert to any possible hazards.

If you're doing this effectively, it should feel like your eyes are moving in a series of rapid movements, pausing briefly between movements on objects located in your intended path of travel. These pauses should be very brief, but long enough to gather any essential information before moving along to another area. This allows you to effectively search the entire path of travel every few seconds.

Bad Effects on the Visual Search Process

Your eyes are sensitive organs, and to be most effective they must be well-rested and not compromised by physical limitations that can potentially hinder eye performance. Fatigue is one enemy of good eye habits. Fatigued operators tend to fixate lower and more to the right than well-rested riders, thus limiting their vision to only a small portion of the overall scene.

Alcohol is also extremely detrimental to good eye habits. "An intoxicated person's pupil will slow down and tend to stay fixed longer on an object," explains Jim Ouellet, author of a research paper that investigated alcohol involvement in motorcycle accidents.

What could be better than an afternoon with your bike, your friend, and a cup of your favorite tea? Taking frequent breaks will help keep your energy high.

"In effect, it takes longer to make sense of the things you're looking at, so you can process less information about the things going on around you."

Alcohol-impaired operators tend to fixate straight ahead and don't move their eyes nearly as much as sober riders, resulting in, among other effects, blocking out peripheral inputs (tunnel vision). This also results in the classic fatal DUI scenario of running off a corner at the end of a long straightaway. Crash data indicates that alcohol is a contributing factor in at least 50 percent of all motorcycle crash fatalities—a decreased sensitivity to visual inputs due to drunkenness is one of the primary elements of this. Alcohol also reduces low-light vision, and makes the eyes more reluctant to focus.

Intoxication and fatigue will degrade your ability to see potential hazards and can cause to you engage in more risky riding behavior because you are less aware of these hazards. Getting good visual information is essential for riders—nearly every action you take when riding a motorcycle is based on information that you collected visually. Because of this, it's very important to take every step you can to ensure good vision habits. Avoid riding when you're tired, and never ride under the influence of alcohol or other drugs. Always ride with proper eye protection, keeping your eyes unaffected by wind and debris. Take special care when environmental factors—darkness, fog, glare, or rain—compromise visibility.

Most important, practice, practice, and practice some more at moving your eyes around in your visual field. Good eye habits are not ingrained—these are learned behaviors, and anyone can improve with proper practice. Since your eyes are your first method of defense in avoiding hazards on the highway, the importance of building these skills cannot be overstated.

VISUAL PERCEPTION: THE MECHANICS

Riding a motorcycle is a relatively complicated process involving several complex operations—not the least of which is visually identifying cues in busy traffic environment. This is the "search" function of the human thought process, and it depends on clear, accurate, visual perception.

When we talk about mental perception, we're talking about using the senses to acquire information about the surrounding environment or

Riders should keep their eyes moving throughout the intended path of travel, avoid fixating on any one spot, and look through curves as much as possible.

situation. Good perception means possessing the ability to see and interpret accurately. Perception generally includes a variety of neurological processes for acquiring and mentally interpreting information from all five senses, but because of the unique situation of riding a motorcycle, visual perception is most important to safe riders. Wind and road noise can compromise a rider's ability to hear things, and no one would say that smell or taste are particularly central to riding safely. Visual stimuli are vitally important to riders.

Good eye habits don't just happen—effectively searching your path of travel is not a reflexive action. Visual perception is an active process, not a passive one. For it to work, you have to purposely move your eyes in a systematic fashion to feed your brain enough data to perceive accurately. The more accurate the information you can feed it, the more meaningful your predictions will be, and the more appropriately you will be able to respond to situations ahead and around you.

Successfully piloting a motorcycle in a low-stimulus environment is a relatively simple task. If traffic is

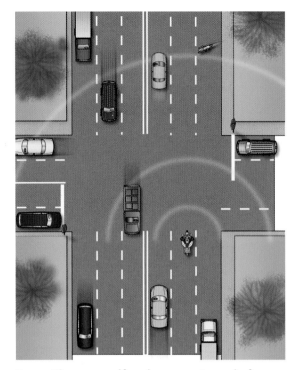

Separating yourself and your motorcycle from other vehicles in the roadway will help you see emerging traffic situations more quickly and accurately, and give you more time and space to respond to any hazards and leave you an escape route.

visual scene. As a result of this, a target-fixated rider tends to steer toward the spot where vision is focused. The result of target fixation is we miss important factors in the riding scene, whether they are debris, another vehicle, or a traffic light.

Lane Positioning

Successful motorcyclists know that capturing other people's attention is affected by how you position yourself within the lane and in the flow of traffic.

The main idea when positioning your motorcycle in traffic is to create a comfortable "space cushion" separating yourself and your motorcycle from the other vehicles on the roadway. This will not only help you see emerging traffic situations more quickly and clearly, but will also give you more time and space to respond to any hazards and leave you the escape route you planned.

Lane Placement

There is no one best lane position—the best position is constantly changing depending on traffic conditions. Here are some considerations that could possibly affect your choice of lane position:

► Increasing your ability to see more

► Increasing your visibility to other motorists

► Avoiding other motorists' blind spots

► Avoiding surface hazards

► Protecting your lane from other drivers

► Communicating your intentions

► Avoiding windblast from other vehicles

► Providing escape routes

► Setting up for and negotiating curves

In general, the best place to be in the flow of traffic is riding near the center of your lane—this position makes you most visible to drivers in front of you, and also leaves a reasonable cushion on both sides for you to respond to any encroachment by surrounding traffic. There are some situations in which you will want to avoid the center of the lane—busy intersections, for example, where oil drippings from cars can make this part of the lane especially slippery. In these cases, you might consider riding in the left portion of the lane. Another time to use this position is when getting ready to

light, weather conditions are good, and visibility and space are favorable, all that is necessary is to choose a clear path and guide your motorcycle along it. Practically anyone with basic skills can accomplish that. It's when a situation becomes more hectic—heavy traffic, bad weather, low light—that the challenge increases and requires excellent mental and physical skills. In situations like these decisions become more critical, and mistakes more costly.

Decisions are based on perceptions and priorities—delayed recognition, attaching incorrect meaning to what you've observed, or any other form of inaccurate perception will start you down a road toward poor decisions, a road that can easily lead to a crash or other unwelcome conclusion.

Keeping your eyes moving, and, more importantly, being able to concentrate in the right place at critical moments, is your best defense against target fixation. Target fixation refers to the phenomenon wherein a rider's vision fixates on an element of the pass. Then again, there are times when you would want to avoid the left track—when riding in the lane to the right of a large truck, for instance. The left wheel track would make you less visible to the truck driver, and more susceptible to the truck's windblast. In this case you might move to the far right edge of the lane, or better, slow down until you were no longer beside the truck.

As you can see, there is not one best lane position—you have to rely on your own judgment and instincts. One absolute is that you should avoid riding in another vehicle's blind spot, the area where you are not visible in any of the mirrors of a vehicle ahead of you. Remember the rule that is helpfully posted on the back of nearly every passing eighteen-wheeler—if you can't see a driver's face in their mirror, he can't see you either.

Following Distance

There's no question when you're following a fire truck or other emergency vehicle—if it says, "Stay back 500 feet," in big letters across the rear bumper, it means "Stay back." Determining the proper following distance behind regular automobiles, in normal day-to-day traffic, takes slightly more care on your part. As a general rule, on good road surfaces in ideal conditions, you should maintain a minimum two-second space cushion between yourself and any vehicle in front of you. Two seconds of space should allow enough time to respond accordingly if the vehicle ahead makes a sudden stop.

In order to establish the two-second space cushion, use a technique called "fixed-object count-off." To do this, pick a fixed object ahead of you—

street signs or light poles work well, as do painted roadway lines. As soon as the vehicle in front of you passes the object, count off: "one-thousand-one, one-thousand-two . . . " If you haven't yet reached the fixed object by the time you finish your two-second count, your following distance meets the two-second minimum. Note the word "minimum." Two seconds is the minimum safe distance to maintain sufficient reaction time. The greater your following distance (there is no rule that reads you must be exactly two seconds behind), the more time you will have to smoothly respond to a situation.

Your following distance should be considered a safety zone, not a safety shield. At highway speeds a two-second window should give you enough time to react to a vehicle you are following. But it will not necessarily give you sufficient space for hazards in front of the vehicle you are following. You'll need much more than two seconds. Remember this and plan your evasive maneuvers accordingly.

Determining an adequate following distance is based in part on a rider's ability to perceive, react, and brake to a safe stop. The more prepared you are, the better you will be able to react in the distance available. Though you should keep a two-second safety cushion between you and the car in front of you, your attention should be much farther ahead. Glancing ahead 12 seconds and actively scanning a four-second immediate path of travel will help you identify hazards before they affect your safety margin.

A two-second following distance is the recommended minimum in ideal conditions. As the vehicle ahead passes a fixed point, count off "one-thousand-one, one-thousand-two"; if you haven't reached the fixed point, the following distance is at least two seconds.

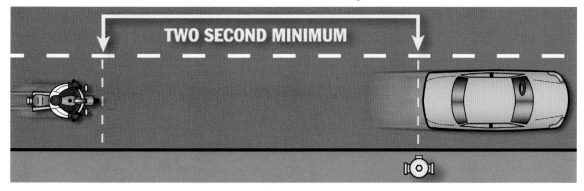

▶ STOPPING DISTANCE

BY RICH OLIVER

Total stopping distance consists of three parts. You can put yourself at an advantage by thinking about how to improve your performance in each of the three parts.

▶ Perception distance is the distance you travel from when factors are developing until you recognize a problem. You can reduce perception distance by seeing the big picture and watching well ahead for factors that could affect your line of sight or a path of travel.

▶ Reaction distance is the distance you travel from when a problem is perceived until braking begins. You can reduce reaction distance by anticipating problems and having a prepared response. For example, covering the brakes or being ready to press in the direction of a swerve can save precious feet that could make a difference.

▶ Braking distance is the distance you travel from when brakes are applied until you are stopped. Braking distance can be improved by having a well-maintained motorcycle and by practicing quick stops often. It is wise to find an empty parking lot to refine good braking skills so an emergency braking response is quick and precise.

A safety margin results mostly from increasing the time and distance to perceive and recognize the often complex interaction of factors. You have the best opportunity to maximize your safety margin by looking for and identifying the factors that could lead to a problem. This way you can adjust speed and lane position to avoid the need to make an emergency reaction.

Keep in mind that carrying a passenger or cargo may increase total stopping distance, because precise operation of the controls may be affected and motorcycle weight distribution is altered. Practice quick stops in a safe area with your passenger to determine the effects on braking and handling.

Realize that, as speed increases, the distance required to stop the motorcycle increases exponentially. It also takes a certain amount of time to react to an emergency situation and make the decision to apply the brakes—that time converts to distance. Given that a motorcycle traveling at 60 mph covers 88 feet per second, you can see that perception- and reaction-time distances quickly add up, emphasizing the importance of considering the three parts of total stopping distance when maintaining your safety margin.

Poor roadway conditions will increase the distance required to come to a stop, so be prepared for longer stops on wet or otherwise slippery surfaces.

To ensure the quickest reaction time and maximum performance in emergency braking situations in real-world traffic, practice the following techniques:

▶ Go to a safe area and practice stopping quickly.

▶ Actively search for potential hazards.

▶ Cover the brakes by lightly resting your fingers over the front brake lever in high-risk areas such as intersections, unfamiliar areas, and any other traffic situations that might require quick stops. This will help to reduce your reaction time when applying the brakes. ■

Rich Oliver is a seven-time national road racing champion with more than 85 professional victories to his credit. He founded the Rich Oliver Mystery School in 2002, teaching his advanced riding techniques to hundreds of professional and recreational riders alike. The Mystery School is located on a 10-acre custom riding facility in Auberry, CA.

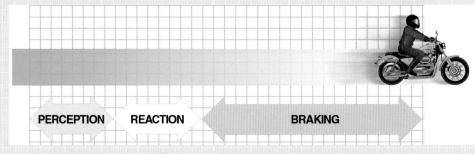

Total stopping distance consists of perception, reaction, and braking distances.

PERCEPTION   REACTION   BRAKING

LEARN TO SEE

SEE is another valuable acronym to add to your mental toolbox. Where T-CLOCS was employed to assist with the pre-ride checking of the motorcycle, and FINE-C gave you a handy way to remember the engine starting routine, SEE gives you the steps to protect yourself in mixed-traffic scenarios. SEE breaks down like this:

► Search

► Evaluate

► Execute

Search

We're already fairly familiar with the "Search" component of the SEE acronym from discussions earlier in this chapter. Search refers to the process of scanning aggressively for potential hazards. Searching provides you with the information necessary for you to make good decisions and take proper action. Remember, good searching extends beyond what is immediately in front of you to include everything 12 seconds in the distance, as well as the areas to the sides and behind you. Check your mirrors frequently as part of your search pattern, and use head checks to monitor blind spots (the areas to the side and behind that the mirrors do not show). Note: many motorcycles have convex mirrors that allow the rider to see farther to the sides, but they can also distort your sense of how far away an object actually is.

Your search efforts are most effective if you are able to prioritize the elements of the traffic environment. There are three primary categories of information that should be monitored as part of your search activity: 1) traffic control devices and markings; 2) road characteristics and surface conditions; and 3) other roadway users. Any one of these three can be more or less important than the others, depending on the situation. Monitor all three of them together, shifting focus as the situation demands, and you will have the information necessary to ride safely.

Remember, the most common area for conflict between yourself and other roadway users is at an intersection. This is where different vehicles cross paths and where communication between roadway users is most critical—and also, most confusing. A

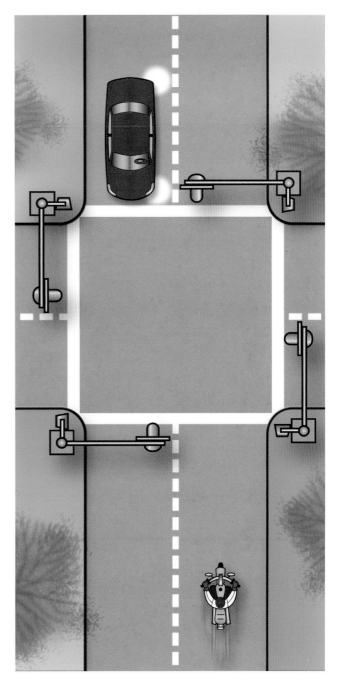

The most common area for conflict between yourself and other roadway users is at an intersection, where communication is most critical—and also, most confusing. A common motorcycle/automobile crash occurs at an intersection when an oncoming vehicle turns left into the path of an approaching motorcycle. Before you enter an intersection, search for oncoming traffic that might turn left in front of you as well as traffic from the left and right and even behind you.

common motorcycle/automobile crash mode is when an oncoming vehicle turns left into the path of an approaching motorcycle. Because of this, using the SEE techniques is especially critical at intersections.

As you approach an intersection, search for the following:

▶ Traffic approaching from behind

▶ Oncoming traffic that might turn left in front of you

▶ Traffic from the left

▶ Traffic from the right

Pay special attention at intersections with limited visibility. Be equally aware of visually "busy" surroundings that could camouflage you and your motorcycle.

Evaluate

To "Evaluate" is to process the information that you gathered using your search patterns. To evaluate means simply to anticipate potential problems and to make plans in your mind to deal with those problems should they actually occur. Evaluating

effectively is a logic puzzle of sorts, a game of figuring out how factors accumulate and interact to create hazards or conflicts.

The fundamental rule of successful evaluation is this: "to get the best results, predict the worst possible outcome." Though this might sound counter-intuitive, predicting a worst-case scenario will help you to best anticipate all possible outcomes. Predict a green traffic light will soon change to red; predict the curve is sharper than it looks; predict that another vehicle will cross into your path.

Evaluate the mix of possible factors that could cause you trouble. Do this by considering potential hazards from these three primary categories:

Traffic Control Devices and Markings Know what your responsibilities are regarding traffic flow as well as what others are supposed to do. But don't count on others being aware of traffic control devices like traffic lights, stop signs, flashing warning lights, etc. Signs and lines help keep traffic separated as well as provide information about lane usage, traffic patterns and pedestrian areas. Get the big picture as you evaluate the situation ahead as well as the space around you.

The minimum safe following distance in dry weather is two seconds. Any closer would be considered tailgating, since you wouldn't have time to brake or swerve in an emergency.

Managing risk while riding means successfully managing time and space to create a safety cushion for you and your motorcycle.

Road Characteristics and Surface

Conditions Consider the type of roadway, such as whether it is hilly or curvy, is made up of two lanes or four, is a one-way or two-way street, is crowned or banked, or has curbs or shoulder areas with minimal or large areas for escape-route possibilities. Also factor in surface conditions in and around your path of travel such as potholes, guardrails, bridges, poles, signposts, or vegetation. Evaluate areas that have fixed objects near the road because they aren't very forgiving if you hit them.

Other Roadway Users Most other vehicles outweigh you and are moving quickly, so think about how they might affect your speed, lane position, or path of travel. Evaluating what might happen well in advance will give you time and space to respond accordingly before you might need emergency reactions. Think too about how pedestrians, bicyclists, and animals may affect your path of travel and space cushion.

Don't think of evaluating outcomes as guessing—think of it as "reading" the situation. Take clues from your surroundings and assemble them into a reasonable scenario as you might assemble random words to create a grammatically correct sentence. Arrange these clues based on the likelihood that they would contribute to a hazard. Ask yourself, "How critical is the hazard? Might it lead to a collision? If so, how probable is that collision? Where would that collision occur? What decisive actions (downshifting, braking, swerving) might I have to take to avoid this sort of collision? What are the potential consequences of this hazard? How might the hazard—or my efforts to avoid it—potentially affect me and other roadway users?" As you can see, your level of riding knowledge and experience is important for this "what if" portion of the SEE process.

This process is called risk management. What risk management really boils down to is successfully managing time and space to create a safety

Executing your decision typically involves changing your speed, your position, or both. Remember to communicate your intentions to other road users whenever possible.

cushion for you and your motorcycle. Categories to consider include: 1) your capabilities and limitations with regard to your skills operating your motorcycle; 2) the capabilities and limitations of your motorcycle; and 3) roadway/traffic conditions. For example, the safety cushion is gone if a required maneuver calls for skills beyond those that you possess or if there is simply not adequate time or space available to complete that maneuver. Your safety cushion evaporates when a situation requires more steering and/or braking than the motorcycle is capable of providing. Your safety cushion is gone if there is no escape path.

Execute

A skilled rider is a decisive rider. Once you've adequately evaluated a situation and decided on a course of action, "Execute" it. Resist the urge to pause or second-guess. Instead forge ahead with your carefully crafted plan of action. Remember, especially in a critical situation, time and space are at a premium. Act decisively and immediately to maximize your response time and keep your safety cushion as large as possible.

Decisions are executed in three ways:

Communication Communication between roadway users is usually initiated through the use of lights or horns, as well as eye contact or other body language. Note that communication is the most passive of all the possible actions that you can take, since it depends entirely on the response of someone else. Use any of these methods to communicate with or attract the attention of other motorists, but don't rely on the actions of others (their response) to ensure your safety.

Adjust Speed Accelerate or slow to avoid a hazard, or, if conditions allow, come to a complete stop.

Adjust Position Change your lane position or change direction.

The degree to which you are able to adjust your lane position or speed depends on how critical the hazard is and on how much time and space you have to make these adjustments. The more time and space available, the less adjustment is required and the less the risk. This is especially important to remember in areas of high potential risk, such as intersections. Give yourself more space and take steps to reduce the time you need to respond when approaching intersections. Remember to cover both brakes and your clutch, and ready your mind with possible escape routes.

Also remember the importance of remaining visible when approaching intersections. One-third of all intersection collisions involve car drivers turning left in front of other drivers. This is especially true with regard to oncoming motorcyclists. The "Hurt Report" states, "The failure of motorists to detect and recognize motorcycles in traffic is the predominating cause of motorcycle accidents. The driver of the other vehicle involved in a collision with the motorcycle did not see the motorcycle before the collision, or did not see the motorcycle until too late to avoid the collision." Remain extra-alert in these situations.

Learn to SEE better. Commit the SEE acronym to memory, and make this strategy second nature for you so that you unconsciously go through the process every time you ride. Gather good information, process that information properly, and make the best decision to ensure your own safety—whether it involves oncoming traffic or not. Take steps to actively manage your situation—don't put yourself at the mercy of other roadway users. Understand completely the importance of timing, positioning,

and the use of space. Ride defensively. Assume that you are completely invisible to other vehicle operators, and respond accordingly. Control your ride—don't let your ride control you.

MOTORCYCLING EXCELLENCE MEANS:

▶ Your mind is active and attentive on every ride.

▶ You make choices to be as visible (conspicuous) as possible in traffic.

▶ You are constantly looking for factors that could affect you, especially around intersections.

▶ You improve your street strategies by learning more about safe riding practices.

▶ You are constantly searching for clues that could affect your choice of speed, lane position, or path of travel.

▶ You understand the best line of defense in avoiding trouble in traffic is to be skilled in the use of your eyes and mind; you search for clues that could affect you, evaluate the interaction of factors, and execute controlled responses with precision.

As an alternative to making a bar their destination, this riding club had an alcohol-free picnic at a local park.

► DETECTION PROBLEMS

There is a reason that all those pro-motorcyclist bumper stickers carry the same simple message (Start SEEING Motorcyclists!)—two-wheeled travelers have a tendency to disappear from the radar screen of most drivers. Why is this the case? There is no solid answer, but there are at least three potential factors that contribute to this lack of detection:

Size differences   Drivers truly fail to detect motorcyclists in a busy, target-rich traffic environment, because motorcycles are narrow.

Human visual-perception limits   Drivers observe the motorcyclist, but fail to attach valid meaning to him or her. As a result, their matching, comparing and association of the information they gather yields inaccurate conclusions.

Associations   Or, more accurately, dissociations. In this case, the driver sees a motorcycle, and then identifies it in the same category as a bicycle or moped. As a result, the approaching motorcyclist isn't viewed as a safety threat.

Defenses Against Faulty Detection

Fortunately, lack of detection (on the part of other drivers) is a treatable condition. A research study completed some years ago by the University of Michigan identified a range of detectability treatments for both the motorcyclist and the motorcycle itself. These treatments were later evaluated in a study funded by the NHTSA titled "Effects of Motorcycle and Motorcyclists' Conspicuity on Driver Behavior." This study found three treatments to be especially effective:

- ► Riding with the motorcycle headlight illuminated

- ► Wearing a bright-colored helmet and high-visibility fabric on the rider's upper torso

- ► Modulating the headlight beam (if legal in your state)

Regardless of what strategies you choose, maximizing your visibility to other motorists should remain a priority whenever you ride. To even stand a chance that other motorists won't turn in front of

Studies show that wearing high-vis clothing, especially on your upper torso, increases your conspicuity considerably.

you, you first have to make sure that they see you. Remember the importance of dressing in high-visibility riding gear, and consider fitting your motorcycle with a headlight modulator (if these are legal in your state). These strategies aren't guarantees that you will be seen, but they have been scientifically proven effective to increase your conspicuity. Every little bit helps.

Increasing this conspicuity is an important part of riding safely, but don't rely on these techniques exclusively. The best advice is still to "trust no one." You are ultimately the only person responsible for ensuring your own well-being in traffic.

In addition to doing everything you can to make yourself visible, master and maintain your own detection skills as outlined earlier in this chapter, so you can create a safety margin and avoid hazardous situations, and successfully escape these situations should you somehow become entangled in one. ■

STAYING SAFE ON A MOTORCYCLE BOILS DOWN TO AVOIDING TROUBLE BY HAVING TIME AND SPACE FOR YOURSELF.

You might expect that interstate highways, twisty back roads, or anyplace else where you might ride at a higher rate of speed are the most dangerous environments for motorcyclists.

Actually, studies indicate that most crashes occur within the first 15 minutes of a ride, at intersections or driveways, and at speeds under 40 mph.

We've all got our own special nicknames we use to refer to dangerous drivers—most of which are not suitable to print on the pages of this book. On the next few pages we've given the most egregious offenders titles more appropriate for polite company, then we've described the situations where you are most likely to encounter these sorts of drivers. We also examined ways that you can use SEE and other safe-riding skills to stay out of trouble when interacting with these caged menaces. The idea is not to call people names or play a blame game, but to maintain a safer riding environment for everyone.

THE SHARK

Imagine a typical scene from a nature-network documentary, one that shows a fur seal frantically swimming with a great white shark in ruthless pursuit, the huge snout of the shark filling the television screen. In the corresponding street scene, you're riding your motorcycle down a wide arterial street when a huge sedan closes in on you, its grille filling your mirrors. Just as you change lanes to get out of this car-shark's path, the tailgater also changes lanes behind you. What are your best strategies for avoiding (or evading) this situation?

Statistics show that intersections are the most dangerous place for a motorcycle. This chapter describes strategies for staying safe.

Strategy: As soon as you notice a tailgater approaching in your mirrors, take steps to get out of the way. Activate your turn signal and make an obvious, decisive lane change to the right or left. If the car is already upon you before you notice its presence, take care before making a move to avoid the "shark pursuit" situation described above. When evading a shark, signal early and pause for just an

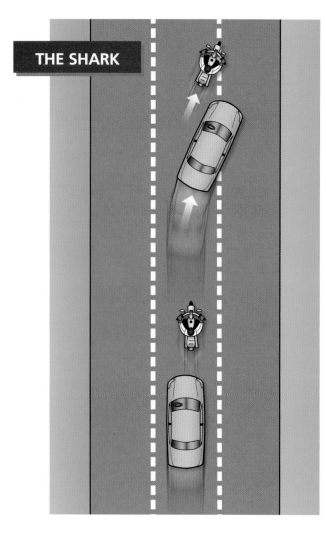

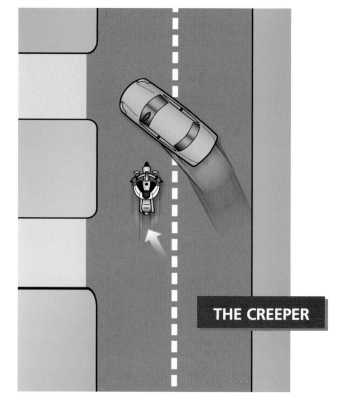

THE SHARK

instant (to make sure that the tailing driver isn't also planning to change into the same lane) before making a definite and decisive move into the other lane. Your actions should clearly communicate your intentions to the other driver so he is fully aware of what moves you intend to make.

THE CREEPER

Riding along a suburban street, you approach a slow-moving car. You would like to pass, but the driver keeps speeding up and slowing down, causing you to delay that action. After following the creeper for several blocks, you become frustrated and decide to accelerate by. As soon as you pull out to pass the creeper, the driver makes a sudden left turn into a driveway, leaving you no room to stop or swerve.

Strategy: The car's erratic pace should have tipped you off that the driver was searching for something (a street address, perhaps) and that her attention was elsewhere rather than on surrounding traffic. Evaluating the situation, you should have predicted that the driver might turn or stop suddenly. Your best strategy in a situation like this is to separate yourself from the hazard. You could have dropped back at least two seconds. If you choose to pass, do so only after clearly establishing contact with the driver, preferably after receiving a hand signal from her. Never pass at an intersection or other traffic situation where the car could turn in front of you.

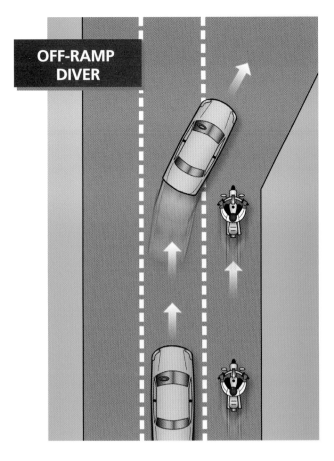

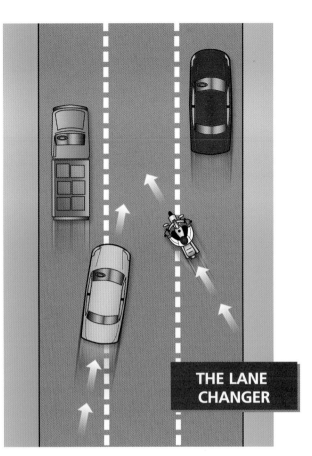

OFF-RAMP DIVER

You are riding along an urban freeway, in the far right lane. Just as you approach an off-ramp, a car in the lane to your left dives in front of you, braking hard to make the off-ramp at the last possible moment. You have very little room to brake or swerve, and a crash may be imminent.

Strategy: When you see an off-ramp ahead, glance around you and evaluate the situation. Do you see any cars around you that might exit? Are you doing anything that might cause other drivers to expect you to exit? Since you are riding along in what is the exit lane, other drivers may assume that you are going to exit as well—an assumption that might affect their movements. Off-ramps (and on-ramps) are prime locations for vehicular conflicts. When approaching a ramp, it is often a good idea to move out of the exit/entrance lane. Take steps to avoid riding in the blind spots of cars traveling around you. In this situation, the driver might not have known that you were even between him and the exit, if you were in his blind spot.

THE LANE CHANGER

While riding in the right lane of a three-lane highway, you decide to pass a slower-moving car by changing lanes to your left. Just as you begin to move left, a car in the far left lane also decides to pass by moving to the right, and suddenly the two of you are fighting for the same lane. When it's car-versus-bike, you already know the outcome.

Strategy: By actively searching the present traffic environment you should have observed the car two lanes over, and predicted that the driver would end up in your target lane if she decided to change lanes and pass at the same time you did. Separate yourself from the hazard: either wait a few moments to pass, until the car in the far left lane has moved ahead, or slow down to drop back a car length. It is also a wise tactic to signal several seconds before making a move, and to turn your head occasionally to check your blind spot to better observe surrounding traffic.

THE REAR-ENDER

It's the soundtrack to every motorcyclist's nightmare: you're sitting astride your bike at an intersection, patiently waiting for the red light to change to green, when you hear the screech of tires. Next you're flying through the air and into the intersection. You've just been rear-ended by an inattentive driver who was too busy dialing his cell phone to notice you stopped at the red light.

Strategy: Remember, even to attentive drivers, motorcycles are difficult to see—especially at night. Remain aware of the fact that drivers approaching an intersection may not see you. Frequently check your mirrors to monitor traffic approaching from the rear, keeping an eye out for fast-moving traffic approaching from behind. Flash your brake light. If you do notice a car speeding toward you, move to one side or another to get out of its way. Don't shift into neutral when stopped at an intersection. Keep your bike in gear, so you can quickly escape if a dangerous situation arises.

(Above) In crowded urban traffic, you should continuously search around you for potential hazards and vehicles changing lanes.

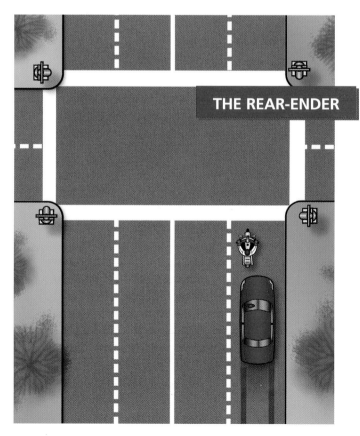

THE REAR-ENDER

THE SLEEPY COMMUTER

You're riding your motorcycle to work just after sunrise, traveling down a typical suburban street lined with car-filled driveways. As you approach one of these driveways a car begins to move and backs out directly into your path. You brake hard and come to a stop just inches away from its rear bumper.

Strategy: Given the hour of day and the type of neighborhood, you could have expected to encounter at least a few drivers backing out of their driveways and heading off to work. Other clues include drivers getting into their cars as you approach, or a tell-tale puff of exhaust warning you that the car has been started and is preparing to leave. Watch for brake lights and backup lights, too.

If you observe any of the above warning signs, take the following precautions: Slow your pace and prepare to stop, if necessary. Keep your eyes up and cover the front brake lever and rear brake pedal. Stabilize your speed so that if the car does begin to move out into your path, you have sufficient space to stop. If there isn't room or time to slow to a stop, scan for an escape route to swerve into. If there is no oncoming traffic, swerve to the left; if this route isn't available, consider swerving to the right.

THE BASIC LEFT-TURNER

Approaching a busy four-way intersection there are a lot of elements to monitor: cross traffic may or may not stop for the light; pedestrians could step out at any time; an oncoming car waiting to turn left could fail to detect your presence and turn left in front of you. Sure enough, just as you approach the intersection, the car in the opposing left-turn lane swings into your path. You brake hard and swerve at the last second, barely avoiding a broadside collision.

Strategy: Without a doubt, this scenario is a frequent hazard for motorcyclists riding in urban areas. A common type of motorcycle crash (for sober riders) occurs during daylight hours, at low speeds (around 30 mph), when an oncoming vehicle turns left into your path. Again, when approaching an intersection with a vehicle waiting in the left-turn lane, your best bet is to assume the worst: that a car will pull out in front of you. Reduce your speed as you approach the intersection,

THE SLEEPY COMMUTER

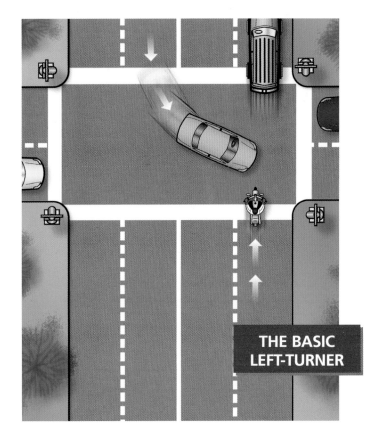

THE BASIC LEFT-TURNER

THE HIDDEN LEFT-TURNER

obscured by another (usually larger) vehicle. For this reason, it is never a good idea to follow too closely behind a larger vehicle. Foreseeing this situation, you should have slowed and increased your following distance, moving back to where you could better see and be seen.

A similar situation can occur when vehicles are waiting on both sides of an intersection to make left turns. Occasionally, if you are passing to the right of a vehicle that is waiting to turn left, especially if that vehicle is a truck or other large vehicle, you and your motorcycle can be obscured from the sight of the oncoming vehicle waiting to turn, causing that person to turn out into your path. Remain aware of this possibility, and prepare accordingly when passing vehicles that are waiting to turn left.

either downshifting or lightly applying the front brake. Adjust your position in the lane to be seen better. Slowing will increase your safety cushion: slowing just 10 mph reduces your stopping distance significantly, and covering your brake greatly reduces reaction time. After you've slowed, continue to visually monitor the car in case it moves and forces you to change position or stop quickly.

THE HIDDEN LEFT-TURNER

You're riding in heavy traffic, in position behind an eighteen-wheeler. The eighteen-wheeler travels through an intersection. You follow behind, when suddenly a car from the opposite direction appears in front of you, attempting a quick turn to go behind the semi. With virtually no time to react, you hit the car just ahead of its front wheel and go sailing over the hood, giving your helmet its first road test.

Strategy: This is a variation of the "Basic Left-Turner," only instead of the offending vehicle failing to distinguish you in the larger traffic pattern, in this scenario you and your motorcycle are

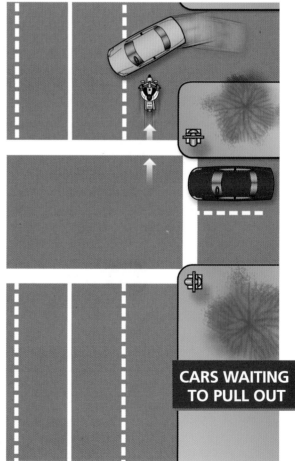

CARS WAITING TO PULL OUT

CARS WAITING TO PULL OUT

Riding along a wide arterial street, with an uninterrupted view of traffic ahead of you, you observe a minivan waiting to pull out of a shopping center parking lot. You make eye contact with the driver, and visually confirm that the vehicle is not moving. But just as you are about to pass the shopping center exit, the driver accelerates into your path.

Strategy: Though we tend to focus our attention at intersections in an urban environment, there are also potential danger zones between intersections, as this example illustrates. These are situations where the small profile of a motorcycle can be problematic. Drivers waiting to pull out may not even see you approaching in the busy traffic environment. Even if they do "see" you, they may fail to accurately judge your closing speed, as occurred in the above example. Eye contact in this situation can be misleading.

Have an open area scoped out in case you need to take evasive action when approaching any vehicle that could pull out into your path. As you approach,

THE ONE-WAY STREET

(Below) Approach every intersection with your senses alert. Search for other vehicles and try to anticipate what each one will do.

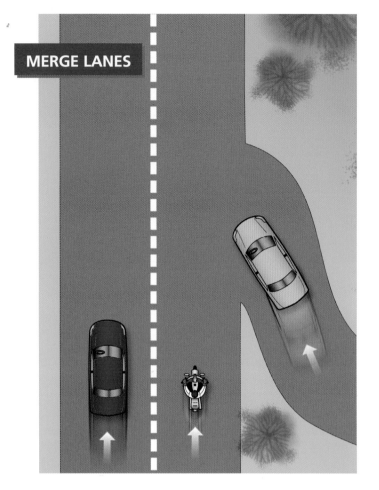

MERGE LANES

(without signaling), inadvertently trapping you in his path. There was no way, short of watching for the non-existent signal, to predict that this driver was going to turn left. But remembering that intersections are always situations of increased risk, you might have prepared for this by taking actions to separate yourself from the other vehicle. By riding so close (and inside the driver's blind spot) you effectively hid yourself from the driver's vision and greatly increased your exposure to danger.

SEE THROUGH DANGER

Successfully negotiating any of the above situations is largely a matter of observing the SEE protocol to decide how best to deal with an approaching hazard, then acting with skill and control to make the proper maneuver. Here are some further examples of how you might apply the SEE approach to some common street situations. Remember that these are just examples—not universal solutions. Every situation you encounter while riding will be different and require its own unique response. What is important here is learning to apply this protocol in order to execute sound decisions. With that in mind, here are some common traffic situations that might pose a hazard to motorcyclists, followed by suggestions of how SEE can be used to best negotiate these.

check the vehicle's front tire, which will provide your first indication that the car is starting to move. Any step that you can take to increase your visibility to other drivers (wearing a bright-colored helmet or jacket and using your high-beam during daytime) is especially helpful in situations like this. If it's clear the other driver doesn't see you, honk your horn! (Just be ready in case the driver doesn't hear it.)

THE ONE-WAY STREET

You are riding along in the left lane of a one-way street, with a car ahead of you on your right. As the two of you enter an intersection, the car swerves left across your path to make a turn.

Strategy: Because traffic was light, the driver may have forgotten that he was traveling on a one-way street and never looked in his blind spot for you. Since there was no traffic in the oncoming lane, he felt free to make a normal left turn

MERGE LANES

Search: You are traveling along a four-lane divided highway, approaching an on-ramp entering from your right. Searching within the traffic pattern, you notice a car passing in the lane to your left, and also a car entering from the ramp.

Evaluate: You determine that that vehicle approaching from the right will enter the lane precisely as you and the adjacent vehicle arrive at the point of intersection. To account for this, you decide to increase your space cushion by reducing your speed, allowing the merging vehicle to enter and also allowing the adjacent vehicle to pass.

Execute: Smoothly roll off the throttle or gently apply the brakes, but not before checking your mirrors and blind spots to make sure there aren't vehicles following close behind. Continue the SEE process.

CURVED ROADS

CURVED ROADS

Search: While taking a Sunday morning jaunt along a curving mountain road, you come upon a series of tight tree-lined curves that you can't see beyond. Recognize that there may be hidden hazards lurking around the next blind curve. Remember, under ideal circumstances you should search 12 or more seconds out. Here visibility is limited to a four second immediate path of travel, so you need to plan accordingly.

Evaluate: Consider any unknown hazards (such as slower traffic, surface irregularities, rocks, animals, etc.) that could be present in the upcoming path of travel. Decide to increase the amount of time and space available for you to react by slowing your speed until you have passed through the section of curves.

Execute: Roll off the throttle to reduce your speed and move to the center lane position, both being actions that increase your space cushion to oncoming traffic or other unseen hazard. Continue the SEE process.

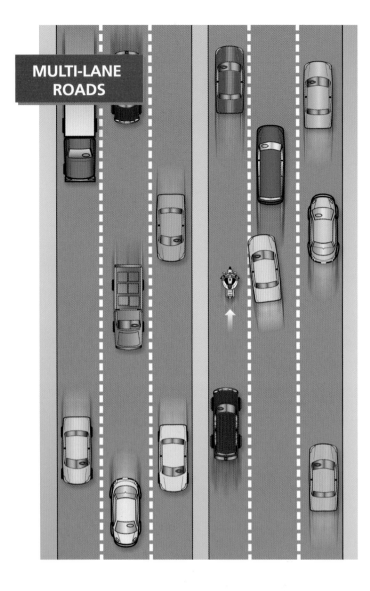

MULTI-LANE ROADS

MULTI-LANE ROADS

Search: You are traveling along a multi-lane highway in heavy traffic. Following distances are very close and your space cushion is reduced. Searching this chaotic traffic pattern, you observe all of the following hazards: other vehicles, reduced space cushion, inadequate following distances, and reduced space to both sides. A hurried-looking driver is in the lane to your right, tailgating the car ahead of him and obviously looking for an opportunity to pass. He begins to change lanes into the space that you presently occupy.

Evaluate: Immediate action is required. Decide to communicate with the other driver and take action to protect your space.

Execute: Execute by sounding your horn. Steer to adjust your position away from the offending automobile, cover your brakes and clutch, slowing or speeding up as necessary to avoid the car. Continue to SEE.

BLIND HILL

Search: You approach a hill. Similar to the "curved road" scenario described above, here the hill again reduces your available field of vision to less than the optimum 12 seconds, and could potentially hide unknown hazards ahead.

Evaluate: Recognizing this reduced visibility, you predict that as you crest the hill an unknown obstacle (a child in the street, for example) might appear

BLIND HILL

in your path of travel. Accordingly, you choose to increase the space and time for you to react by reducing speed and moving to the center of your lane.

Execute: Roll off the throttle to slow slightly; cover the brakes and clutch in case braking or downshifting will be required to make a more drastic reduction in speed. Steer to the center of the lane. Continue the SEE process.

PASSING OTHER VEHICLES

Search: Traveling again along a two-lane state highway, you approach a slow-moving vehicle and make a decision to pass. Passing on a motorcycle is not substantially different than passing in a car, though (as is always the case on a motorcycle) taking steps to ensure your own visibility is more important when you are riding. Take every possible step to be sure the driver you are overtaking is aware of you.

Evaluate: Make sure there is a good opportunity to pass. Check for oncoming traffic, and gauge whether or not there is sufficient clear roadway available to complete the passing maneuver safely.

Execute: Once you have determined that it is safe to pass: move to the left portion of the lane, at a safe following distance. This will increase your line of sight, and also make you more visible. Signal and perform a final traffic check, remembering to glance in your mirrors and also make a head check to look for traffic approaching from behind. Move into the left lane and accelerate. Select a lane position that maintains a sufficient space cushion between you and the car you are passing, but that also leaves you the space to avoid hazards that may appear in the oncoming lane. Signal to return to your lane, and check your mirrors and perform a head check to make sure you won't cut off the car you just passed before returning to your lane. Resume SEEing.

TAILGATERS

Search: Traveling along a crowded, multi-lane highway, in your mirrors you notice a truck following very, very closely.

Evaluate: Traffic is very heavy, and slowing and speeding up somewhat erratically. You predict that

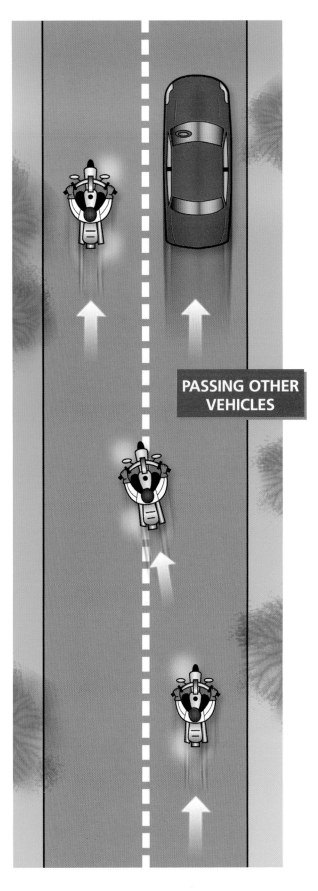

PASSING OTHER VEHICLES

It all comes together when you're in sync with your surroundings: proper lane positioning, adequate following distance, and continuous application of Search, Evaluate, Execute.

you may need to brake hard and that the vehicle behind you might not have enough room in which to brake hard without hitting you. With traffic to both sides, you are unable to change lanes. You decide that alternate actions must be taken to increase the distance between you and the tailgating driver.

Execute: In this situation you have a range of options available to you; some will be better than others depending on the individual situation: 1) flash your brake light to communicate to the tailgater; 2) gradually reduce your speed, which will increase your space to the front, lessening the likelihood of your having to brake dramatically; 3) look for (or

create through signaling or manipulating your speed) an opportunity to change into another lane, allowing the tailgater to pass you and continue on his hurried way.

MOTORCYCLING EXCELLENCE MEANS:

▶ You keep plenty of time and space available to respond to traffic.

▶ You are quick to spot trouble and have a defensive strategy to deal with hazards and conflicts in traffic.

▶ You assess the big picture (bird's eye view) in traffic by searching at least 12 seconds ahead.

THE UNEXPECTED HAPPENS.
ARE YOU READY FOR IT?

"Expect the unexpected"—this is an important phrase to keep in mind whenever you ride a motorcycle. We've already established, through the numerous examples cited earlier in this book, that the street is an unpredictable place for a motorcyclist. Unaware motorists, dirt and debris, animals, pedestrians and other hazards give motorcyclists plenty of reasons to pay attention. The street can be a scary place to ride if you don't have the necessary traffic management and hazard avoidance skills, and the confidence that comes from practicing those skills, in order to control your machine in any situation.

Helping you to build a comprehensive motorcycle riding skill set that can be applied effectively in most riding situations is the purpose of the material presented in this book, and each individual basic riding skill that we have presented up to this point forms the solid foundation on which the entire skill set rests. While these basic skills are essential for safe, confident performance in ordinary situations, sometimes—when any of the above-mentioned hazards come into play, for example—events shift beyond the parameters of ordinary and become extraordinary, and potentially dangerous if you're not prepared to respond defensively. Such extraordinary situations demand refined riding skills with specific techniques used in emergency and hazard-avoidance maneuvers that will help you better handle the unexpected on the road when things get hairy. A cool head, a bit of common

With factors such as inattentive motorists, animals, pedestrians, and dirt and debris, the road an be a scary place if you don't have adequate searching and hazard-avoidance skills, and the confidence to use them in any situation.

sense, and knowledge of how your bike behaves at the extremes will go a long way toward avoiding the ill effects of these common surprises. Here are some of the special situations that you might encounter, and tips on how to negotiate or prepare for them.

SWERVING

You typically have two choices when confronting an obstacle in your path—stopping or swerving. A motorcycle's maneuverability makes swerving a

A swerve is basically two consecutive quick countersteers. The first of these turns is to swing out and avoid the obstacle; the second turn is made after you have cleared the hazard, returning you back to your original direction of travel.

valuable and primary hazard-avoidance technique that all riders need to practice and use. In situations when you are traveling at higher speeds or when you aren't confident that traffic behind you will also stop, swerving around a hazard (if space allows) may be your best solution.

Think of a swerve as two consecutive quick turns (countersteers). The first of these turns is to swing out and avoid the obstacle; the second turn is made after you have cleared the hazard, returning you back to your original direction of travel. You'll learn more about countersteering in later chapters.

Remember, especially in a situation that requires immediate action (such as swerving around an obstacle), that a motorcycle steers by countersteering. To swerve left, press the left handgrip first, then press the right handgrip to complete the swerve and return to your original path of travel. To swerve right, press the right handgrip first, then press the left handgrip to complete the swerve. No matter which way you wish to swerve, the initial press must be deliberately firm to cause the motorcycle to lean and swerve quickly.

Allow the motorcycle to lean independently of your body when you swerve, by keeping your torso upright and letting the motorcycle to move freely beneath you. This will allow the motorcycle to turn more quickly. Stabilize your body by bracing your knees against the fuel tank, and keep your feet planted on the footrests. Avoid target fixating on the hazard you are attempting to avoid; instead look directly where you want to go (your escape path).

Finally, maintain constant throttle and never brake while you swerve. Swerving requires a quick turn, which demands maximum traction—any braking input at this point could overwhelm available traction and cause a skid or crash. If you need to slow, separate your braking from your swerving. Brake before you initiate the swerve while the motorcycle is still upright, or swerve first, then brake once the swerve is complete and the motorcycle is again upright.

Swerving is a very useful skill for a safe rider to possess. Remember, the likelihood that you will need to employ this skill could be greatly reduced if you consistently practice SEE to identify potential obstacles before you reach them—before a last-minute swerve is your only alternative.

MAXIMUM OR EMERGENCY BRAKING

Stopping your motorcycle in the shortest possible distance is another valuable skill that street riders need. When an obstacle appears in front of you and swerving is not an option because there are no escape routes available (a piece of furniture falls off of the truck in front of you), then stopping becomes your only option to avoid a collision.

The term "maximum braking" is used when both brakes are applied as firmly as possible without locking up either wheel, typically in an emergency situation. To achieve maximum braking, simultaneously squeeze the front brake and clutch levers, and press the rear brake pedal with firm pressure. Apply the brakes smoothly—avoid "grabbing" or "stabbing" the brakes, as the harsh application is more likely to cause a skid or other upset to the chassis. During maximum braking, keep the motorcycle in as straight a line as possible to reduce lean angle and the likelihood of the wheels losing traction. Remember, if either wheel is skidding, maximum braking power is not being applied to the road surface. Keep your body centered over the motorcycle and look well ahead, not down.

Maximum braking, like swerving, is a critical skill that should be practiced. It is wise to occasionally go to a clear (not wet or oily), safe area and practice maximum braking maneuvers to accustom yourself to how much braking force can be applied before your wheels begin to skid. This is especially the case if you have recently purchased a new or different motorcycle and need to discover its unique braking characteristics.

STOPPING IN A CURVE

Braking in a curve requires special care because any time the motorcycle is leaned over, the amount of traction available to transfer braking force is reduced. The more extreme the lean angle, the greater the possibility of the tires losing traction (see Chapters 11 and 12 for a more detailed discussion of traction). The secret to stopping quickly (and safely) in a curve is to have enough room to get the motorcycle perpendicular to the road as quickly as possible to maximize the traction available for braking. If road and traffic conditions permit, stand the motorcycle upright, "square" the handlebars, and apply the brakes just as you would for a maximum-braking, straight-line stop.

Of course, conditions might not allow for a straight-line stop—doing so in a left-hand curve might find you running off the road; in a right-hander you might meet oncoming traffic. If either of these situations is present, your only course of action is to apply the brakes as smoothly and gradually as you can while the bike is still leaning. As you slow, your lean angle can be reduced, and as the lean angle reduces you will have more traction available for braking and you will be able to more firmly apply the brakes. By the time you come to a stop, the motorcycle should be straight up and down, handlebars squared.

CONTROLLING SKIDS

Though the first time it happens it will no doubt be alarming, a skidding tire isn't necessarily a hazardous situation, and certainly no reason for undue panic. Knowing what actions to take will help you avoid a panic response, and allow you to correct the skid with a minimum of drama. Which particular corrective action you should take if your motorcycle does start skidding will vary depending on which wheel is skidding.

If you need to make a quick lane change—to avoid vehicles that are slowing or merging, or objects in the roadway—swerve with two quick countersteers (see Chapter 13).

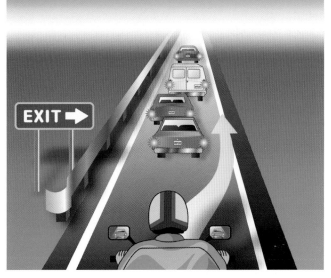

Always remember that traction is limited. If you must brake and swerve, separate the two.

Rear-wheel skids are more common during sudden, maximum braking. In simplified terms, this is because during deceleration (due to braking force) much of the load on the rear wheel transfers to the front wheel, decreasing the amount of traction available to the rear tire, making it easier for the rear wheel to lose traction and stop spinning (skid).

Every braking situation is unique, depending on the geometry and mass of the motorcycle involved, the road surface, the tires, and the speed. It's difficult to recommend one ideal solution to every rear-wheel skid.

If you lock up the rear wheel under heavy braking, try to relax—the rear wheel may "fish-tail" a bit while skidding, but by looking well ahead to maintain a straight-ahead path, you are likely to be able to bring the motorcycle to a stop without problems.

However, the key to safely recovering from a rear-wheel skid is gauging the alignment of the bike's wheels and anticipating the effect that alignment will have if the braking dynamic is changed. As a rule of thumb, the farther out-of-line the rear wheel is relative to the front wheel, and the greater the momentum (a function of speed and mass) of the motorcycle, the more sensitive the situation is.

For example, if under hard braking from highway speed the rear wheel skids and becomes substantially out-of-line ("sliding out"), then suddenly regaining traction on the rear wheel (by releasing the rear brake pedal) can have dire consequences. Upon regaining rear-wheel traction, the momentum of the now-sideways motorcycle can force it to quickly straighten up and "high-side," or crash by falling over in the direction of the skid. Not an ideal outcome!

If you find yourself in this situation, keep the rear wheel locked (skidding) until the motorcycle has come to a complete stop (see illustration). Try to relax—the rear wheel may "fish-tail" a bit while skidding, but by looking well ahead to maintain a straight-ahead path, you are likely to be able to bring the motorcycle to a stop without falling victim to a "high-side" crash.

You should only consider releasing the rear brake in the event of a rear-wheel skid at low speeds if the motorcycle is nearly upright with the front and rear wheels very nearly aligned.

Front-wheel skids are a different matter. The front wheel may lock up, or skid, if the brake lever is grabbed abruptly and high braking force is applied before the front tire gains extra traction due to the load transfer from rear to front wheel. As the weight then transfers forward on a tire that has broken traction (is skidding), the front wheel "washes out" and can cause a "low-side" crash in which the motorcycle and the rider fall over together away from the direction of the skid.

In this situation, immediately release the front brake to allow the front tire to regain traction. Then reapply the front brake. Use a firm, progressive squeeze on the brake lever, applying more pressure as weight transfers to the front wheel, making more traction available.

While front- and rear-wheel skids can be controlled, it is clearly better to avoid them altogether. Practice your maximum braking technique—especially on a new or unfamiliar motorcycle—in an empty parking lot or other safe area with a good road surface, and use SEE to deal with potential hazards before they cause you to skid.

SURMOUNTING OBSTACLES

In some situations, neither braking nor swerving is a reasonable option. While a motorcycle is clearly no match for another vehicle or even most animals, some obstacles that appear suddenly in your path can be easily surmounted. You can easily ride over a piece of lumber that falls off a truck or a small pothole, for example, if you take proper care.

Once you have determined that there is no other recourse but to ride over the obstacle, prepare as follows: adjust your path of travel so that you approach the obstacle at as close as possible to a 90-degree angle. As you near the object, rise slightly off the seat. Next, shift your weight rearward and roll on the throttle slightly. This will lighten the front end and let you use your legs as an "extra set of shock absorbers" and allow you to ride over the obstacle. Keep your knees bent slightly and braced against the tank. Roll off the throttle after the front wheel crosses the obstacle. When the rear wheel comes into contact with the obstacle, expect the rear of the motorcycle to rise also as it clears the hazard.

STARTING ON A HILL

Skill and coordination are required to start out on an uphill grade. A good technique is to apply a brake to prevent the motorcycle from rolling backward while you move the clutch lever to the friction zone. Often the rear brake is used. But if you need to keep both feet down for balance, you could use the front brake while easing out the clutch lever into the friction zone until you can release the brake and apply some throttle. Keeping the clutch lever in the friction zone can hold the motorcycle in position until you are underway. It may be helpful to use more throttle than when starting out on a level surface. Also, you may have to stay in the friction zone longer to get moving. Practice the technique in low-traffic areas to develop the skill and coordination.

POOR ROAD SURFACES

A public highway is an unpredictable place. Even familiar stretches can seem like a foreign land at times. Conditions can change from day to day, depending upon weather, road use, or other unpredictable factors. When it comes to surfaces on new or unfamiliar roads you must be prepared and

To surmount an obstacle, slow as much as traffic and time permit, approach at a 90-degree angle if possible, rise slightly off the seat and keep your knees bent. Squeeze both handgrips firmly, shift your weight to the rear, and slightly roll on the throttle just before the front wheel contacts the obstacle. Upon contact, roll off the throttle. Keep your eyes up looking well ahead.

Special skill is required to start out on a hill. A good technique is to apply the rear brake to prevent the motorcycle from rolling backward while you ease out the clutch into the friction zone. If you need to keep both feet down for balance, use the front brake lever while easing out the clutch until you can release the brake and apply some throttle.

ready for anything. You never know what surprises lurk around yonder bend. Sound knowledge combined with a good riding strategy is essential for handling some common poor roadway surface conditions that you should be prepared to encounter:

Loose Surfaces/Debris This not only includes the obvious variations in roadway surfaces like gravel roads, but also corners on twisty back roads where other vehicles may have kicked up gravel and dirt from the shoulder and into the cornering line, wet leaves, or the areas near the bottom of

Bridge surfaces often present changes in road surface, and can be slippery when wet. Use SEE and slow before reaching the bridge, and avoid sudden changes in speed or direction while on the bridge surface.

hills where sand and other debris tend to gather after a rain. Reduce speed to create a margin of safety and stay upright, minimizing lean. Also watch for glass, metal, or other sharp debris in these areas that could cause a puncture.

Spills Sand, gravel, diesel fuel, oil, coolant, or any number of other liquids and that could spill out of another vehicle and onto the roadway and create a slick spot. Make it a regular part of your SEE process to search the road for spills like these, and if you do notice anything irregular, make any speed or direction adjustments before you reach the spill.

Rain Grooves Rain grooves that cut into the surface of the pavement do not reduce traction, but they will give a slightly loose feel to your motorcycle as you cross them. Scan for them and adjust accordingly so that they don't take you by surprise and cause you to overreact.

Bridge Gratings The coefficient of friction between rubber and steel (like that which bridge gratings are made from) is significantly lower than that of rubber on asphalt, especially when wet. In other words, less traction is available. Slow as you approach these, and make any speed or direction changes before you reach the grating. Once you are riding across the bridge grating, keep your speed steady and don't make sudden changes in speed or direction.

Bumps, Cracks, and Tracks Although most bumps and cracks are small enough that you barely notice them, sometimes they can be big enough to be considered obstacles, such as where winter ice

and tree roots break up the pavement. If you encounter a bump like this, prepare just as you would for surmounting an obstacle and cross at as close to a 90-degree angle as possible. If necessary, rise off the seat as you go over them. For railroad crossings, it is usually safe to ride straight within your lane to cross the tracks. For track and road seams that run parallel to your path, move far enough away from the tracks to cross at an angle of at least 45 degrees, then make a quick, sharp turn.

Crowned Roads/Worn Pavement
Heavy traffic often creates tire wells in the lane where automobile and truck tires meet the pavement, and a corresponding crown in the center of the road between the two tracks. Rain (or debris) can accumulate in the low spots. A crowned road can reduce the amount of available lean angle in some corners or otherwise affect cornering. Adjust your path of travel accordingly.

Icy or Slick Surfaces Ice and snow, moss, wet leaves, mud, crack sealant, tar snakes (tar-filled surface cracks), and some road paints—can be slippery, especially at extreme (hot or cold) temperatures. Avoid them whenever possible.

Rain The first few minutes after rain begins to fall is the most hazardous time for motorcycle riders—any oil or other foreign matter on the roadway surface combines with the first raindrops to create a slick sheet. It may be wise to avoid riding during the first few minutes of a rainstorm, or at least greatly reduce your speed until the rain has had an opportunity to rinse the slick coating from the surface. When riding on wet surfaces, ride along in the tire tracks left by vehicles in front of you—water levels will likely be lowest in the area where a car tire has just passed, lowering the likelihood of your motorcycle hydroplaning. Surface oils will be most prevalent at intersections.

CARRYING PASSENGERS

Carrying a passenger is a great way to increase the utility of your motorcycle, as well as introduce other people to the magic of motorcycling. However, it is important to realize that carrying a passenger changes the dynamics of handling and stability of your bike. Adding this weight behind the operator sometimes shifts the weight distribution of the motorcycle higher and somewhat to the rear, increasing the distances needed to slow, stop, and accelerate. The additional weight will also affect the cornering characteristics of a motorcycle.

As the rider, you'll need to take the changes in handling and stability into account. Before you saddle up with another person on the pillion, make sure that you have enough riding experience on your own to be able to deal with the added complexities of "two-up" riding. Adjust tire pressure and suspension settings as described in your owner's manual. When you are confident enough in your abilities to take on a passenger for the first time, get a feel for how your motorcycle will handle with the added weight by practicing in an empty parking lot before you head out into traffic. Remember to be as smooth as possible. Avoid accelerating, shifting, or braking and decelerating abruptly or unexpectedly to help your passenger brace in anticipation of the movements of the motorcycle.

The passenger is the rider's responsibility. Don't assume your passenger knows anything about the motorcycle or motorcycling—take time to help them understand the do's and don'ts of riding on the back of a motorcycle.

Here are some guidelines to ensure that the ride goes well for both you and your partner. Discuss these guidelines before your passenger even mounts the motorcycle:

▶ Your passenger wears protective gear. This includes, at a minimum: helmet, eye protection, jacket, gloves, long pants, and boots. But you knew this already.

   Caution your passenger about touching the hot parts of your motorcycle (such as the mufflers) or interfering with moving parts (the wheels and drive chain).

▶ Your passenger should not climb onboard until you are on the bike, side stand up, bracing the bike vertically with both feet flat on the ground. When you are ready, the passenger should grasp your left shoulder and climb aboard using the left passenger footrest, paying attention to keeping weight centered over the motorcycle. You should squeeze the front brake lever while the passenger mounts and dismounts to keep the bike from rolling.

▶ Your passenger should hold onto your waist or hips, or the bike's hand-holds, for maximum security and keep his or her feet on the passenger footrests at all times for maximum stability.

▶ Remind your passenger to never stand and to avoid turning around or making any sudden moves that could upset the motorcycle's stability. Your passenger's motions should mimic yours, especially whenever you're leaning into the turns. Looking over your shoulder into the direction of turns will help this happen.

▶ If you're taking your child along as a passenger, there are a few additional points to consider. Ensure that he or she is mature enough to handle the responsibilities, tall enough to reach the footrests, wears a properly fitted helmet and other protective gear, and holds onto you or the passenger hand-holds. Check your state's laws; a few states have set minimum ages for motorcycle passengers.

An important part of being a responsible rider means never showing off or otherwise trying to impress your passenger, especially if he or she is new to the sport. A passenger on a motorcycle can feel particularly vulnerable, and it is important for a safe experience that they trust you completely. This is especially true with first-time passengers—for them, your most impressive feat will be a smooth, relaxed ride.

Motorcycles can carry more than you might think if the load is distributed appropriately. Common carrying methods include a rear luggage rack (left top), tank bag (left), and saddlebags (above). Keep the weight as low as possible and evenly distributed front to back and side to side.

OTHER LOADS

Despite their small size and minimalist accommodations, motorcycles are capable of carrying fairly sizable loads—people regularly ride motorcycles around the world, for months on end, carrying all the necessary equipment for such extended trips safely on the back. The key to using a motorcycle's pack-animal characteristics is understanding the dynamics of the vehicle, then taking care to pack loads on the bike in a way that will not upset these dynamics. The three important factors to consider when loading a motorcycle are: load weight, load location, and how the load is fastened to the motorcycle.

Weight

Every motorcycle has a maximum load rating specified by its manufacturer; you can find this number in your owner's manual. The maximum allowable load is the difference between the weight of the motorcycle itself and the maximum allowable weight of the motorcycle and its load, including rider and passenger (if you are carrying one) and any other cargo.

To calculate how much load you can carry, subtract your weight (in riding gear), your passenger's weight (if you will be carrying one), and the weight of the motorcycle from the maximum load capacity number specified by the manufacturer. Whatever is left over is the maximum load you can carry.

Finally, before riding a loaded bike, check your owner's manual for suggestions on tire pressure and suspension adjustments—loaded motorcycles will often require added pressure in the tires and/or firmer suspension settings to handle well.

Location

The rule when locating a load on your motorcycle is to keep the weight as low as possible, and evenly distributed from front to back and side to side. It's helpful here to think of your motorcycle's load triangle—a space formed by imaginary lines connecting your head to the motorcycle's two axles. To maintain as much stability as possible, try to contain the heaviest items within the load triangle. Avoid carrying heavy items in a tail trunk.

Carrying weight high and far back can lighten the front end and cause handling instability. If you ride with a tankbag, be sure that it doesn't interfere with your comfort or ability to steer the motorcycle. Avoid the temptation to strap your sleeping bag or any other gear to the front fork or handlebars of your motorcycle. Even if the suspension travel is unaffected, the extra weight over the front wheel can cause dangerous front-end instability.

Fastening

This one is simple—make absolutely certain that the load is fastened securely to the motorcycle. Use racks and luggage that are designed specifically for use on your type of motorcycle. Secure all items with tie-down straps or web nets, taking care not to block any lights or moving suspension parts. Check and double check that there are no loose items that could shift and fall off, or worse, get caught in the wheels or drive train. Having your tailpack or a loose strap get caught up in the rear wheel or chain of your motorcycle will definitely impede your forward progress, not to mention complicate your trip. Also take care to keep luggage away from mufflers and other hot motor parts. Check the security often.

Finally, use common sense. Even though these might not exceed the weight limit, items like surfboards and bicycles (don't laugh, we've seen both!) have no business being transported on the back of a motorcycle. When in doubt, leave stuff home.

OTHER SPECIAL SITUATIONS

Tire Blowout

There is likely nothing that comes on so suddenly, and nothing that is more terrifying, than suffering a tire blowout while riding your motorcycle. If a blowout should occur, keep a firm grip on the handlebars, steer smoothly, and gently ease off of the throttle. Avoid downshifting or braking—the sudden weight shifts of these actions can upset the now-unstable chassis. If traffic permits, slow gradually and move off to the side of the road. If you must brake, limit your braking to the wheel with the good tire. Applying the brake to the wheel with the bad tire can cause the tire to separate from the rim, leading to a loss of control.

Aftermarket hard luggage is increasingly available and popular for a wide variety of bikes, making it possible to turn standard and sport bikes into highly serviceable tourers.

Concentrate weight low and to the center of the motorcycle (in the "load triangle" determined by your head and the two axles). Keep the weight even, side to side.

Fortunately, blowouts are uncommon and generally preventable, especially with modern, tubeless tire technology. Carefully inspect your tires for undue wear or aging as part of a T-CLOCS inspection before each ride. The most common cause of tire failure is underinflation—check your tires often and keep them inflated to the specified levels outlined in your owner's manual.

Broken Clutch Cable

Routine inspection and lubrication of the clutch cable will help prevent it from breaking. If it breaks while you're in motion, it's possible to shift the motorcycle without the clutch—just roll off the throttle and press hard on the lever. It will be jerky

It is not uncommon for dogs to chase motorcycles. As you approach it, slow down, shift to a lower gear, and when it gets near, accelerate by it. Don't kick at it.

and probably not quiet, but it will get you into the next gear.

Stopping smoothly with a broken clutch cable is more complicated. If possible, travel to a place where help will be available, or where you will at least be able to pull off and park the bike in a safe place while you go to find help. Slow the bike gradually, downshifting one gear at a time until you arrive at first gear. If possible, shift the bike into neutral before you come to a stop (though this will be difficult on some bikes). If you are unable to find neutral, wait until you're ready to stop, then shut off the engine using the engine cut-off switch. Be prepared—with the engine and transmission still engaged, this stop will be anything but smooth.

If the clutch cable breaks while the motorcycle is stopped, quickly apply the brakes, forcing the engine to stall. Some motorcycles are equipped with hydraulic clutches that use fluid pressure instead of a cable to engage and disengage the clutch. A rapid loss of fluid will cause a problem identical to a broken cable: you won't have control over the clutch mechanism, and the same emergency procedures will apply.

Animals

Depending on the situation, nearly any animal can present a danger to a motorcyclist. An errant bird could collide with you or a squirrel could dart out in front of you. Colliding at speed with a deer can yield the same amount of force and damage as colliding with an automobile. How you respond to an animal that appears in your path depends on the size of the animal, and the type of risk that it presents to you.

The first line of defense against animals in the roadway is to use SEE and slow in areas where such critters are likely to be crossing the road. Proper swerving and stopping techniques can help you avoid collisions with our fellow mammals. Hitting a small rodent is upsetting, but if handled correctly it is unlikely to result in a crash—a motorcycle can run over a small animal and stay upright. Such an outcome may be preferable to swerving into oncoming traffic or colliding with a tree or other fixed object off the roadway.

Dogs often chase motorcycles. Whatever you do, resist the urge to kick at the dog, as this could throw you off-balance. A good plan of action when approaching a dog (especially one that that seems intent on chasing you) is to slow, downshift, honk, and then accelerate past the point of interception. This will throw off the dog's planned point of interception and confuse it.

Larger animals like deer or elk present larger problems. All animals are unpredictable, so extra care should be taken in rural areas where encounters with these creatures are more common. Use more aggressive SEE tactics in areas where you are most likely to come across deer, elk, or moose, especially at the edge of wooded areas late at night. Leave additional time and space to react to a sighting. If you do encounter one of these animals on the roadway, the only reliable avoidance tactic is to stop completely before you reach it. Then wait for the animal to leave, or move past it at a very slow speed.

Wind

Light, steady winds are no reason for concern. If necessary, lean the motorcycle gently in the direction of the breeze and continue your forward course. Strong gusts of wind, however, can drastically affect motorcycles and often demand immediate corrections to avoid developing into problems. Be aware of these possibilities, and take proper precautions in situations where you are likely to encounter gusting winds—when crossing exposed bridges or overpasses, when overtaking large trucks, or when coming around large buildings in urban environs, for example.

Wobbles and Weaves

These two terms refer to related (but distinct) handling problems, and although rare, you might encounter one of them on a motorcycle. Though they might look similar to the uninitiated observer, wobbles and weaves affect different ends of the motorcycle—the term weave refers to an oscillation of the rear, and is usually relatively slow-cycling; a wobble, on the other hand, refers to a shake in the motorcycle's handlebars, and is typically more violent and faster-cycling than a weave. Wobbles are often called by another term—tankslappers—a reference to the fact that it looks like the rider's hands are "slapping" the fuel tank when the handlebars shake violently from side to side.

Wobbles and weaves stem from a variety of causes, but most often they result from excessive weight located in the wrong place on the motorcycle or odd handling inputs that upset the chassis—accelerating out of a bumpy corner while the bike is still leaned over, for example. Mechanical problems can also create these situations—extremely worn steering head or swing arm bearings, for example, or underinflated or severely worn tires.

Differences between wobbles and weaves are mostly academic, though, since the corrective action for both of these is the same. As soon as the bike begins to wobble or weave, grip the handlebars firmly without locking your arms or fighting the steering. Then smoothly roll off of the throttle to slow gradually. Do not apply the brakes, and do not accelerate. In some cases, especially with a rear-end weave, it helps to shift your body weight forward by leaning over the tank.

One thing you really don't want to hit is a moose.

MOTORCYCLING EXCELLENCE MEANS:

▶ You are prepared for unusual situations that may happen during your ride.

▶ You practice your swerving and braking skills often, and in a safe area.

▶ You are constantly alert for roadway features and conditions that could affect your riding decisions.

▶ You ensure you are a very capable rider before choosing to carry a passenger, and you practice in a safe area with a passenger before riding two-up in traffic.

▶ You review emergency procedures in your mind so you have an arsenal of prepared, almost automatic responses.

▶ You take special care at night to ensure your visibility (conspicuity) to others.

▶ You take into account how age and experience affect your riding skills.

To pick up a relatively light machine such as this training bike, simply use your legs (not your back), take hold of the low side of the handlebar, and lift. Be prepared to put the side stand down once the bike is upright.

▶ RAISING A FALLEN BIKE

Most of the time you manage to keep your motorcycle upright, but every now and then you may have to raise a machine that has toppled over. You're most likely to drop a bike at very slow speeds, or even when standing still. Perhaps when stopping at a red light you put your foot down on a small puddle of oil, and as your foot slipped sideways you couldn't hold the bike up. Or perhaps you merely stopped for a drink of water on a hot day, and came back to find the side stand had sunk into the hot asphalt and permitted the machine to fall over.

Whatever the size of your bike, the trick to raising a fallen machine is to use leverage and avoid straining your back. You may be so embarrassed at dropping your bike that you quickly grab hold and attempt to wrestle it upright by brute force. Even a middleweight bike can cause injury if you don't pay attention to how you raise it. And keep your gloves on to protect your hands from hot or sharp parts.

If the fallen machine has engine-protection bars, the technique is to grasp both handlebars, rock the bike *toward* you on the engine-protection bars, and use momentum to roll it back upright. Bend your knees, not your back, and use leg power to push the machine upright. If the bike has fallen on a slope, pivot it around if possible, so that it points uphill and shift the transmission into first gear before attempting to raise it.

If your machine isn't equipped with engine-protection bars, you'll either have to get some additional muscle, or use leverage. If you're on your own, grasp the low handlebar, turn the front wheel toward you, grasp something solid along the frame, and work your knees up under the saddle to help lever the bike upright. Use your legs to push. If the machine has fallen on its right side, it's a good idea to extend the side stand before raising the bike, just in case you lose your balance and can't keep it from falling the other way as you get it up.

One enterprising woman, Carol Youorski (a.k.a. Skert), has become somewhat of a celebrity by traveling around to motorcycle gatherings and giving demonstrations on lifting even large touring bikes using leverage and proper techniques—and Skert can't weigh an ounce over 120 pounds, soaking wet!

When attempting to raise any machine, remember that gasoline may have spilled from the tank or carburetors. Not only is spilled fuel a fire hazard, it can also make the pavement very slippery. Avoid smoking near any fallen bike, and watch where you step when attempting to lift it. There are two other fluids that can spill and cause damage. Battery acid may leak from vent holes or fill caps while the machine is on its side. Acid can cause burns to skin, eat holes in your riding gear, and corrode the frame. After a spill, smart riders make a point of flushing the battery area with lots of water. Brake fluid won't burn your skin, but it can be disastrous for paint and plastic parts. Immediately wipe clean any spilled brake fluid and wash the area with soap and water as soon as possible.

Of course, your immediate concern after a spill is the cosmetic damage to paint, chrome, and plastic parts. But you should also be concerned with hidden damage that could cause serious problems as you ride away. Brake, clutch, and shift levers can be bent in a fall, and can subsequently fracture when you don't expect it. Sometimes you can straighten bent levers without cracking them, but it is a wise precaution to replace any bent lever as soon as possible. It also makes sense to check the running gear after a fall, to be certain a fender isn't rubbing the tire, or that a brake cable or hose hasn't been damaged. If any brake fluid has been spilled, refill the fluid in the reservoir to prevent air from being pumped into the brake system. Likewise, check the battery electrolyte level.

Lessen the chances of dropping your bike by practicing some simple habits. First, whenever you climb on or off the bike, always squeeze the front brake lever to prevent the machine from rolling. Second, when you stop, keep the handlebars straight and make a smooth, *complete* stop, using lots of front brake. Riders who have to make several dabs with their foot while the bike creeps to an unpredictable stop are very likely to drop the machine.

Finally, park your bike sensibly. Point the front end uphill, even if you have to roll backward into a parking spot. If you can't lodge the rear wheel against a curb, leave the transmission in first gear. Be sure the bike leans over against the side stand so that it isn't likely to topple over the other way should someone bump it. And place something solid and flat under the side stand if the asphalt pavement is hot, to prevent the stand from sinking. A small piece of metal such as a flattened can will help keep a side stand from sinking when parking on grass or dirt.

Since it is more difficult to balance at slow speeds, you can reduce your chances of dropping your bike by practicing slow-speed maneuvers. If you haven't yet taken an MSF Experienced *RiderCourse*, it's an excellent place to start your slow-speed practice. ∎

Heavier motorcycles require a different technique, but still rely on the muscle power in your legs to right a fallen machine. With your back to the bike, take hold of the handlebar with your right hand and the frame with your left, then simply walk the bike up with your legs.

►RIDING AT NIGHT

There are times when you must continue riding at night, or times when you choose to go for a ride after the sun goes down. You may find yourself miles from home as it gets dark, or you may choose to ride at night to cross the desert and avoid the daytime heat. Whatever the reasons for riding at night, there are some special considerations for motorcyclists.

Vision is one of our most important considerations. If you can't see where you are going, you can't stay on the road. If you can't see the hazards ahead, you can't take evasive action. The human eye is not well adapted to nighttime vision. Human eyes often take several minutes to completely adjust physiologically from very bright surroundings to dim light levels. Consider what happens when your photograph is taken with a flash. You are momentarily blinded until your eyes can adjust. The same thing happens when going from a brightly lit restaurant to a dark parking lot, or if you stare at the headlights of an oncoming vehicle. There are several tactics you can use to maximize your nighttime vision:

► Use only *clear* eye protection (not tinted), and keep it clean and free of scratches.

► Wait a few moments after leaving a bright area before riding away. Allow your eyes time to adjust to the low light level.

► Practice *avoiding* bright light sources as you ride along. Look to one side of street lights, signs, or headlights. For example, as a car approaches, shift your vision from the headlights to the white line along the edge of your lane.

Fatigue is a common problem at night, especially on longer rides. It is easy to get weary while riding, so work in rest breaks. Failing to acknowledge fatigue can create a situation that leads to a crash. Smart riders take more frequent rest breaks at night. They get off the machine and do some exercises to get the blood flow refreshed. At a minimum, consider walking briskly to the other end of a parking lot and back. Rest stops are beneficial, not only for rejuvenation, but also for the change of pace.

If you just can't seem to stay awake, find a suitable spot and take a short nap, or even stop at a motel and check in for some sleep. Booking a room for the night is a lot cheaper than a crash. (For security purposes, try to get a room on the ground floor where you can park your bike within earshot, or in a well-lit area.)

Wild animals are more likely to be roaming the highway at night, especially during the spring and fall. Animals such as deer are difficult to see at

When riding at night, remember that it takes several minutes for the human eye to adjust from very bright surroundings to dim light levels.

Be wary of overriding the headlight when driving at night. This is when your total braking distance (based on your speed, reaction time, and the road conditions) exceeds the distance you can see ahead. The solution is easy—slow down.

night, and hitting a deer with a motorcycle can be disastrous for both animal and you. The correct tactic for avoiding a deer strike is to brake quickly to a slow speed when a deer is seen. Deer eyes reflect light much as a glass reflector. If a "reflector" alongside the road winks off and on, it is very likely a deer or some other animal. Remember that deer travel in families, so one deer indicates that others are nearby.

Of course, it helps to spot wild animals if your headlight is bright and aimed correctly. Your high beam should strike the road surface at its maximum range, yet allow the low beam to be below the eye level of approaching motorists to avoid blinding them. If you make frequent nighttime trips, consider adding an auxiliary driving light, wired into the high-beam circuit. Remember, all vehicle lights must conform to the equipment laws of the state in which you are riding.

You will also help yourself be more readily seen by adding reflectors or reflective tape to the rear and side panels of tail trunks and saddlebags, or adding extra taillights. The human eye has trouble judging the distance at night, which may contribute to an increase in risk. Reflective clothing and added lights can help other drivers to see you better.

When riding in traffic, try to maintain more space around you, and be especially wary of vehicles approaching from behind. Adjust your riding tactics. When approaching a stop signal, adjust speed so that you don't have to wait a long time for the light. When making a left turn, consider going around the block to the right, rather than waiting in the left turn lane where a sleepy driver could pick you off. Flash your brake light often when stopped. It gets attention better than a steady light.

You may decide to follow another vehicle at night to take advantage of the additional lights, or to help avoid animal strikes. By observing when the lights of the vehicle in front of you bounce up and down, you can get an idea of where potholes are. If you do follow a car or truck, keep an adequate following distance. (Recall that we recommend a minimum following distance of two seconds.) Make a point of counting out your following distance in seconds, rather than just guessing. When the car ahead passes by a stationary point such as a street light, start counting, "one-thousand-one, one-thousand-two . . . " If you can count to two before passing the same street light, you are at the minimum distance.

Be aware of other vehicles that seem to pace you at night. Some drivers are merely curious, but there are also "weirdos" looking for a little entertainment, and you could be the victim. Change speed or lanes to create space around you and separate yourself from possible problems. When pulling into rest areas or restaurant parking lots, scrutinize the night life there before shutting off the engine. If you don't like the looks of the place, move on, and find someplace more friendly.

Take into consideration how aging affects night vision. The eyes gather less light as a person ages, making it more difficult to see clearly. Also, the eyes become more sensitive over time, which makes adjusting to light sources and handling glare more difficult.

Some riders enjoy night riding, some tolerate it occasionally, and some motorcyclists can't stand it at all. If you have reservations about night riding, or can't seem to keep your eyes open after dark, don't ride at night. ■

Hazards come in all shapes and sizes—and from all directions.

CHAPTER 10
Group Riding

RIDING ALONE, YOU ONLY HAVE TO ACCOUNT FOR YOURSELF. RIDING WITH OTHERS, YOU MUST TAKE INTO ACCOUNT THE NEEDS AND ABILITIES OF THE OTHER RIDERS.

Motorcycling is essentially a solo activity—even with a passenger onboard you're somewhat isolated from others when you're in the saddle, alone inside your helmet. This isn't to say, however, that motorcycling isn't an excellent group activity and a great way to spend time with friends. For many, riding as part of a group—whether a small bunch of friends on a Sunday morning ride or with an organized rally—is the epitome of the motorcycle experience. Reliving the highlights of a great ride over dinner at the end of a long day in the saddle is what makes motorcycling a satisfying social activity for so many of us.

Group rides can be categorized into three basic types: destination-oriented rides, route-oriented rides, and benefit-oriented rides. A destination-oriented ride focuses on specific place, like a restaurant, motorcycle hangout, or organized event. Route-oriented rides tend to be more free-form, usually without a fixed timetable, endpoint, or plan, organized only for the joy of riding together. This type of ride is ideal for small groups of similarly matched riders. Benefit-oriented rides are usually organized to raise money for a charity or other special interest group. These rides are typically large in scale with plenty of publicity. The type of group ride you choose to participate in (if you choose to participate in any at all) says much about you and your opinion toward the motorcycling experience.

A staggered formation during group rides helps maintain a proper space cushion between motorcycles, takes up less space on the highway, is easier for other motorists to see, and protects the lane better to lessen the chance of the group being split up by other traffic.

There are some things you should keep in mind before embarking on a group ride, no matter whether you're headed out with one other rider or hundreds. Riding alone, you only have to account for yourself. Riding with others, you must take into account the needs and abilities of the other riders—especially their riding experience, skill level, and general comfort on the road and around other motorcycles. Everything from where to position your bike on the roadway to how to effectively communicate with others in your group takes on a larger significance when riding in close proximity to others. You're not only responsible for your own safety and enjoyment, but you also share partial responsibility for ensuring that the ride is safe and fun for everyone else involved. From this perspective, what follows is a discussion of group-riding dynamics to help you keep safety first and foremost in mind as you participate in your next group ride.

ARRIVE PREPARED

Make sure you are ready to go when you show up for a group ride. Nothing annoys other riders more than standing around, eager to get going while waiting for an unprepared rider to get his act together. Arrive on time, with a full gas tank and everything that you will need to complete the ride. Introduce yourself to the designated leader and sweep rider, who brings up the rear of the group. If there is a route map offered, take one and study it, making special note of any fuel, meal, and rest or lodging stops. Pay attention during the pre-ride meeting for any changes in the route or map, and note these accordingly. Ask what hand signals will be used during the ride, and remember to use them. Riding in a group can be overwhelming—

Arrive on time and prepared with a full tank of gas at the start of a group ride. Pay attention during the pre-ride meeting, and if there is a route map, take one and study it, making note of fuel, meal, and rest stops.

preparing properly will help you avoid problems and make the group-riding situation less stressful and more enjoyable.

Resist the temptation to show off—such plans usually backfire, anyway. Ride responsibly and impress other riders with your cool-headed safety mindedness and self-control. If an unchecked ego on the part of another rider rears its ugly head and you find a group ride becoming overly competitive, aggressive, or dangerous, find a way to improve the situation safely or remove yourself from it before you become caught up in it.

RIDING IN FORMATION

A group's riding formation on the road plays a huge part of maintaining safety during a group ride. The staggered riding formation includes maintaining a proper space cushion between motorcycles so that each rider has plenty of time and space to maneuver and to react to any hazards that may be encountered.

Compared to a single-file line, a staggered formation takes up less space on the highway, is easier for motorists to see, and protects the lane better to lessen the chance of the group being split up by other traffic. Side-by-side formations are never preferred, as these greatly reduce the space cushion to the side. For example, if you suddenly needed to swerve to avoid a hazard, in a side-by-side formation you would not have room to do so. You don't want your handlebars to get entangled with your buddy's. The only time that a side-by-side formation might be required is during a parade or other slow-speed event, where other safeguards would be in place to minimize the threat from traffic or other hazards.

An ideal staggered formation will give each rider plenty of room to maneuver and still maintain the riding formation. A staggered formation can be tight or loose, depending on traffic conditions. During heavy traffic a tighter staggered formation is best, to keep riders together within traffic. However, the integrity of the formation is always secondary to safety—you don't tighten it up to keep traffic from breaking it up. It's okay to relax the formation to let cars in between bikes of the group—after all, even if a few riders are separated from the group, everyone has a map and knowledge of the next destination, right?

How do you best gauge the ideal following distance? In good riding conditions, a minimum space cushion is considered to be a two-second following distance between a rider and the rider directly in front of them (see the first photograph in this chapter). In a staggered formation, the leader rides in the left third of the lane, while the next rider stays at least one second behind in the right third of the lane, the rest of the group following the same pattern behind. If the formation is correct, the third rider is two seconds behind the leader, but only one second behind the second rider.

In certain situations a single-file formation is preferred. These are situations where more room to maneuver might be needed, such as on a curvy road, under conditions of poor visibility, entering and leaving highways, on roadways with poor surfaces, or any other situation where an increased space cushion is preferable. Riding single file, each rider can use the entire lane and choose his or her own line through a turn. When riding single file, remember to maintain an adequate space cushion (a two-second or more following distance) between riders.

No matter what formation you are riding in, pay careful attention to the riders in front of and behind you. Periodically check the riders following in your rear view mirror. If you see a rider falling behind, slow down and allow them to catch up. Think of the group like a rubber band—the line of riders may stretch out or tighten up from time to time, but overall, if all the riders in the group use this technique, the group should be able to maintain a fairly steady speed without some riders feeling pressured to ride too fast to catch up.

In some situations, such as a curvy, two-lane road, a single-file formation would be preferred. In this case, with little or no shoulder to the right, single-file riding would increase the space cushion and allow each rider to use the entire lane and thus choose his or her own line through the turn.

INTERSECTIONS

You should remember from earlier in this book that intersections are the area of highest risk to a motorcyclist. This, of course, remains true for groups of motorcyclists riding together, despite the increased visibility of a large group. Here are some tips to help groups successfully negotiate some of the more hazardous situations that you might encounter in instances where two or more roadways intersect.

When turning at protected intersections (those with traffic light turn arrows), tighten the formation to allow as many riders as possible to pass through. Do not ride side-by-side, however; maintain a single file or tight staggered formation. Despite your best attempts, if your group is more than a few bikes strong there is a good possibility that not all riders will make it through the traffic light arrow. For this

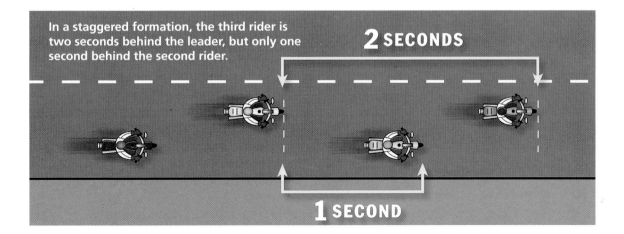

In a staggered formation, the third rider is two seconds behind the leader, but only one second behind the second rider.

2 SECONDS

1 SECOND

reason, it is important to discuss beforehand what to do if some riders get separated at a light. Having a plan to stop at a predetermined point up ahead will keep each rider from feeling pressured to run the light or speed to catch up.

At unprotected intersections riders should proceed with caution and in single file, only turning when it is safe and legal to do so. Lead riders should slow down after unprotected intersections to allow the group to reform after everyone has ridden safely through the intersection. Respect the rights of other motorists; blocking an intersection without permission or without an appropriate escort is illegal in most circumstances.

At two-way stop intersections where you are required to stop, move through only when it is safe and legal. When stopping at an intersection that you intend to proceed straight through (without turning), it may be appropriate to close formation and sit side-by-side while waiting to proceed. When the light changes, the rider on the left leaves

Know ahead of time the planned rest stops and destinations of the group. That way, should you get separated from the rest of the group, you can rejoin the other riders without riding over your limits to catch up.

first, then the following riders, in order to reestablish the staggered formation and space cushion as they depart. Again, how the group will handle such situations should be determined at a rider's meeting before the ride begins.

INTERSTATES AND FREEWAYS

High speeds and the increased potential for hazards make riding in a staggered formation essential on freeways and interstates. Enter these roadways single file and form up after safely merging. Once on the highway, be alert for entering and exiting cars that might cut through your formation. Resist the temptation, especially in heavy traffic, to close up the formation too much. Maintain your space cushion and at least your one-second/two-second staggered-formation following distance. Exiting an interstate requires a single-file formation that allows you to better merge and respond to whatever is at the end of the exit lane.

PASSING

Group passing dynamics differ depending on the type of roadway on which you are traveling. Whether on a freeway or interstate, it's acceptable for the group to pass as a unit, provided this pass is safe and legal. When the opportunity arises, the lead rider should signal the lane change once it has been determined that the group can pass as a unit. The other riders should then follow this lead and signal one at a time and move into the next lane.

Passing slower-moving traffic on a two-lane roadway presents a greater potential for complications, so in this situation the members of the group should pass one at a time. The leader should signal his intention first and then pull out and pass only when it is safe and legal. After the pass is completed, the leader should return to the left lane position and continue at a speed that leaves room for the next rider to tuck in between him and the vehicle being passed. The next rider should then move up to the left position and wait for a safe chance to pass—each rider should pass only when he or she feels it is safe to do so. The rest of the group should follow the same pattern. Of course, such passing maneuvers should be limited to marked passing zones only.

SEPARATION ANXIETY

Signals, traffic, a mechanical problem—there are any number of reasons that you might suddenly find yourself separated from the group you are riding with. If this situation arises, don't panic. Your group should have a pre-planned procedure in place to regroup. Don't feel pressured to catch up, especially if it means breaking the law or riding beyond your skills. It's always preferable to finish a group ride alone than it is to finish in trouble.

If you have plans to separate from the group before the end of the ride, make sure to notify the group leader in advance to avoid creating anxiety for the leader. Make sure they know where and when you plan to depart so they know that you haven't had a problem and aren't in need of assistance. When you do depart, the rest of the riders should adjust the formation to maintain the proper space cushion and following distance. This may require some riders to change their position to the opposite side of the lane.

TROUBLE AHEAD

Reacting properly to hazards in the roadway is especially important in the context of a group ride, as it is more likely that there will be other motorcyclists in close proximity to you. For this reason, maintaining a proper space cushion and following distance throughout the ride is essential to allow riders to adjust their lane positions if debris is encountered. If while riding in a staggered formation you come across a hazardous area—a construction zone, for example—it is best to transition to single file. Avoid riding over debris unless you have no other choice. Not only could you damage your tires or bike, but you also risk throwing debris into another rider's path. Ride as smoothly as possible and avoid sudden changes in speed or direction. The same is also true of traveling on wet roadways.

If a member of the group does have a bad interaction with one of these hazards, the following riders should all stop, including the designated sweep rider at the back of the pack. It's best for the riders ahead of the incident to continue on to the next scheduled stop area, since turning around and doubling back could cause additional safety problems. It should be the responsibility of the sweep rider to assess the situation and, if it appears there

Avoid bunching up like these riders when riding in a staggered formation. Allow a full two-second following distance between you and the rider directly in front of you. Ideally, the leader should ride in the left side of the lane, while the second rider stays one second behind in the right portion of the lane, and so on.

will be a delay, send another rider ahead to inform the rest of the group. If medical assistance is necessary, use a cell phone to call 911.

A successful ride with a group of like-minded individuals is one of the ultimate motorcycling experiences. Taking part in a group ride is a great way to share the fun and camaraderie of motorcycling. Having the proper attitude—knowing your limits and the limits of the group, and taking responsibility to ride within them—is the key to making this social form of motorcycling fun for everyone. Following these simple guidelines will help make your participation in group rides safer and more satisfying for everyone involved.

MOTORCYCLING EXCELLENCE MEANS:

► You ensure you are a safe and capable rider before riding in a group.

► You ride your own ride and are not affected by pressure to ride inappropriately or beyond your comfort or skill level.

► You familiarize yourself with common group riding signals.

► You honor group ride procedures as communicated by a group leader.

▶ HAND SIGNALS FOR GROUP RIDING

Hand signals are an easy and effective way to communicate with other riders and keep everyone together and on-task during a group ride. Hand signals will vary from group to group, which is why it is especially important to inquire about what signals will be used at the rider's meeting before you embark on a ride with any new or unfamiliar group. To get you started, here's a review of the most commonly used hand signals. ■

STOP

Arm extended straight down, palm facing back.

SLOW DOWN

Arm extended straight out, palm facing down, swing down to your side.

SPEED UP

Arm extended straight out, palm facing up, swing upward.

TAKE THE LEAD

Arm extended upward 45 degrees, palm forward pointing with index finger, swing in arc from back to front.

FOLLOW ME

Arm extended straight up from shoulder, palm forward.

HAZARD IN ROADWAY

On the left, point with left hand; on the right, point with right foot.

SINGLE FILE

Arm and index finger extended straight up.

DOUBLE FILE

Arm with index and middle finger extended straight up.

FUEL

Arm out to side pointing to tank with finger extended.

REFRESHMENT STOP

Fingers closed, thumb to mouth.

COMFORT STOP

Forearm extended, fist clenched with short up and down motion.

PULL OFF

Arm positioned as for right turn, forearm swung toward shoulder.

HIGHBEAM

Tap on top of helmet with open palm down.

TURN SIGNAL ON

Open and close hand with fingers and thumb extended.

The MSF Group Riding kit can help a club organize its rides. The video and handbooks explain safety strategies, hand signals, and proper riding formations.

►TIPS FOR GROUP RIDE LEADERS

Plan ahead. Planning ahead is essential to the success of any group ride, no matter whether your group numbers two or 200. Organize the route well ahead of time, and pre-ride it if possible to assess the conditions. Planning in advance is especially important if you are putting together a large-scale ride. Parade and street closure permits, security, donation procedures and policies, route mapping, and participant waivers are all things that should be straightened out well in advance of a large event. For best success with events like these, form a planning committee to assist.

Designate a lead rider and a sweep rider (who brings up the rear of the group). To ensure a safe ride, both of these roles should be filled by experienced riders well-versed in the dynamics of group riding.

Hold a riders' meeting. Before departing, discuss things like route, rest and fuel stops, hand signals, and who will act as ride leader and sweep rider. Introduce yourself. Be friendly—the key to a successful, communicative group ride is everyone being comfortable. Before setting out, do your best to assess everyone's riding skills, experience and stamina (asking questions, if necessary) and try to choose roads and speeds that match those abilities.

Arrange the group. Some groups put slower riders at the back, so they don't hold the group up. This works fine as long as you remember to regroup periodically so these riders aren't left behind. Other groups prefer to put slower riders up front, so no one falls too far back. This is your choice, depending on the preferences of the group—both are equally functional as long as there is an experienced rider in the lead and another experienced motorcyclist riding sweep. No matter how the group is arranged, a good lead rider will set a pace that follows traffic laws and accommodates the skill levels of all the riders in the group.

Keep the group to a manageable size, ideally five to seven riders. If necessary, break the group into smaller sub-groups, remembering to designate a lead rider and sweep rider (both with the requisite experience) for each individual group.

Ride prepared. Pack a cell phone, first-aid kit, a full tool kit, and be prepared to deal with any problem that the group might encounter. This will enhance the safety and experience for the entire group.

Keep the group together. Plan ahead and signal changes early to make sure that the word gets back through the group with time to spare.

Consider the peer effect, both positive and negative, and take this into account. Remind everyone to ride within their personal skill and comfort levels, at their own pace and well within their own experience level, and assure them that the group will pause and regroup at regular, pre-selected intervals so they will not feel pressured to ride beyond their limits to keep up. ■

CHAPTER 11
Traction

When operating a four-wheeled automobile we have certain expectations regarding if, or how much, our tires will slide on whatever surface we happen to be traveling. We exit the interstate at speeds that we know from experience will safely allow us to complete the turn without giving any thought to the car spinning out of control and into the guardrail. The tendency for our car's tires to "stick" to the road, and the way that tendency is influenced by vehicle speed and the roadway surface we are driving on, is an example of traction at work. Traction can be defined as *the potential for friction between two surfaces in contact with each other.* In the case of motorcycles, traction can be thought of as the amount of "grip" between the motorcycle's tires and the road surface.

WHY IS TRACTION IMPORTANT?

When driving a car, you usually don't concern yourself with traction until your tires actually start to slip. A patch of oil or a little sand may cause one of the car's tires to slip for an instant, but with three other tires gripping the pavement, a slight slip of one tire isn't usually a concern. On a motorcycle, with only two tires gripping the pavement, one tire slipping can have serious consequences. Because of this, piloting a motorcycle along the highway requires that a fair amount of the rider's attention be focused on maintaining traction.

Motorcycle tires are relatively narrow, which makes traction a limited commodity. What's more,

The greatest demands are placed on a motorcycle's available traction while in a turn, under acceleration or deceleration.

this limited amount of traction is divided up among multiple forces created when braking, cornering, and accelerating. The farther you lean in a corner, for example, the less traction is available for braking; the harder you accelerate, the less traction is available for turning. If any one of these actions uses an excessive share of available traction, the result will be a loss of control of the motorcycle. A thorough understanding of traction, and the way that traction is affected by braking, cornering, and accelerating, is essential to safe motorcycling.

Road surface makes all the difference when it comes to traction. Gravel roads provide far less available traction, making it important to avoid sudden changes in speed or direction. If you inadvertently lock up the front wheel while braking, release the front brake lever to allow the front wheel to regain traction, and then carefully re-apply progressive pressure to the brake lever.

WHAT AFFECTS TRACTION?

Earlier we defined traction as the potential for friction between the tire and the road surface. This potential for friction is expressed in engineering terms

by the formula $F = C_F \times N$, which says that friction force (F) between your tires and the roadway is equal to the coefficient of friction (C_F) multiplied by normal force (N), the force pressing the tire to the roadway. To make this discussion relevant to motorcycle dynamics, you can substitute the words "traction" for friction force and "tire loading" for normal force. Coefficient of friction, in the simplest terms, is a measurement of potential traction according to how two surfaces interact with each other. For example, if you take a polishing cloth and wipe your motorcycle's gas tank, the coefficient of friction between the tank and cloth would be low. That is, for a given force pushing the polishing cloth against the tank, relatively little force is necessary to move the polishing cloth parallel to the tank's surface. Now replace the cloth with 80-grit sandpaper—not only is the coefficient of friction much higher, but you'll need to get the tank repainted as well.

Coefficient of friction can be expressed in one of two ways: as *static friction* or *sliding friction*. Static friction refers to the friction value of two surfaces that are not moving relative to each other. This is called the *coefficient of static friction,* and this value remains constant. As soon as the surfaces start to move or slide against each other, the coefficient of friction value is reduced; this new, lower value is referred to as the *coefficient of sliding friction*. Coefficient of sliding friction will vary slightly at speed, due to the multiple forces at work on a sliding tire.

Motorcycle tires normally roll without any sliding between the rubber and the road surface; as long as the tires are rolling and not sliding, tire adhesion (static friction) is the major contributor to the amount of friction that can be generated between tire and road surface. If the tires do begin to slide, however, adhesion can be compromised. Other factors, such as rubber deformation, "tearing" (small bits of rubber separating from the tire's surface due to high traction and contact stresses) and "viscous behavior" (vibrations in the tire tread caused by sliding over an uneven surface) can all have an effect on adhesion.

Coefficient of friction between your tires and the road you're traveling along is determined by three factors: 1) Road surface material and condition; 2) Tire construction and condition (tread

Tires made for off-road use have a deep tread pattern, to better grip soft road surfaces and increase traction.

compound, temperature, condition, and age are all determining factors); and 3) Tire load or stress (inflation, passenger or luggage load, and whether the tire is rolling or sliding). In the next few pages we will discuss all three of these in detail.

Road Surface

If you could ride exclusively on smooth, dry asphalt, it would be easy to predict the amount of traction available between your tires and the road. Unfortunately, road surfaces usually vary widely on every ride. Asphalt, concrete, gravel, and dirt all have distinctly different traction characteristics, and these variations, coupled with the debris that collects on roads, make it a challenging task to predict and monitor available traction. The best thing you can do to avoid traction trouble is to remain alert to the roadway conditions and stay well within the safety margins.

Be on the lookout for changing road surfaces; railroad tracks, metal construction plates, bridge expansion joints, tar snakes, wet wooden planking, and rain-soaked bricks will all provide less traction than dry asphalt. And, otherwise ideal road surfaces are often made troublesome by sand, gravel, soil, water, anti-freeze, and oil. Any of these factors results in a less-than-ideal surface for your tires to grip onto, and can result in reduced traction.

Tire Construction and Condition

Modern motorcycle tires run the gamut from super sticky "racetrack-only" tires to touring tires that

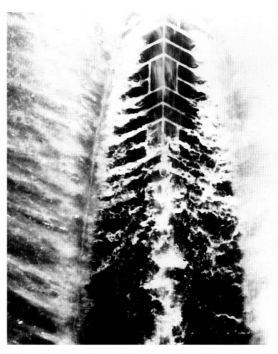

This photograph, made through a glass plate, shows how water is squeezed from the path of a tire.

can go 12,000 miles (or more) between replacements. Advances in compound materials and tire design mean that even riders of cruisers and large touring motorcycles can choose rubber that provides nearly as much traction as the "full race" tires of the 1980s. There are even tires on the market that use two different rubber compounds in the same tire: a harder compound in the center of the tire for extra life when riding in a straight line and a softer compound on the outer edges for extra traction while leaning through turns.

Both tire profile and tread design affect the shape and size of a tire's contact patch. With normal force pressing your tires against the road, an elliptical contact patch is formed. The larger a tire's contact patch, the more potential it has for traction. Many modern tire profiles are designed to produce a small contact patch while the tire is upright (for quick turn-in and steering action) and a larger contact patch when the tire is tilted for increased traction when leaning through a turn. Inflation pressure likewise affects a tire's contact patch. Let air out and the contact patch grows (but remember, too little air can cause the tire to overheat or slip off the rim).

Rubber is harder when it's cold than when warmed up. Motorcycle tires are designed to provide maximum traction at specific temperatures.

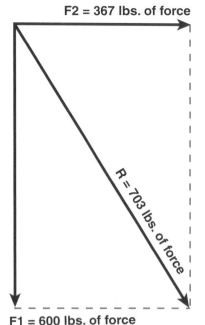

F2 = 367 lbs. of force

R = 703 lbs. of force

Diagram 11-1: Multiple forces acting on an object can be combined to find their net effect. This diagram shows two perpendicular forces, F1 and F2, acting on a point. Their net effect (the "resultant") is force R. Notice that it is easy to find the resultant force of two perpendicular forces by drawing this kind of diagram. Force R has exactly the same effect (amount of force and direction) as the combination of forces F1 and F2.

F1 = 600 lbs. of force

Riding moderately for the first few miles on the street will allow your tires to come up to proper operating temperature. Don't take that interstate on-ramp near your home at maximum lean angle and cornering speed before your tires come up to temperature.

Other factors that affect tire temperature are inflation pressure and load. Manufacturer-recommended tire pressures are calculated precisely to provide optimum performance and longevity. If you run your tires at a pressure that is lower than the manufacturer's recommendation, you run the risk of overheating your tires, leading to increased tire wear and diminished performance. Be sure to check your owner's manual for proper tire pressures and carrying capacity—especially if you ride two-up on a large touring bike and tend to pack everything but the kitchen sink.

If motorcycles were never operated in the rain or other inclement conditions, all motorcycles would be equipped with slick tires used on the racetrack. Racing slicks have no tread in order to maximize the amount of rubber in contact with the pavement. The grooves and channels on street tires only subtract from the available surface area that contacts the track. When it starts to rain, the racers simply make a pit stop and replace their slicks with treaded rain tires that provide better traction in wet

conditions by channeling water out from under the tire. As you can imagine, riding on the street and carrying two sets of tires with you on a cloudy day is utterly impractical—so street tires feature a treaded surface that is designed to be a compromise between acceptable traction in both wet and dry conditions.

The tread on a street tire is designed to provide channels for water to escape from the area of the tire that contacts the road (the contact patch). As tires wear and the tread depth is reduced, less water can be squeezed out between the tire and the road and the tire will start to ride up on the thin film of water left behind. This is called hydroplaning, and can result in a complete loss of traction. If your tires wear to the point where the tread depth is between 2/32 and 3/32 inches deep, it's time for new rubber.

Age and use are two factors that affect tire compound and performance. Every time we ride, our tires go through a "heat cycle" as they go from ambient to operating temperature and back down again. Each successive heat cycle slowly hardens the tire. In addition to heat cycling, tires "age" and slowly harden during non-use. So beware when you come across low-priced closeout deals on tires that may have been stored for a few years. Inspect your motorcycle's tires often and replace them if they show any signs of aging: cracking, worn tread, hardening, etc.

Tire Loading

Tire loading is largely a result of the "normal force," which pushes the tire against the roadway. You'll recall the term "normal force" as one part (N) of the traction formula ($F = C_F \times N$) discussed earlier in this chapter. The word "normal," in engineer-speak, means that the force occurs at 90 degrees (perpendicular) to the surface. Normal force is the force pressing the tire and the roadway surface together to produce friction. The force pushing your tires against the road is provided by gravity, and is proportional to the weight of your motorcycle distributed between front and rear wheels—usually about 50 percent on each tire.

The higher this downward force, the more potential traction is available. Remember, the distribution of this normal force between the two tires is somewhat variable, and is something that you have control over from one moment to the next because

The centrifugal force acting on a motorcycle is high when it makes a tight turn, wanting to tip the motorcycle toward the outside of the turn. The angle the motorcycle makes with the ground allows gravity to pull the motorcycle in the opposite direction. In a beautiful symphony of physics, the two tipping forces exactly balance one another.

it is directly affected by speed, lean angle, turning radius, throttle control, shifting, and braking.

For example, the 50/50 front-to-rear weight distribution of the average motorcycle only exists when your bike is on a level surface, and only when the motorcycle is stopped or moving at a constant speed. Twist the throttle hard in first gear on a 1000cc sportbike, for instance, and the front tire will lift off the road's surface and into a wheelie, transferring all the weight of the bike to the rear tire. Conversely, squeezing the front brake lever hard enough can lift the rear tire off the ground as the motorcycle's weight is transferred to the front tire.

While such dramatic examples of weight transfer may not happen to the same extent on cruisers or other types of motorcycles, acceleration and braking forces will always alter the amount of load force pressing your front or rear tires against the road's surface. Realize that the total amount of load force doesn't change in these instances, only how that load force is distributed between front and rear tires. This is yet another complication in the elusive game of measuring traction. How much traction you have available depends not only on your tires and road conditions, but also on how you ride your motorcycle.

Centrifugal Force

The weight of the motorcycle and rider (normal force) is one major component of force that makes up the total load the tire is subject to; another component is centrifugal force. The difference between normal and centrifugal forces concerns the direction that these forces act on the moving motorcycle in relation to the road surface. Normal force operates perpendicular (or normal) to the road surface; centrifugal force operates parallel to (or along) the road surface. Tire load is primarily a result of these two component forces acting together against the tire.

Normal and centrifugal force both apply a load to the tire by acting on the motorcycle's center of gravity (CG). Center of gravity refers to the point where the motorcycle's mass would balance front-to-rear and side-to-side if an imaginary point were drawn through it. For the purpose of this discussion, we're only concerned with the combined center of gravity with the rider (and passenger if applicable) sitting on the bike, fuel level, and placement of luggage. Note that, except for the effect of the weight of gasoline in the tank, the actual center of gravity for your motorcycle never changes. Cruisers tend to have a low CG, while tall dual-sport bikes will tend to have a higher CG—this is constant, and is determined by the layout

This photo and Diagram 11-2 show the forces acting on the center of gravity (CG) of a motorcycle in a turn. The force of gravity, W, and the centrifugal force, CF, both act on the CG, perpendicular to one another. Their resultant force, TL, passes in a direction exactly aligned with the CG and contact patch, keeping the motorcycle stable in a turn, even while it is leaned over.

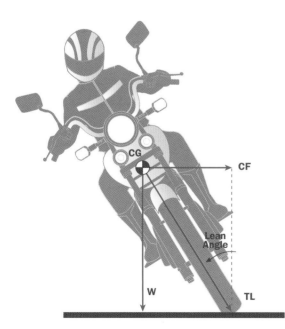

Diagram 11-2: Forces acting on the center of gravity while turning on a level surface.

and design of the motorcycle. But for the purposes of this discussion we're concerned with the combined CG of rider and motorcycle together, and this CG is variable. When you change your body position while riding, the combined CG of the bike and rider will change as well. Standing on the footrests, for example, raises the combined CG; when roadracers hang off the seat and toward the inside of a turn, the CG is shifted lower and to the side of the motorcycle.

Diagram 11-2 illustrates how normal and centrifugal forces act on a motorcycle's CG while turning on a level road. The weight (W), or normal force, pushes the CG downward; centrifugal force (CF), on the other hand, acts horizontally on the CG to keep the bike from falling over as it turns. The result of these two component forces combines to produce tire loading (TL). The angle of the resultant force TL is the lean angle necessary to keep the bike turning at your selected radius.

Even though they might not be able to articulate the formulas presented above, skilled riders know when and how much they can load the contact patch of each tire if the demand for traction is high (in other words, if maximum braking or swerving is required for a particular situation). Conversely, when riding in situations with reduced traction, an alarm bell goes off in a skilled rider's head. These riders carefully control tire loading by precise throttle and braking inputs, in order to minimize tire loading in low-traction situations. Now that you have a basic understanding of the mechanics of traction, understanding how to control tire loading is the next step toward safe riding. The finer points of traction management are the topic of the next chapter of this book, The Traction Pie Analogy.

MOTORCYCLING EXCELLENCE MEANS:

► You know the limits of traction and what affects those limits.

► You maintain maximum traction reserve to minimize risk and preserve the ability to respond to ever-changing road and traffic conditions.

► EFFECT OF SURFACE SLOPE ON TRACTION

The slope (or incline) of a road can have a major effect on a motorcycle's traction as it travels through a turn. You will find one of two types of inclines within a turn: "on-camber" inclines (also called a positive-sloped, or "banked," corner) and "off-camber" inclines (negative sloped). On-camber turns are turns in which the slope of the road angles downward toward the inside of the turn. An on-camber slope can help the motorcycle travel through the turn faster with less lean angle (it's like the road has done some of the required "leaning" for you). An off-camber turn slopes away from the inside of the turn, and makes more demands on the motorcycle with regard to traction and lean angle.

In diagram 11-3 you can see an example of an on-camber corner, and how a positive slope can assist the motorcycle in negotiating the curve. In that diagram, each of the two major component forces—weight (W) and centrifugal force (CF)—is further broken down into components that act perpendicular to the road surface (w1 and cf1) and parallel to the surface (w2 and cf2). These subcomponents are then added or subtracted to come up with the perpendicular and parallel components of tire loading. The results of these forces are shown on the right side of the diagram, where the resultant tire loading (TL) is shown along with the net results of the perpendicular force (w1 + cf1) and the results of the parallel forces (cf2 – w2).

On a non-level surface, the perpendicular component of tire loading due to weight alone is reduced. This includes traveling directly up, down and across hills. The steeper the slope, the greater the loss of total traction due to the weight. But in a turn with positive cross slope, centrifugal force makes up for this loss in traction by adding a greater perpendicular component of its own. Also notice that the parallel components (cf2 – w2) act

Diagram 11-3: Turning on a surface with a positive slope

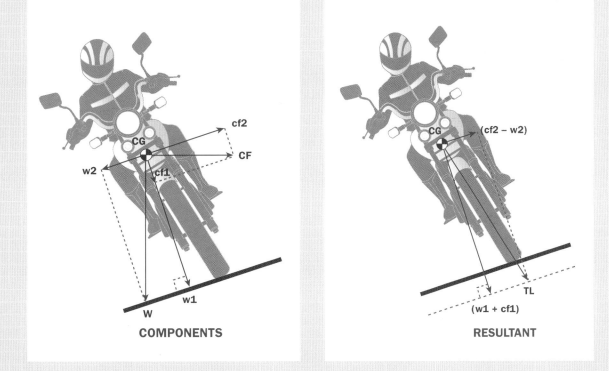

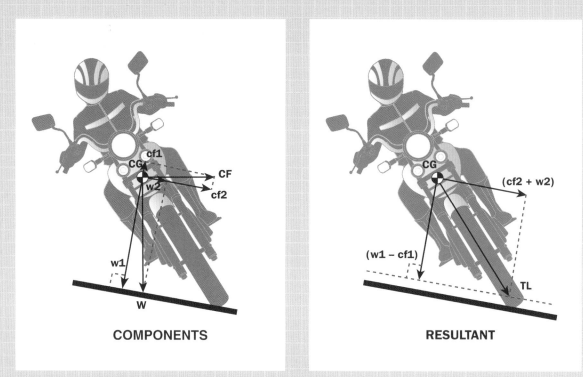

COMPONENTS

RESULTANT

Diagram 11-4: Turning on a surface with a negative slope

in opposing directions so the demand for overall traction is reduced. An extreme example of centrifugal tire loading can be seen at so-called "Wall of Death" carnival shows. This side-show act features a motorcycle ridden around and around a cylindrical cage until enough centrifugal force is created to make the motorcycle "stick" and ride up the vertical walls of the cage.

On turns with a negative or "off-camber" slope, the weight of the rider and bike produces less traction and the centrifugal force reduces traction even further because its perpendicular component (cf1) acts in a direction away from the surface. The net component that produces traction (w1 – cf1) is smaller than on the positive camber turn. The parallel components (cf2 + w2) now both "push" the bike downhill and unload the tires even more, even though the demand for traction in an off-camber situation is high. Because of this combination of factors, off-camber turns can be especially tricky and should be approached with caution. ■

CHAPTER 12

The Traction-Pie Analogy

KNOWING HOW MUCH TRACTION YOU HAVE LEFT IN ANY GIVEN SITUATION IS AN IMPORTANT PART OF LEARNING TO RIDE WITH CONTROL.

The next step toward becoming a safer, more controlled rider is to use your understanding of the factors that influence traction to determine how much traction you need in any given riding situation. Accelerating, decelerating, braking, and cornering all use a portion of your motorcycle's available traction. Furthermore, traction is affected differently at the front and rear tires, depending on your riding technique. Add to this the changing condition of the roadway surface and any of the other variables that regularly confront motorcyclists, and it would seem that figuring out exactly how much traction you have available at any given moment is impossible, or at the least very challenging.

Rather than trying to explain the concept of traction management with complicated formulas and numbers, let's simplify the matter with a series of pie chart graphics that make it easier to visualize traction usage as different-colored slices of the available traction pie. Each pie chart presented on the following pages represents traction usage under different conditions (constant speed, acceleration, deceleration, turning, etc.). Comparing the slices of pie in the different charts should help you to visualize how the traction potential is added, subtracted, and distributed between front and rear tires under varying load conditions. You'll notice that exact figures aren't used on these pie charts— that's because the pie slices are roughly proportional to the primary forces acting on the tires, and these don't always add up to 100 percent. Precise

Now that we have a basic understanding of traction, we'll see in this chapter how various riding situations affect available traction and how it is used.

math isn't essential here—what is more important is the general concept of how traction may be used so you can be a safer rider.

The three dominant "consumers" of traction are driving force, braking force, and side forces. What is left over is traction reserve. Traction needed by each of these consumers is variable (from zero to 100 percent of available traction) depending on what maneuver you are attempting, as well as the nature of the tires and road surface. Experienced riders have learned to manage how much traction each force is consuming. Each of these forces is under your direct control, and as long as you don't "eat" more of the traction pie than is available (use up all of your traction reserve), you will ride without having to think about formulas. The strategy is to anticipate how much traction you will need for any situation, and keep some extra in reserve for safety margins and emergencies.

DRIVING FORCE = ACCELERATION

Driving force is another term to describe acceleration. Driving force acts only on the rear tire and is produced both when you accelerate and when you maintain a steady speed. The added demands of driving force are the primary reason that rear tires wear out before the front tires. Roadway orientation can also influence the effect of driving force—traveling uphill at a constant speed increases driving force, for example, while traveling downhill decreases it.

BRAKING FORCE = SLOWING

Braking force is produced any time you apply the front or rear brakes of the motorcycle. Another form of braking force is "engine braking." Engine braking refers to when you "roll off" or close the throttle while moving in gear, and the slowing engine speed produces what is, in effect, a braking force to the rear tire. Engine braking can be quite strong on some high-powered motorcycles. Rolling friction between the tires and the road will also produce a small amount of braking force. Pushing your bike with a flat tire will give you firsthand experience with this type of braking force. For this reason, tire pressure and how much load you are carrying can affect rolling friction.

SIDE FORCE = CENTRIFUGAL FORCE

Side forces push your bike's tires sideways or perpendicular to the direction of forward motion. The most obvious side force is created while negotiating a turn. The faster you go through a turn, the greater the side force and the greater the lean angle required to counteract the side force. Other factors that contribute to side force are steering forces required for tracking and balancing, cross-sloping surfaces (off- or on-camber turns) and crosswinds. Any one or a combination of these side forces can be major consumers of available traction in a cornering situation.

SLICING THE TRACTION PIE

When a motorcycle is standing still on level ground, both the front and rear tires have 100 percent of their traction available to the rider—there are no driving, braking or side forces at play. It isn't until the motorcycle is underway, and these forces begin to take effect, that the traction pie analogy becomes useful. Available traction for each tire is constantly changing, but remember that the combined effect of the two traction pies remains constant. Explaining how traction is affected in situations of steady speed, acceleration, braking, cornering and other forces is the purpose of this next section.

STEADY SPEED

Riding at a constant speed, in a straight line, on a clean, dry, level road, both the front and rear tires will offer the same amount of available traction (assuming that the motorcycle's front-to-rear weight distribution is 50/50). Both pies will have small traction slices removed for each force acting minimally on the tires (as shown in Diagram 12-1), but the vast majority of total traction will be held in reserve and available for any changes in direction, speed, or braking that might be necessary.

Breaking down the small slices: braking force (due to rolling friction) consumes a bit of available traction on both pies, but the rear tire's slice is canceled out by the driving force from the engine. To keep a constant speed, the throttle has to be opened slightly thereby applying driving force to the rear tire to overcome rolling friction and wind resistance. Even though you are traveling in a straight line, you unconsciously make small steering corrections to maintain balance and tracking. Side forces used for these steering corrections accordingly take a small slice from both pies. The large portion left in each traction pie is held in reserve. These traction reserves provide you with the control options necessary for safe riding.

ACCELERATION

When you open the throttle to accelerate in a straight line, you create a driving force that uses a portion of the rear tire's traction reserve to provide forward motion. The more you twist the

Diagram 12-1: At steady speed on a level surface, traction available at both tires exceeds the force consumers, leaving plenty of reserve traction.

Diagram 12-2: Under acceleration, available force at the front tire is reduced as weight is transferred to the rear tire. Driving force consumes more traction at the rear tire.

throttle, the larger the slice of the rear tire traction pie that is used. The driving force, acting through the motorcycle's center of gravity, causes a rearward weight transfer that increases the load on the rear tire while decreasing the load on the front tire. Rapid throttle openings can make this transition (and its result on available traction) significant. Instead of a 50/50 balance, the rear tire might suddenly carry 100 percent of the bike's weight as the front tire lifts off the road surface in a wheelie. Diagram 12-2 demonstrates available traction under an acceleration situation. Notice that the traction pie for the rear tire is larger than that for the front tire. This reflects the fact that more loading of the rear tire makes more traction available there, while a load reduction on the front tire leaves it with less available traction. Notice also how proportionally more of the available traction is held in reserve in the front tire pie, because its traction consumers are relatively small.

BRAKING

Braking forces on the tires can be created in two ways: applying the brakes or rolling off the throttle to create engine braking (engine braking mostly affects the rear tire). Both the front and rear tires consume a portion of their respective traction pies in response to braking force. Because braking forces also act through the motorcycle's center of gravity, in the opposite direction as acceleration forces, the front tire now becomes more loaded than the rear. As a result, the front tire has more traction available for braking than the rear.

Diagram 12-3 shows weight transfer to the front tire under braking. Notice that almost all of the traction reserve at the rear tire is used up in a deceleration situation. Rear tire unloading under heavy braking reduces available traction and can cause the rear tire to lock up more easily.

In addition to creating engine braking, getting off the throttle abruptly and reducing acceleration

Diagram 12-3: Under deceleration, available force at the rear tire is reduced as weight is transferred to the front tire. Braking forces consume more traction at both tires.

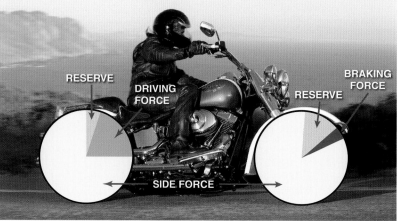

Diagram 12-4: In a high-speed turn, available traction increases, as turning forces load both tires. However, side forces rise to consume traction.

force can also cause an extreme weight transfer from the rear to the front tire. This can be potentially dangerous in corners, for example, when "chopping" the throttle (quickly closing the throttle). This action causes a weight shift that could either overwhelm front tire traction or unload the rear end and cause the rear tire to break traction. Smooth throttle inputs, both on and off, are the safest way to keep adequate rear tire traction in reserve.

CORNERING

Each time you lean your motorcycle into a turn, extreme side forces are generated between the tires and the road. Traction pie slices that represent side forces increase dramatically when entering a constant-speed turn, and even greater quantities of traction are used when corner entry speed is high. Cornering force increases as the square of velocity. In other words, it takes four times as much

traction to ride through the same radius turn at 30 mph as it does at 15 mph; at 45 mph, nine times the traction is required! This is important to note because nearly half of all solo motorcycle crashes occur when cornering.

Diagram 12-4 represents traction use as a motorcycle travels through a turn. As you can see from the traction pies, almost all of the available traction is used by cornering side forces. In this instance, any increase in lean angle (either because of increased speed or a tightening turn) would quickly use up what little reserve traction is available to both tires. A motorcycle's lean angle can be a useful indicator of cornering forces at work, because lean angle is directly affected by both speed and turn radius. Sharper turns and/or greater cornering speeds require additional lean angle. And as lean angle increases, greater slices from the front and rear traction pies must be allocated to the resulting side forces.

Because of the extreme traction demands in cornering, choosing an appropriate corner entry speed is very important. Special caution is needed for decreasing-radius turns. If you do happen to enter a corner too "hot" (fast), with too high an entry speed, it's important not to panic—you do have options. You could reduce your lean angle to reduce side force, though this comes at the expense of a wider turn—you could find yourself crossing over into the oncoming lane of traffic or running onto the shoulder. Another choice is to reduce your speed. As your speed decreases, side force and lean angle would diminish as long as the radius of the turn remains the same.

Attempting to slow your motorcycle while already leaned over in a turn is complicated, and you need to keep several points in mind to ensure your safety. First, remember to make smooth inputs. Getting off the gas too abruptly can create a chain of events that reduce, not increase, available traction. Once the driving force disappears from the rear tire, it's replaced by a braking force (engine braking). At the same time, weight is transferred forward, unloading the rear end of the motorcycle and reducing rear tire traction even further. Using the front brake presents similar complications. Weight transfer from rear to front likewise unloads the rear tire. The front tire is now loaded and using more traction to absorb braking forces, leaving less available for side forces. Remember, doing anything that requires another slice of the traction pie inside of a turn—for example, over-accelerating or decelerating—increases the likelihood of a skid. This is why a conservative corner entry speed that leaves plenty of traction in reserve is wise strategy!

Balancing the demand for traction between braking, driving, and side forces becomes more difficult when any combination of the three forces brings a tire near its traction limit. To best manage traction, try to separate the demands for traction in time and space so that only one or two forces are eating from the traction pie at any given time. For example, try to set your cornering speed before you enter the turn, so that heavy braking forces aren't competing with side forces for traction in the early part of the corner. If you find that you need to stop quickly mid-turn, separate the traction demands by first straightening the motorcycle to reduce lean angle (and the resulting side forces), then apply both brakes for a controlled rapid stop. The fewer forces at work at any one time, the more traction will be available for any critical maneuver.

WELCOME TO THE "REAL ROAD"

So far, our discussion of traction management has assumed that the action was taking place on a smooth, dry, consistent surface. Of course, riding in the real world is different; ideal conditions are seldom present all of the time. Anything other than dry, clean concrete or asphalt offers less than optimal traction, and thus, smaller traction pies. Riding in the rain is a useful example: clean, wet pavement provides about 80 percent the traction of clean, dry pavement, so when you ride in the rain your available traction pies are effectively 20 percent smaller. Braking, driving, and side forces do not vary with road surface condition—these still eat the same amount of traction pie wet or dry. Only overall traction reserves are reduced in the wet. Less traction in reserve translates into a smaller safety margin for emergencies, and demands slower speed to accommodate the difference. The rules for riding your bike in the rain are no different than driving your car under the same conditions—drive more slowly, increase your following distance, and do not enter turns as fast.

Extremely slippery conditions require even more caution and forethought. Ice patches, metal plates on bridges, gravel, sand, wet leaves, and moss/algae ("green slime") are several examples of extremely slippery surfaces you might encounter on the road. Even just maintaining a constant speed on these road conditions is difficult. Slight differences in driving force (from acceleration or engine braking forces) could exceed the traction reserve at the rear tire. One technique that is helpful in these situations is to disconnect the engine from the offending surface by squeezing the clutch and coasting through the slippery mess. When doing this, though, remember that approach speed must be high enough to permit coasting without the need for significant steering inputs to maintain tracking and balance. If your motorcycle is moving so slowly that it begins to tip or lean, the necessary corrective steering inputs (side forces) could exceed the available traction.

While tire tread will channel water away from the tire to facilitate traction in the wet, deeper puddles can raise the spectre of hydroplaning. Use SEE and slow before the puddle, then ride through cautiously. Avoid braking or steering (braking force and side force reduce available traction) while riding through the puddle if at all possible.

Uneven or bumpy roads continually change the amount of traction available. Such "vertical accelerations" can cause tires to unload and load rapidly. Any time tire loading is decreased the traction pie becomes smaller. The motorcycle's suspension will attempt to smooth out these surfaces, though tire unloading will still affect traction. Any sudden reduction in traction may affect the front and rear tires differently and can cause skids on bumpy surfaces.

Even experienced riders have to constantly think about traction management. It's a complicated process with a dizzying number of variables at play. The traction pie is just one analogy to help understand how this process works. What's important is that you understand the concept of maintaining traction reserves under ever-changing riding conditions. Smooth operation of your motorcycle's controls provides the base for applying your traction management skills. Knowing how much traction you have left in any given situation is an important part of learning to ride with control.

MOTORCYCLING EXCELLENCE MEANS:

► You become aware of the interrelated dynamics of your motorcycle's suspension and tire characteristics, the road surface, and your speed.

► Your make decisions to ensure adequate traction reserve.

► You apply a riding strategy that considers the consumers of traction in braking, swerving and cornering maneuvers.

► You take into account road surface features and conditions.

COUNTERSTEERING IS A KEY ELEMENT OF RIDING WITH CONTROL. PRESS "HERE" TO TURN.

Countersteering is the technical term used to describe the unique way that a single-track vehicle like a motorcycle changes direction in order to negotiate corners or swerve.

In the simplest terms, a motorcycle steers opposite (counter) to how a two-track vehicle (an automobile, for example) steers. When you turn your car's steering wheel to the right (clockwise), the car turns to the right. If you turn a moving motorcycle's handlebars to the right, the motorcycle will actually go left. The differences between regular steering and countersteering are related to centrifugal force and differences between how a single-track and a two-track vehicle respond to the changes in centrifugal force that are created after a turn is initiated.

If you have ever pedaled a bicycle faster than 10 mph (the speed beyond which the momentum of the bicycle becomes a significant factor for steering) and then turned, you have experienced countersteering firsthand. Most of us performed this action reflexively at a young age, without any understanding at all of how a bicycle actually steered. Similarly, many motorcyclists who have never received any formal rider training have been riding for years without any awareness of the countersteering phenomenon. Because the concept of initially turning left to go right is inherently confusing, both beginning and experienced riders sometimes have trouble coming to terms with the idea of countersteering. Breaking down this idea requires a bit of background on the act of steering

Steering a motorcycle is a lot like steering a bicycle. Once you learn the basics, it just feels natural. This chapter will help you develop a smooth, confident style for better control.

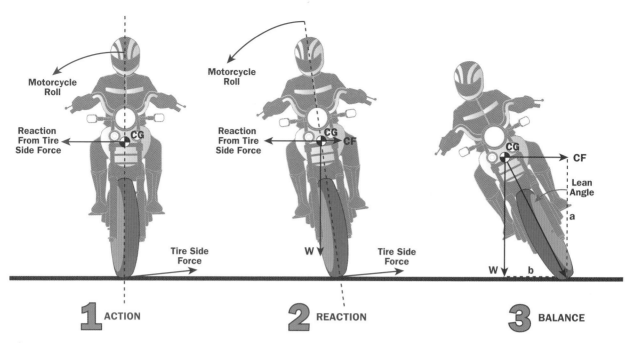

Diagram 13-1: ACTION – Steering force applied by countersteering. REACTION – Tire side force continues to cause motorcycle to roll. BALANCE – Resulting lean stabilizes motorcycle in the turn.

a vehicle (single- or two-track), and the physical properties at work.

In the simplest terms, changing the direction of any vehicle is accomplished through centrifugal force acting on the vehicle's center of gravity. In the case of turning an automobile, the automobile counters the effects of that centrifugal force by transferring weight to the outside track or tires, causing the car to turn in the direction in which the steering wheel is turned.

Motorcycles must lean to turn, and this leaning introduces an additional dynamic. Where an automobile transfers weight to the outside of a turn during steering, a single-track motorcycle counters the centrifugal force generated in a turn by leaning, which moves the center of gravity toward the inside of the turn. As a motorcycle leans into a turn, it is balanced between the force of gravity trying to pull the machine farther toward the ground and centrifugal force tugging the mass of rider and machine toward the outside of the turn.

Turning a motorcycle is done by initiating and controlling the lean angle. Accelerating and braking have no effect on turning when the bike is vertical and traveling in a straight line. Changing your motorcycle's center of gravity by moving your body does not cause turning either (though it may be used to adjust lean angle after the turn has been

initiated). Getting a bike to turn quickly and precisely without using a countersteering input at the handlebars is impossible. A moving motorcycle must lean to turn, even at slow speeds. Turning is a result of lean angle, and countersteering is an effective way to initiate the lean that begins a turn.

As complicated as the concept of countersteering is, the actual procedure is easy—"Press left, go left. Press right, go right." In other words, gently pressing outward on the left handgrip will cause the motorcycle to turn left, and gently pressing outward on the right handgrip will cause the motorcycle to turn right. Applying more pressure to the bars causes the motorcycle to lean more quickly; pressing longer results in a greater lean angle. Turning forces are created by the motorcycle's lean angle without any significant additional rider input. Once turn-in has been initiated, the motorcycle seems to turn almost effortlessly.

The illustrations in Diagram 13-1 will help make sense of these seemingly contradictory concepts. Imagine that you are riding a motorcycle at 40 mph in a straight line, and you momentarily turn the handlebars to the left by pressing against the right grip. This press against the right grip is the "Action" referred to in the first illustration. In that image you can see the front tire's contact patch will immediately steer to the left. Momentum wants to make the motorcycle continue in a straight line. Steering the front tire to the left causes the mass of bike and rider to roll about the center of gravity, which results in the bike leaning to the right—this

THE CAMERA NEVER LIES

1. Slowing and looking.

2. Pressing on the left handlebar.

3. The rolling moment resulting from the countersteer produces a lean.

4. The lean, in combination with steering trail, steers the front tire in the direction of the turn.

5. And away we go!

is the "Reaction" in the second illustration. The resulting lean and gyroscopic precession *(see next section)* instantly turns the front wheel to the right and causes a right turn. In effect, countersteering "trips" the bike: when you momentarily press right, the bottom of the bike actually turns left for an instant causing the bike to lean to the right, leading into a right turn. The entire process happens so quickly that you may never even notice the initial left turn.

Once the turn has been initiated, the rider continues to use countersteering techniques to control the lean angle and maintain balance. When pressure on the bars is relaxed, lean angle will stabilize at the point where the centrifugal force that pulls the bike outward and the weight that pulls the bike downward are equalized. This is the point of "Balance," as illustrated in the Diagram 13-1. If the rider were to keep pressing against the right handgrip, the motorcycle would lean more and more to the right until the motorcycle chassis contacted the ground or the traction limits were exceeded and the front tire "washed out" from underneath the motorcycle.

Once you develop the technique for countersteering, you'll see how easy it is to make the motorcycle lean just by pressing forward on that side of the handlebars.

"GYROSCOPIC PRECESSION" AND OTHER BIG WORDS

The preceeding pages cover the simple explanation of countersteering—here's a slightly more technical discussion of the physics behind the phenomenon for readers who remain less than convinced of the effectiveness of countersteering. Start by considering a motorcycle's rotating mass. The mass of the spinning wheels, tires, and brake rotors together experience what is called "gyroscopic precession," a force that causes the front wheel to turn in the direction that the motorcycle is leaning. Precession is the behavior of a gyroscope that causes it to tilt when an attempt is made to turn its axis. Precession can easily be demonstrated using a bicycle wheel (see diagram on next page). Hold the bicycle wheel by its axle and have another person spin the wheel. Holding the wheel out in front of you, turn it to the left, as though you were steering to the left. Notice that the wheel wants to tilt (lean) to the right. Here's another experiment: Holding the spinning wheel out in front of you in the same way, lean it as if you're entering a turn. Notice that the spinning wheel wants to turn (steer) toward the direction in which it is leaned. Both experiments show gyroscopic precession in action. It is this important effect that contributes to the stability of bicycles and motorcycles when they are moving.

Rotating wheels on a motorcycle have more weight and spin faster (at higher speeds) than bicycle wheels, and as a result, motorcycle wheels carry more rotary momentum (in other words, are subject to stronger gyroscopic effects). The faster the wheels are turning, the more rigid the steering becomes and more pressure on the handlebars is required to produce the same rate of change in lean angle. As speed increases, the front wheel acts as if there were two big springs on either side trying to hold the steering in a centered position. Motorcycle racers use lightweight wheels and brake rotors in order to minimize gyroscopic momentum and produce quicker steering response on the race, improving control at speeds higher than normal traffic.

The steering effects discussed above operate at any lean angle. Once you have created a given lean angle through countersteering you can lessen the pressure on the bars, and the chassis' steering trail (see diagram on page 146) will tend to stabilize the bike through the turn because the weight and centrifugal force are in balance. This illustrates why the duration of the steering input determines both the amount of lean angle and the radius of the resulting turn. The force of the steering input only controls the rate of change in lean angle—the harder you turn the handlebars, the more initial side force acts on the front tire and the more quickly the motorcycle will lean into the turn.

PRESS OR PULL, IT'S STILL COUNTERSTEERING

Whether you "press" on the right handgrip to initiate a lean to the right or "pull" the on the left handgrip to initiate a lean in the same direction, you're countersteering. Given the choice, it's more natural to press the handlebar in the direction that you want to turn. You'll have the feeling that by pressing down on one side of the handlebars, the motorcycle just falls away toward that side. It's a very natural effect. You want your outside arm and hand to always be relaxed and not "fighting" your "steering" arm for adjustments in steering corrections. This practice will allow you to produce a smoother arc through a turn without wobbling from point to point within the same turn.

To summarize the process of countersteering, think of it as the most efficient way to generate the necessary forces to initiate a change in lean angle. Conscious and deliberate use of countersteering might take some getting used to. Try to overcome any uncertainty by practicing the technique in an open parking lot. Travel in a straight line at 25 mph and then press gently on either the right or left handgrip, paying attention to the effect it produces. You'll find after consciously practicing countersteering several times that you have actually been doing it all along. Feeling comfortable with the technique of countersteering will allow you to corner more confidently and safely, and to execute quick and precise changes in direction, actions that could allow you to safely avoid objects in your path of travel. Countersteering is a key element of riding with control.

MOTORCYCLING EXCELLENCE MEANS:

► You frequently practice countersteering for cornering and swerving.

► You are able to visualize what happens when you press (or pull) on the handlebars.

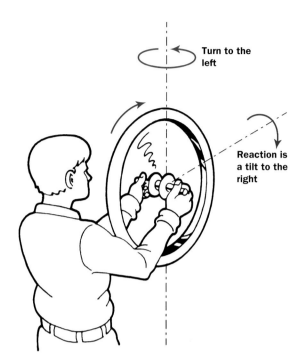

A motorcycle wheel behaves like a gyroscope. As you steer toward the left, gyroscopic forces cause the motorcycle to tilt (lean) to the right and turn to the right, tending to cancel the steering input. This effect gives motorcycles great stability when they are moving.

► MOTO-MATH

MOTORCYCLE GEOMETRY EXPLAINED BY ERIK BUELL

Let's forget for a moment about countersteering and traction management and instead turn our attention to geometry. "Wait!" I can hear you saying, "I thought this was a book about riding motorcycles, not a math text!" Never fear—first, this is the "fun math" that your high school geometry teacher told you that you'd find useful some day. Second, a decent understanding of the basics of motorcycle chassis geometry will add much to your mastery of your machine.

Chassis geometry—the various angles and distances between the chassis components of your motorcycle—is what largely determines the "feel" of your motorcycle at speed. Sitting down at the computer-aided design station, designing motorcycles is a very complex science. But for you, the rider, it doesn't need to be that complicated; just understanding a few basic terms and principles can be very useful.

Starting at the front of the motorcycle, the two most important terms to grasp are "rake" and "trail." Rake refers to the angle of the steering axis from vertical, and is usually expressed in terms of degrees (e.g., 24 degrees of fork rake). Cruiser-style bikes tend to have more rake; sport bikes usually have less. In general, a chassis with more fork rake will tend to be more stable in straightaways, but will require a greater effort to turn, compared to a chassis with less rake. In the old days, when motorcycle frames were flexible and could twist more easily, a lot of fork rake was necessary to keep the bike stable at speed. Nowadays, with much stronger and stiffer chassis designs, it is possible to have much less rake and still have excellent stability.

The second front-end geometry measurement is trail: the distance between where a line drawn through the steering axis intersects the ground and the center of the tire contact patch. The tire contact patch is always behind ("trailing") the steering axis. This dimension influences the self-centering tendencies of the wheel. More trail causes the tire to generate more self-centering force and, therefore, creates more stability but also requires a higher turning effort.

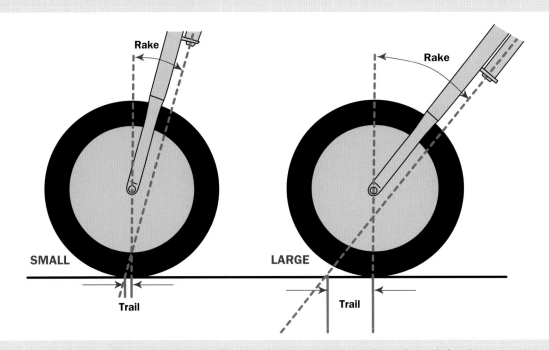

A larger amount of trail creates a greater distance between the steering axis and the tire contact patch, making the motorcycle more stable, but requiring higher steering effort.

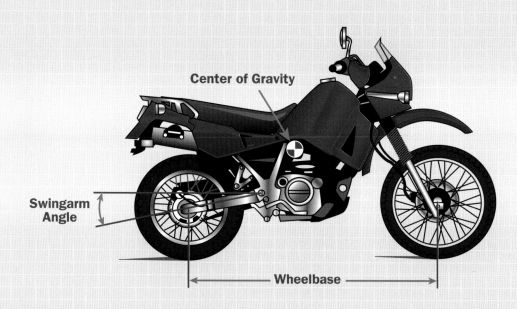

Center of Gravity

Swingarm Angle

Wheelbase

Moving toward the middle of the motorcycle, center of gravity is the important term to come to terms with. The center of gravity refers to the point where, if you picked up the bike at that point, it would stay perfectly balanced without tipping backward, forward or sideways. Where exactly the center of gravity is located depends on the layout of that particular motorcycle, and varies (sometimes significantly) between different models and motorcycle types. Center of gravity also has a significant effect on how the bike handles—generally, a low center of gravity right underneath the rider's body will make the motorcycle feel the lightest and most nimble.

At the back of the motorcycle chassis there are two significant geometry figures: wheelbase and swingarm angle. The wheelbase is the distance between the front and rear axles. A bike with a shorter wheelbase tends to be more nimble and - require less lean angle for a given cornering speed. A longer wheelbase gives the rider more room on the motorcycle, and gives the bike a solid, substantial feel going down the road. Swingarm angle refers to the angle off horizontal of a line drawn from the rear axle to the swingarm pivot. A greater swingarm angle contributes more "anti-

squat" properties to the chassis, which means when you accelerate hard the bike doesn't squat down at the back, but instead lifts up and pushes the rear tire into the ground. In addition to better traction and power transmission, this also helps maintain ground clearance when coming out of a corner. Too much angle and anti-squat, however, can make the bike's suspension too stiff to function properly under hard acceleration.

One important aspect of motorcycle chassis geometry is the angles formed by the position of the seat, handlebars, and footrests—the components that determine how you fit on your motorcycle. This is why it is important to make sure that you ride a motorcycle that fits you comfortably. I like to think of a motorcycle and rider as being one unit, which makes you, the rider, the most important and sophisticated part of the motorcycle chassis geometry equation. ■

Erik Buell is chairman and chief technical officer of Buell Motorcycle Company, which he began in 1993 with the help of Harley-Davidson Motor Company. Buell owns a minority interest in the company, with Harley-Davidson owning the rest.

▶ FALSE START

COUNTERSTEERING, TRICYCLES, AND TRAINING WHEELS, BY KEITH CODE

Blame your parents if you hit a car with your motorcycle. They are the ones who bought you a tricycle in preparation for later riding a bicycle with training wheels and it laid a false foundation for what you are now trying to achieve in confidently controlling your motorcycle.

Even though body positioning can help fine-tune a motorcycle's path through a turn and maximize traction, the No BS bike demonstrates that handlebar input is the primary way to initiate a turn.

Lean To Turn

To this day uneducated riders around the world still contend they "lean" to turn their motorcycles. As far back as the Wright brothers it has been observed that pressure on the handlebars initiates the lean of the bike—not the movement of a rider's body mass in his intended direction of travel. Unfortunately, the steering is opposite that of the tricycle or bicycle with training wheels. OK, excuse your parents; they didn't know that.

Countersteering

These are magic words for the counterintuitive process (counterintuitive because of the tricycle training) of applying pressure to the bars in the opposite direction of the intended turn. It is the only way to achieve quick and efficient directional changes on a motorcycle.

No BS (Body Steering) Bike

My research led me to create the "No BS" bike. It has the normal handlebars plus an additional set which are mounted to the frame and do not rotate. The second bars are equipped with a throttle so the rider can maintain the bike's speed and stability.

Riding the bike with hands on the solid mounted bars is frightening. The tiny, subtle inputs into the bars we do unconsciously to direct our bikes and maintain control over them become unavailable and the rider feels about as effective in turning the motorcycle as a railway passenger trying to turn a train from the caboose. The rider soon realizes that body inputs are, at best, a secondary influence in steering the bike.

Your final parental rebellion is learning to turn. Practice countersteering on every ride, at every corner. It will give you confidence in cornering and help you make that quick swerve when you need it. ■

Since the 1950s, Keith Code has dedicated himself to riding, understanding, and teaching the art of riding motorcycles. His California Superbike Schools have trained more than 100,000 riders worldwide.

CHAPTER 14
Safe Cornering Techniques

FOR MANY RIDERS, GRACEFULLY ARCING THROUGH A SUCCESSION OF SMOOTH TURNS IS THE ULTIMATE MOTORCYCLING EXPERIENCE. CURVE AHEAD!

When first learning to ride, basic skills like accelerating, shifting, and stopping demand a rider's full attention. During the first days of learning, the finer points of cornering and countersteering begin to make sense. And when a rider ventures out into the real riding world, and encounters his or her first twisty road, the dynamics of cornering become apparent. For many riders, this is where the fun starts. Riding a motorcycle in a straight line is certainly exhilarating, especially for a new rider. However, for many riders, gracefully arcing through a succession of smooth turns is the ultimate motorcycling experience.

Just like riders, no two turns are exactly alike. And because corners often are connected one to another, entering and exiting each corner requires thinking ahead, anticipating your next move, and making use of multiple riding strategies. Use the "SEE" (Search/Evaluate/Execute) protocol introduced earlier in the book. Analyzing visual information and acting accordingly is key to learning how to successfully and safely negotiate corners. This is an essential point: cornering is a learned skill. It takes time to develop and refine safe cornering techniques. Single-vehicle motorcycle crashes account for nearly half of all crash fatalities, and many of these involve cornering. The information on the following pages is intended to help you master this important and satisfying skill.

Cornering involves a lot more than steering. In this chapter, we'll explore the skills you need to put it all together.

VISION

Most of the information that we need to ride safety is received visually. The eyes provide the data for the brain to interpret and evaluate. Consequently, anything you can do to optimize your vision will enhance your riding performance. Wearing quality eye protection at all times, using prescription glasses (if needed) that are up to date, and keeping your face shield clean, scratch-free, and not tinted too darkly, will all aid your assessment of the road.

When you've mastered the skills of cornering, hairpin turns will become a joy you'll look forward to.

Having the ability to see clearly is only the beginning; choosing where to look, and paying attention to what you see, is also vitally important. Less-experienced riders have a tendency to focus their sight an unnecessarily short distance ahead of the bike. Experienced riders, on the other hand, maintain a sight path that is much longer and broader. Using a more "open" sight pattern by looking at least 12 seconds ahead helps these riders notice a greater number of details farther ahead, helping them to better anticipate actions that might become necessary down the road.

You might think of this as the difference between driving your car using the low-beam lights compared to using the high beams. Inexperienced motorcyclists too often ride in "low-beam" mode, and tend to focus too much on small details—roadside objects, potholes, or other objects that are immediately in front of them. While those details do need to be evaluated, switching to high-beam mode increases your visual horizon and allows you to take in information earlier—things like multiple vehicles approaching an intersection, or oncoming hills, curves, or surface conditions—leaving you more time to evaluate and respond to the situation.

LOOKING

Riding safely demands that you keep your eyes moving to get the big picture ahead. Look for factors that could develop into a hazard or cause you problems.

Coming up to a curve, allow your eyes to take in as much information as possible. Is the radius of the turn tight or wide? Are there objects on the side of the road—animals, people, or cars—that might demand attention? Is this a single turn, or the first in a series of curves? Is it a decreasing radius curve? Will traffic complicate your line through the curve? These are all important concerns; keeping your field of vision as open as possible is necessary for you to gather the required information to answer these questions.

Once you've assessed the overall layout and situation of the curve, your vision should be seeking out more discrete details: Where is the best entry and exit point for the turn? Where is the apex? Is your path clean, or littered with gravel and fallen leaves? Is there anything else in the roadway—rocks, road kill, an oil patch—that might cause trouble mid-corner? Momentarily focusing your vision on discrete points of the corner will allow you to note these important details. These hazards should be "noted," not stared at, or else you run the danger of target fixating. You'll remember from earlier in this book that a motorcycle has a tendency to go in the direction that the rider is looking. In extreme cases, target fixation can actually cause you to ride right into that object you are trying to avoid. Note the obstacle, alter your ride pattern if necessary, but take care not to let your eye linger on that object for too long. Look where you want to go.

LINE SELECTION

When choosing the best line of travel though any given corner, it's helpful to think back on the lessons learned in our discussion of traction management and consider how the line we select will affect the amount of traction available to us. Remember, the major consumers of traction in turns are cornering speed and the radius of the turn. Tighter turns and higher speeds require a greater lean angle and more traction; wider turns and slower entry speeds allow your motorcycle to remain more upright, demanding less traction.

Carefully selecting the proper line through a corner is the best way to reduce the side forces on your tires, thereby reducing their ultimate traction demands. Choosing as wide a line as possible, for example, can maximize available traction by widening the turn's radius, reducing lean angle as well as the amount of time spent at maximum lean. When you're riding on the street, you've got an entire lane at your disposal—use all of it. As shown in Diagram 14-1, enter standard corners from the outside of the turn, follow a path of travel that takes you to the inside of the turn, and exit to the outside. In right-hand turns, this means entering and exiting the turn near the center line of a two-lane road; in left-hand turns you'll enter and exit near the outside of your lane. By entering and exiting a turn on the outside, you make the best use of the available lane surface, taking the most moderate line and minimizing the amount of time spent at maximum lean, plus your line of sight is improved.

When choosing the ideal line, it's also important to determine where the "apex," or center, of the turn will be. The term apex describes the point where you are closest to the inside of the turn. Where you choose to locate the apex (you choose this point) is important to the smoothness and efficiency of your turn. It is not always located exactly at the "middle" of the turn. You have some flexibility in positioning the apex of any particular turn, and you can choose an early apex or a late (delayed) apex, depending on the particular type of corner you are attempting to negotiate.

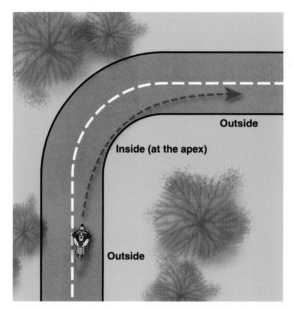

Diagram 14-1: Simple, constant-radius turn

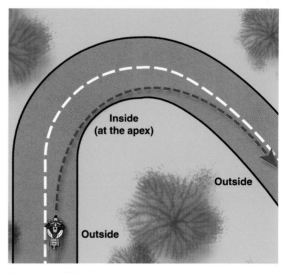

Diagram 14-2: Increasing-radius turn

DIFFERENT TYPES OF CURVES

Turns can be generally grouped into three types: constant-radius, increasing-radius, and decreasing-radius. In constant-radius turns (Diagram 14-1) the radius remains constant through the duration of the corner. In a constant radius corner, the path with the greatest practical radius begins as far toward the outside of the lane as possible. Following a smooth path through a constant-radius turn will

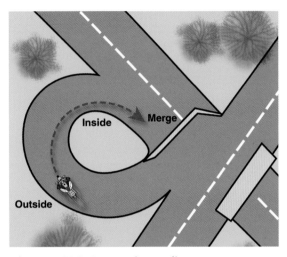

Diagram 14-3: Decreasing-radius turn

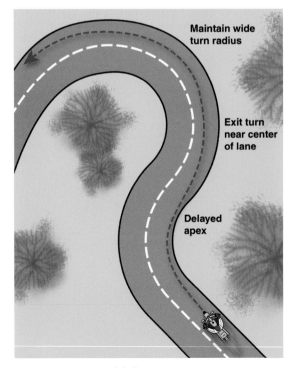

Diagram 14-4: Multiple turns

take you near the inside edge of the corner (the apex) at the corner's midpoint, then as far to the outside as is practical at the exit. Remember, your goal is to "widen" the radius of the turn in order to maximize traction and reduce lean angle. Use this type of turn as a general baseline, and compare the apex point in this constant radius turn to other types of turns.

Increasing-radius turns (Diagram 14-2) are turns that "open up" (the radius widens) as you approach the exit point. These turns are not particularly challenging and are the most forgiving type of turn if you happen to misjudge and enter at too high a speed. The greatest practical radius for an increasing-radius turn is one that places the apex before the midpoint of the turn. This is called an early apex, and this allows you to carry a smoother line in the first half of the corner because it requires a less-aggressive turn in. If you were to use the same apex, as though in a constant-radius turn, here, the first part of the turn would have to be overly sharp and you would be making poor use of the extra room available at the exit of the corner.

One common pitfall that traps inexperienced riders, especially in increasing radius turns, is making multiple apexes in a single corner. This is usually a result of not evaluating the complete turn through to the exit. Because these riders don't evaluate the whole turn, they end up steering toward each discrete point within the turn. This requires the rider to adjust steering multiple times, and often results in "wobbling" through the corner. To prevent multiple apexing, keep your eyes up and looking through the turn, and use a conservative entry speed.

Decreasing-radius turns (Diagram 14-3), are turns that "tighten up" (decrease in radius) as they approach the exit. These are significantly more challenging and cause many riders trouble. The most common problem riders have with decreasing-radius turns is selecting too early an apex. This requires some sort of mid-corner correction—a line adjustment and/or a speed adjustment—to prevent running wide at the exit and crossing into the oncoming lane of traffic. The best strategy in a decreasing-radius turn is to choose a late or delayed apex, one that is located beyond the midpoint of the turn. In the instance of a decreasing-radius turn, a late apex will require a lower entry speed and result in less ultimate lean angle, leaving more traction available in reserve and more room to correct your line if the turn ends up to be even tighter than you anticipated.

Decreasing-radius turns are especially treacherous because many times the nature of these corners (turning back on themselves) means that they are blind, so you don't know what to expect until you are well into the corner. If you enter a corner with visual obstructions, it is best to assume the worst, and expect that the corner will tighten up on itself with a decreasing radius. At best, you will be pleasantly surprised by a constant or increasing radius; at worst, you will have a greater chance of correcting your line or speed to accommodate the decreasing radius. Either way, a delayed apex gives you an increased margin of safety when entering a blind corner, because you can see farther through the corner at the time you enter it.

So far we have only discussed selecting apexes in the context of single turns. Selecting the best apex becomes slightly more complicated when you are entering a series of multiple turns, because the point where you exit one turn is going to determine your entry point for the next turn. The ideal line of travel through individual turns, like those discussed previously, is not always the best line for a series of linked turns. Consider the sequence of two turns where the first has a constant radius and the second is a decreasing radius in the opposite direction, as illustrated in Diagram 14-4. In this instance, if you select a normal or center apex for the constant-radius section, you wind up on the wrong side of the lane to enter the decreasing-radius turn that

follows. In this case, delaying your apex for the first turn will allow you to exit the first turn nearer the center of the lane and in a better position to enter turn two.

This last example illustrates why it is so important to keep speed under control and search the road 12 seconds ahead. In this case, note upcoming corners before you decide on a path (and an apex) through any given turn. Even then, in some cases the "ideal" path or line to take through linked turns is not going to be visible because roadway or traffic conditions interfere with your line of sight. In situations like this, especially on unfamiliar roads, slower entry speeds are the only consistent way to avoid trouble.

APPROACH SPEED

As discussed in Chapter 12, motorcycle tires have the most traction available when positioned straight up and down, at 90 degrees to the roadway. Take advantage of this by finishing all of your braking while the bike is still straight up and down, before you turn into the corner and increased side forces reduce the amount of traction available for braking maneuvers. As you approach the turn, gradually roll off the throttle instead of snapping it closed abruptly. Smooth throttle control will keep weight from abruptly transferring to the front tire and upsetting the front suspension. As needed, apply both brakes smoothly with gradual pressure as needed. If your speed drops sufficiently, you'll need to downshift as well—concentrate on smooth movements with the clutch to avoid upsetting the chassis as you set up for the corner.

Note the late apex chosen by the rider in this decreasing-radius turn.

Multiple turns can be great fun to ride, but they require your full attention to the road ahead, and extra care when you can't see around the next turn.

ENTRY SPEED

Selecting an appropriate entry speed is a complex decision based on your observations as you approach the corner. Line-of-sight, turn radius, grade, and road surface condition and slope, as well as oncoming traffic, all influence this decision. The ideal entry speed into a flat or uphill turn is one that allows you to gradually roll on the throttle from the entry point through the exit of the turn. Barring any unforeseen hazards, if you find yourself having to brake or roll off the throttle mid-turn, then your entry speed was probably too high. Ideally, you want your entry speed to be slow enough for you to safely respond to your worst-case predictions.

Take special care selecting entry speeds when riding with a group of other motorcyclists. Many riders tend to unconsciously follow the lead of the rider in front of them, a hazardous practice that can result in a rider unintentionally overriding his (or his motorcycle's) abilities. The most common mistake in this situation is for a rider to enter a corner too hot because he or she is blindly following the leader, causing that rider to panic and sometimes crash. Remember that the "leader" of your little group may be a more experienced rider willing to brake much harder and lean his or her motorcycle farther than you are. Or alternately, he

could be in the process of making a mistake regarding his entry speed! Follow blindly and you'll be making the same mistake right behind him. When riding in a group, always ride your own ride—only you know your, and your bike's, braking and cornering abilities.

LEAN

Once you've selected your turn-in point and arrived at a suitable entry speed, you need to lean the motorcycle into the corner. Remember from the discussion of countersteering in Chapter 13 that lean is needed to turn. Use a countersteering input—pressing smoothly on the handgrip that corresponds to the direction that you wish to turn (press right, turn right) to initiate this lean.

In addition to initiating the turn, leaning also maintains the balance of the motorcycle through the corner. In a cornering situation, centrifugal force acts on the motorcycle's center of gravity to push the bike toward the outside of the corner, while gravity pulls the bike downward, toward the inside of the corner. Controlling your lean angle with steering inputs is the way that you maintain this balance. Countersteering is the best way to initiate a turn, and also the best way to control your smooth line in that turn after it has been initiated.

THROTTLE CONTROL

After you reach the entry point and press on the handgrip (countersteer) to lean the motorcycle and initiate the turn, you need to roll on the throttle slightly to maintain a constant speed through the turn. If you don't begin to add at least a bit of throttle, your speed will begin to drop and you will lean more, changing your anticipated path of travel through the corner.

Ideally, you want to use a steady speed through the middle of the turn and then gradually roll on the throttle to increase speed as you near the exit of the corner. Getting on the gas too soon (or too hard) when the bike is still at full lean can cause the rear tire to lose traction. The rate at which you choose to accelerate while turning is mostly affected by lean angle—generally, the greater the lean angle, the less throttle you can safely apply. As you approach the turn's exit point and your lean angle decreases, apply more throttle. The acceleration will actually assist your steering, standing the bike upright as you exit the turn.

Another benefit of smoothly rolling on the throttle through a turn is that the both the front and rear suspensions will work in your favor. The suspension will be closer to the middle of its travel, the so-called "sweet spot," so it can more effectively absorb irregularities in the road's surface.

While leaned over through a turn take special care to avoid any sudden "on" or "off" throttle changes. Snapping the throttle shut mid-corner can cause a sudden weight transfer to the front tire. The additional force on the front tire caused by such an abrupt deceleration, combined with the side forces already present from cornering, could also cause the front tire to "wash out," or skid. Also, on some motorcycles, engine braking is pronounced enough to cause the rear tire to actually lose traction and skid when the throttle is abruptly rolled off. Know your motorcycle's handling characteristics, and constantly work toward becoming a smooth operator.

PUTTING IT ALL TOGETHER

The keys to effective cornering techniques are to plan ahead, leave an adequate safety margin, and operate your motorcycle's controls smoothly. Look throughout the turn to identify your entry, apex, and

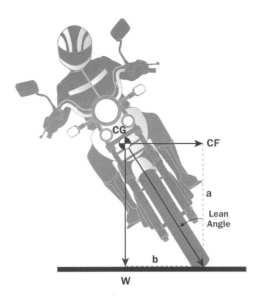

Diagram 14-5: Basic balance condition

exit points. If you can't see through a corner, use a conservative entry speed—speeding up mid-corner is always easier than slowing down. Apply both brakes smoothly and downshift into the gear you'll need before you enter the corner. To increase ground clearance and settle your suspension, smoothly roll on the throttle through the corner, steadily increasing this input as you approach the exit point. Be mindful of your speed, lean angle, road surface, path of travel, and always keeping some traction in reserve. Do this and cornering will becoming second nature—and probably one of your favorite parts of the motorcycling experience.

MOTORCYCLING EXCELLENCE MEANS:

► You recognize that most single-vehicle motorcycle crashes occur in cornering situations.

► You recognize it takes time to refine cornering skills.

► You keep your head and eyes up, and look through corners.

► You pick a line through a curve to maximize visibility and safety margins.

► You recognize the value of a conservative entry speed.

► You practice to make your cornering smooth and precise.

► REG PRIDMORE IS ONE SMOOTH OPERATOR

Safe riding is more a skill of the eyes-and-mind than of the hands-and-feet. This means the safest rider is one who maximizes the time and space margins by using effective decision-making tactics (SEE). A good rider uses a riding strategy (eyes-and-mind) so as to never need superior riding skills (hands-and-feet). The excellent rider has both types of skills, of course. This section provides information about superior hands-and-feet skills.

"Be smooth . . . be smooth"—this should be your mantra in the quest to become a skilled, experienced motorcycle pilot. All the traits that are commonly associated with skilled riders—speed, safety, and control—grow directly out of the ability those riders have to operate the motorcycle's controls in a smooth, regulated manner. Such smoothness is an essential part of being a safer rider, and it will enhance your riding in ways you never thought possible. Smoothness isn't just an artful touch to add to your riding, it's an essential component of being safe and being in control. Smooth operation is a result of early and proper searching and evaluating. So, what does it mean to "be smooth"? Here are some elements of smoothness, as they relate to particular systems on your motorcycle:

Reg Pridmore has coached thousands of riders to become smoother and more proficient. His advice can help you too.

THROTTLE

Modern street bikes, sportbikes especially, are very powerful machines. Riding on the street you need to be constantly aware of the ramifications of this power, and as a rider you need to constantly monitor yourself with regard to how you use that power. Apply too much of that adrenalin-producing horsepower in the middle of a turn, for instance, and you might find yourself in the bushes. Think of throttle action as being on a gradient, not as an on/off switch. Take care to roll on the throttle as you apply it—don't snap it. It's also important to relax your hand and arm muscles so you don't have any tension on the twistgrip—keeping your arm relaxed will make your throttle inputs smoother and less abrupt.

CLUTCH

You need to squeeze in the clutch smoothly, and release it smoothly—especially during downshifts. Here's how to do this:

► Don't squeeze the clutch all the way to the handgrip. I recommend that you pull the lever in no more than one-third of its total throw—just enough to disengage the clutch and allow the gear to shift. If you pull the lever all the way to the bar, you'll tend to "dump" the clutch when you release the lever—not good for smoothness, or traction at the rear wheel. Make sure your clutch is adjusted properly, according to the specifications listed in your motorcycle's owner's manual, for best results.

► Do it right now. Don't be lackadaisical about your clutch work. Master the timing so you can engage and disengage the clutch proficiently for best results. Don't procrastinate!

► For downshifting, err on the side of more rpm. Much of good, smooth clutch technique involves "matching" engine rpm to your road speed before you ease out the clutch lever. When you squeeze in the clutch lever, be careful not to let the rpm drop as you shift or the engine will act as a brake when you release the clutch lever, and you'll risk locking the rear wheel. In fact, you can often achieve a smoother transition by raising engine speed slightly (called "blipping the throttle") before releasing the clutch lever, to better match the rpm needed for the lower gear.

BRAKING

Many novice riders tend to treat the front brake as an on/off switch and grab the brake lever on initial application. If traction conditions are anything less than optimal this could result in the front tire locking up, which might lead to a crash. The initial squeeze of the front brake lever should be gentle—just enough to achieve contact between the pads and rotor. Then, immediately following that initial contact, squeeze the lever progressively harder until the requisite level of braking pressure is achieved. Be very conscious of the amount of pressure you're applying at any given time, and its effects on tire loading and front-wheel traction.

BODY POSITION

I'm sure you've seen racers "hanging off" their bikes in corners. This isn't just theatrics—even on the street, correct body position will help you get through corners more smoothly and safely, using less lean angle with less demand on the motorcycle chassis. The key to moving around smoothly on the bike depends on your staying relaxed and reducing tension in your body. Tension causes abrupt movements and overreaction. To be smooth, you need to move with your entire body, not just your arms or just your legs. Many riders are understandably cautious about moving around on the bike at higher speeds. Get accustomed to the sensation of moving around on the bike by just moving the top half of your body at first. Work on positioning your chin at an angle approximately lined up with your right wrist for a right turn, or your left wrist for a left turn. Keep your arms relaxed. As this process becomes comfortable, make an effort to move the lower half of your body as well. Imagine a pivot point where the seat meets the fuel tank. Pivot right or left around this point, and see if this doesn't help take the bike transition into corners more easily. Once you have your upper and lower body working in unison—

and it may seem like a lot to monitor at first—you'll find that the bike will work for you, rather than against you, on twisty roads.

Put all of the above steps together—smooth inputs to the throttle, clutch, and brakes, as well as smooth body movements when entering and exiting corners—and you will find yourself well on your way to becoming a confident, controlled rider. All the other attributes of an experienced rider—things like quick reflexes and safe, efficient maneuvering—will come naturally once you master the art of being smooth in the saddle. ■

Three-time AMA Superbike Champ and AMA Hall of Fame member Reg Pridmore has been teaching motorcyclists of all skill levels how to ride quickly, safely, and smoothly since 1974. His CLASS (California's Leading Advanced Safety School) riding school was founded in 1986 and today is conducted at leading racetracks all across the country.

Pridmore's techniques involve the use of his entire body to control the motorcycle. "Hanging-off" is one application of that idea.

▶ FREDDIE SPENCER ON TRAIL BRAKING

Trail braking—nearly everyone has heard the term, yet few of us, if pressed, could accurately define it. This is unfortunate; even though it's generally considered an advanced skill, a basic understanding of trail braking is a valuable addition to any rider's skill set. However, novices should not try this technique until they have perfected their basic riding and braking skills over many miles in a wide variety of traffic conditions. To help you understand trail braking, we asked Freddie Spencer, three-time world roadracing champion, owner of the Freddie Spencer's High Performance Riding School, and acknowledged master of trail braking, to explain the concept.

Having a working knowledge and familiarity with trail braking—especially understanding load factors and how much or how little brake you can safely use when leaned over—allows you to more confidently correct your speed or your line in the corner should something appear in your path—an important skill for any safe street rider to possess.

Trail braking, according to Spencer, refers to the technique of gradually "trailing off" the brakes after the motorcycle enters the corner. Most novice riders, Spencer says, do all their braking with the bike straight up and down, and lean the bike into the corner only after releasing the brakes. When trail braking, the rider continues to brake well after turn-in and while the bike is leaned over, gently "trailing" off the brakes as the bike approaches the apex.

"Think of it in terms of percentages," Spencer says. "Imagine that you initiate braking and go to your maximum brake pressure—say 30 percent—fairly rapidly. Still on the brakes, you turn in and then start trailing off the brakes as you enter the corner. Thirty percent, then 20, 10, 5, 4, 3, 2, 1 . . . until you near the apex, get off the brakes entirely, and roll on the gas."

Trail braking offers many benefits: improving front wheel traction, reducing the maximum brake pressure necessary to slow the bike (because you're braking for a longer period of time), and allowing the bike to turn faster with less lean angle. All of these benefits stem from the fact that trail braking maintains a proper forward weight bias deeper into the corner. "When you do all braking with the bike straight up-and-down," Spencer says, "the front suspension is actually unloading when you turn in, increasing the likelihood of the front tire losing traction."

Trail braking keeps the front suspension and front tire loaded, helping the motorcycle to change direction more easily and with less steering input. Trail braking into the corner can also help you better judge distances. Human beings judge distances better the closer they get to a target. Trail braking lets you brake later and deeper into the corner, so you can often wait longer before turning and you can see farther into the corner. Continuing to brake after turn-in also lets you adjust your pace mid-corner. Braking only when aimed straight lessens your options for controlling your speed after the turn has been initiated—you're at the mercy of speed judgments that you made 50 feet back. ■

Expert racers use trail braking to make fine adjustments to their path through a corner. This advanced technique is an important skill but requires very sensitive control of the rear brake.

CHAPTER 15

Low & High-Speed Turning

HOW CAN YOU USE YOUR BODY WEIGHT TO ADJUST YOUR LINE?
WHEN IS SHIFTING YOUR WEIGHT OFF-CENTER ADVANTAGEOUS
IN CONTROLLING YOUR MOTORCYCLE THROUGH A CURVE?

We've already established that countersteering is the best way to initiate a lean for turning and balance. We've also discussed how shifting your body weight is relatively ineffective as a turning tool, beyond making fine adjustments to your line once the turn has been initiated. That said, how exactly can you use your body weight to adjust your line through a corner? And, in what cornering situations is shifting your weight off-center especially advantageous to controlling the behavior of the motorcycle? This chapter addresses how this technique applies to both tight, low-speed turns, and higher-speed corners.

TIGHT TURNS

If you've ever watched a motorcyclist successfully execute a tight U-turn on a narrow, two-lane road, you know that this can be every bit as impressive as watching a professional roadracer drag his knee on a racetrack. This is especially true if you are familiar with the alternative—wobbling across the lane at a slow speed, with both feet sliding along the pavement, only to end up with the front tire well off the other side of the road stuck in gravel or mud. Having the ability to make a quick, clean U-turn is an important riding skill, and a safer alternative to the tedious, multi-point turns that many riders use in order to get their bikes turned around on narrow roads.

Leaning in toward the center of the turn— a technique also called "hanging off"—moves the combined center of gravity toward the center of the turn, and allows the motorcycle to make the turn with less lean angle.

ZERO LEAN ANGLE **30-DEGREE LEAN ANGLE**

Diagram 15-1: When a motorcycle leans toward the center of a turn, the distance to the turn center is shorter than its effective turn radius. At low speeds, leaning out allows the motorcycle to lean at a greater angle, thus decreasing the distance to the turn center.

LEANING OUT

Slow, tight turns are intimidating to many riders because they require relatively large lean angles at low speeds—an uncomfortable proposition. The key to making these motions comfortable is to lean the motorcycle, using your body weight to counterbalance and control the extreme motions. By way of explanation, it is helpful to first understand why large lean angles are necessary for the tightest turns.

Imagine that you are standing next to your motorcycle. Turn the handlebars full-lock to the left and then walk it around in a circle without leaning the motorcycle. In this case, the turning diameter of the circle created by the motorcycle's wheels is entirely determined by the motorcycle's steering geometry. This is the minimum turning radius of your motorcycle without leaning. The only way to further decrease this turning radius is to lean the motorcycle while turning. To understand why this is the case, look at Diagram 15-1, which illustrates why increasing the lean angle decreases turning radius.

The image on the left in Diagram 15-1 shows a motorcycle tire pivoting around its turn center with zero lean angle, just like in our walking example. The center of the curve and the turn radius (R_0) are shown. On the right is a similar view with the tire at a lean angle of 30 degrees. The distance to the center of the circle is still the same in this diagram, only now the "center" is effectively below the surface of the road. The effective turn radius (R_{30}) is measured from the point on the surface that is directly

above the center of the turn. You can see that (R_{30}) is shorter than (R_0) the distance from the turn's center. As the lean angle of the tire increases, the "cone" becomes sharper and the effective turn radius becomes smaller.

On the road, turning radius is determined by the motorcycle's steering geometry coupled with the amount of lean at the motorcycle's wheels. Because leaning is involved, the weight of the motorcycle being pulled downward by gravity has to be balanced by centrifugal force acting on its center of gravity (CG) to pull that CG outward. This is where counterbalancing with your body can be used to improve slow-speed maneuverability. The angle of the composite center of gravity (motorcycle and rider together) is the "effective" lean angle. Because leaning your body outward (away from the center of the turn) will have the effect of moving the composite center of gravity away from the center of the motorcycle, leaning outward can be used to influence the balance (and speed) of the motorcycle without changing its turning radius. This allows you to maintain balance at ever greater motorcycle lean angles because changing your body position (effectively moving the overall CG) allows you to lean the motorcycle farther without actually increasing the effective lean angle.

Diagram 15-2 illustrates how leaning your body outward in a tight turn can decrease effective lean angle compared to the motorcycle lean angle. In this diagram, ML stands for motorcycle lean, measured from vertical to the motorcycle centerline. EL

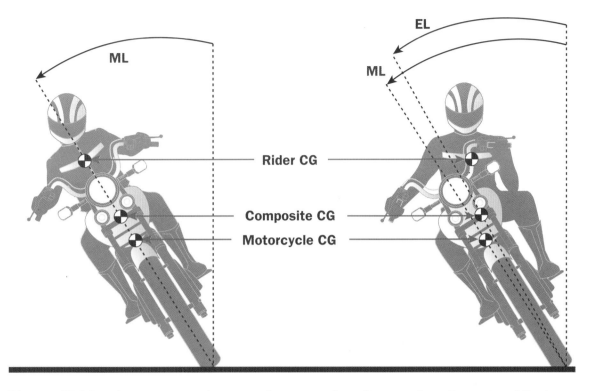

Diagram 15-2: Leaning out moves the composite center of gravity away from the center of the turn, allowing the motorcycle to assume a greater lean angle and therefore make a tighter turn at a given speed.

stands for effective lean, measured from vertical to the line through the composite center of gravity. The motorcycle lean angle and effective lean angle are the same when you lean with the motorcycle, shown in the illustration to the left. Leaning outward (as in the illustration to the right) shifts your weight (and therefore the composite center of gravity) slightly to the outside. This decreases effective lean angle and allows you to lean the motorcycle farther (thereby reducing turning radius) without requiring more speed. This last part is key because the lean angle required to tighten up slow-speed turns often cannot be offset by more acceleration because of the danger of losing traction.

There are still limits to how tightly you can complete low-speed turns—ground clearance, for one. In general, leaning outward in slow-speed turns provides better control and balance, and increases confidence because you feel like you are leaning less as your body is upright compared to the motorcycle.

MAKING IT HAPPEN

Now that we've established that counterbalancing is the best way to safely complete a low-speed turn, let's consider the actual mechanics of performing this maneuver on the bike. Proper counterbalancing begins with your legs, lifting and shifting your body weight outward, supporting most of your weight on the outside footrest. Just like a normal corner, look where you want to go. In this case of a tight U-turn, your chin should be pointed over your shoulder and almost looking backward at the inside of the turn. Lean the bike away from you, using both arms to push the handlebars down toward the inside of the turn. The farther away from the motorcycle's centerline that you position your body weight, the greater the lean angle and the tighter the turn you can make. Move your upper body around gently until you find the balance point for your given speed and turning radius.

Keep the engine driving you forward throughout the turn. Under no circumstance should you

These two views show a rider leaning out toward the outside of the turn. This posture allows the motorcycle to make tighter turns at low speed.

snap the throttle shut or squeeze in the clutch lever—this loss of driveline power will let the motorcycle fall inward, causing you to lose balance. Alternately, if you find that the motorcycle is leaning too far inward and you can't shift your weight any farther outside to correct, add a little throttle. This will cause the bike to "stand up" in the turn. Practice these techniques in a parking lot, starting with a fairly large diameter circle. As you become increasingly confident, narrow the circle's diameter. Most motorcycles should be capable of making a turn within a diameter of 24 feet—less than the width of a two-lane road.

HIGH-SPEED TURNS

Unlike slow-speed turns, in high-speed corners there is usually enough outward centrifugal force available to counterbalance the lean angle required to negotiate a corner at any given speed or turning radius. The primary concerns with high-speed corners are traction (covered in Chapters 11 and 12) and ground clearance. What can you do if you have to tighten your turn radius when there isn't enough ground clearance or available traction to lean over farther?

Slowing down so that you require less lean angle is an obvious answer, though this often isn't an

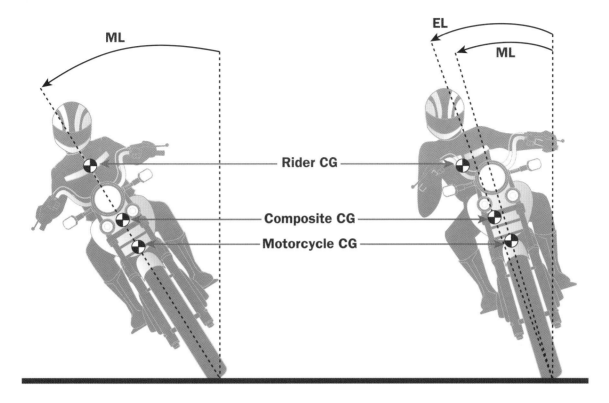

Diagram 15-3: Leaning in moves the composite center of gravity toward the center of the turn, allowing the motorcycle to lean less for a given turn radius. This technique increases your lean angle reserve, providing a greater safety margin for adjustments in the turn.

option—rolling off the throttle or braking while leaned over in the middle of a turn could upset the chassis and might aggravate your ground clearance issues more by further compressing the suspension. Here again, the best solution is to reposition your body weight so that the composite CG is moved away from the centerline of the motorcycle. In slow-speed corners we talked about leaning outward, to increase the motorcycle lean angle without changing the effective lean angle of the composite CG. High-speed corners call for the opposite action, leaning inward to decrease motorcycle lean angle compared to effective lean angle, so the bike is in a more upright position and ground clearance increases and traction demands decrease. Diagram 15-3 shows how this works.

LEANING IN

Moving the combined center of gravity of rider and machine toward the inside of the turn results in less motorcycle lean angle needed to offset the centrifugal force that is trying to pull it toward the outside of the turn. Using less lean angle in a turn increases your lean angle reserve, providing an increased safety margin if you enter a corner too fast or encounter an unexpected hazard in the middle of the turn.

You don't need to move your backside entirely off the seat to lean into a corner. Other more subtle methods can be just as effective, especially at slower speeds. For instance, just dipping your head inward of the motorcycle's centerline can have a pronounced effect on cornering. As you look through a turn, consciously shift your head toward the inside of the turn, taking care to keep your eyes up and level with the horizon, and you should feel the motorcycle lean angle decrease slightly. Another subtle method for leaning in is to swing your inner knee away from the bike toward the center of the turn.

At higher speeds or at more extreme lean angles, it can be useful to shift your entire upper body inward. Do this by pivoting your hips around the fuel tank to move your body closer to the inside of the corner, and at the same time bend slightly at the waist and drop your inside shoulder down. The most extreme variation of this technique is hanging your entire body off the bike, like you might see a professional roadracer do. Approaching a corner, a racer might move half of his backside (or more) entirely off the saddle and position his body as low and close to the racetrack as possible, dragging a knee (and sometimes even toes and elbows) along the surface. Such posture is only necessary at very high speeds or very extreme lean angles—never the case during sane, safe, street riding.

Generally, the more body weight you lean in with, the more the center of gravity is moved inward, reducing necessary motorcycle lean angle and also reducing the amount of countersteering required. With less pressure on the handgrips for countersteering, your arms and hands will remain more relaxed, facilitating smoother throttle and braking inputs and making your overall riding performance more fluid.

Whether you're leaning out for a tight U-turn or leaning in for a high-speed freeway off-ramp, using your body's weight to counterbalance centrifugal force and adjust lean angle is a practice that experienced riders often use to provide an extra margin of safety on the open road. Both of these skills are not difficult to learn, and with some practice you will master them in no time.

MOTORCYCLING EXCELLENCE MEANS:

► You practice turning techniques often, and in a safe area.

► You know how to use lean angle and body position to help make turns safe and efficient.

► KEVIN SCHWANTZ ON CONTROL

Ask head instructor Kevin Schwantz what is the biggest problem for students at his advanced riding school (the Kevin Schwantz Suzuki School) and the answer comes quickly: "defeating the panic response," says Schwantz. "This is something that seems to hit home with a lot of my students. They get into a corner and something doesn't go as planned— they get on the brakes too late, or the corner tightens up or something—and instead of staying calm and regaining control, they slip into panic mode and turn their street bike into a dirt bike."

Fighting panic response is as much a concern for the average street rider as it is for Schwantz's students. It is challenging to keep your wits about you when you come upon an unexpected situation on the road, like gravel in a turn, an animal in the roadway, or a car pulling out of a driveway in front of you. Instead of remaining calm and in control of the situation, it is too easy to panic, freeze up, and ride yourself right into a dangerous situation.

Fortunately, with the right combination of preparation, practice and skill building, you can train yourself to overcome the urge to panic and instead remain in confident control in even the most confusing or challenging situation. Here are some tips that Kevin Schwantz gives his students to help them avoid the peril of panic.

The most important aspect of maintaining control, Schwantz says, is keeping your eyes up and continuing to look through the corner, or wherever else it is that you want to go. Your first instinct when you come upon trouble is often to focus your attention directly on the hazard in front of you. The problem with this is that your motorcycle tends to go where you look, and if you're fixating at the trash can lying in the middle of the road, you just might run right into it. You need to keep your eyes up and looking toward your escape route, not at the obstacle or the edge of the road, to get past it successfully.

Racing champion Kevin Schwantz observes that maintaining control of your response to unexpected situations is difficult for many riding students. Self-discipline, and building the confidence of knowing your motorcycle's limits and your own limits, are important ingredients in the mental mix for learning to control panic responses.

Many riders take to the track at one of the advanced riding schools to learn their own limits as well as the limits of a particular motorcycle. In the protected environment of a closed racetrack, it is possible to explore those limits more safely than you can on the street.

Looking away from the obstacle can also decrease the intensity of the situation. "The hazard is what's making you panic, so obviously you want to avoid fixating on it," Schwantz says. "Take your focus off of the chaos and put it on something that you can count on, your apex and your line, something that isn't going to change."

Another important aspect of avoiding panic is being aware of your limits—both your skill limits and the limits of your motorcycle. If you have a firm idea of the maximum amount of braking pressure you can apply and still maintain traction, or how far you can lean the bike without touching the pavement, you can comfortably approach those limits in an emergency situation without panicking. This is one place where on-track instruction, like that offered by Schwantz's and other advanced riding schools, is useful. The racetrack is a controlled environment where you can safely and predictably approach those limits in order to prepare for the unexpected on the street.

Perception of speed, and trusting the motorcycle to negotiate a situation at speed, is another source of panic that Schwantz frequently encounters in his students. "I hear this all the time," says

Schwantz. " 'I managed to get the bike *stopped* before I ran off the track.' What that tells me is that the cause of the problem was the rider panicking, not the bike's speed."

The problem here is that riders aren't aware of the limits or capabilities of their machines. "It's always a challenge to get a person to realize how hard they can brake, for example," Schwantz says. "They think that the front of the motorcycle is going to slide away really quickly—it isn't." Applying the front brake really hard usually doesn't cause a slide. Even if the front tire starts to skid, control can be maintained by immediately releasing and re-applying the front brake with less pressure on the lever.

There are many different ways to realistically tell the rider that they really weren't going too fast, and that if they hadn't panicked they likely would have negotiated the situation without trouble. The key, Schwantz says, is increasing the rider's confidence. Knowing your bike, and knowing your abilities (and the limits of those abilities) on *that bike*, is a highly effective way to maintain presence of mind and keep from panicking in a hectic situation. Practice defeats panic every time. ∎

EVEN WHEN THE PAVEMENT ENDS, THE FUN CONTINUES

There's a whole world waiting to be explored beyond where the paved road ends—and a good portion of the off-road world is available to explore from the saddle of a dual-purpose or dedicated off-road motorcycle. Off-road riding is a great way to see places normally not accessible to other road-going vehicles, as well as a way to sharpen your general riding skills. With proper preparation, trail riding can show you how a motorcycle feels in low-traction situations, and help you learn other useful skills like surmounting obstacles. And if you do happen to fall over (which happens to all off-roaders), the consequences of falling in the dirt are generally much less severe than falling on pavement.

Off-road riding is also an excellent family activity. There are small-displacement dirt bikes available for riders as young as six years of age, and with parental supervision and proper training young riders can have a fun and safe experience.

Off-road riding uses many of the same skills, knowledge, and strategies previously outlined for street riding, but it also requires some specialized skills and techniques that are outlined in this chapter. Consider this chapter an introduction to the off-road world—it's by no means a complete discussion of all that there is to know and understand about off-road riding, but it is enough to introduce you to the basic techniques and make your first adventure a successful one. Remember also that the Motorcycle Safety Foundation offers the MSF *DirtBike School*, an excellent option for a hands-on introduction to the finer points of off-road riding.

A wide range of people turn to off-road riding as a healthy and challenging recreational activity. It's also a great way for families to enjoy quality time together in the great outdoors.

Before venturing off road, understand that off-road riding involves certain risks. While the risk of colliding with other road users is much lower off the highway, you must be aware of other potential risks such as rocks, ruts, holes, and trees. Off-road riding also entails certain responsibilities, especially with regard to land use. The amount of land available for legal off-road riding has been radically reduced over the past two decades, and the land that remains open is monitored carefully. Ride responsibly. Restrict your riding only to legal, designated off-road riding areas. Never trespass on private property, or knowingly ride on land marked off-limits to motor vehicles. Tread lightly, and act to protect and preserve your riding areas in order to keep off-road riding options open for the future.

GETTING STARTED

When you ride off the highway, you meet the landscape on its terms. There are no lights to control traffic, no speed limit signs, no painted lines to follow, and no road signs warning you of what's ahead. Only you have control over what happens when you ride.

Off-road-style protective gear is similar to street gear, but modified for the rigors of the intended environment. No rider should venture out without a DOT-compliant helmet, face shield or goggles, over-the-ankle boots, long pants (look for sturdy pants with integral kneepads), long-sleeved shirt or jersey, and full-fingered gloves with knuckle padding. Some riders wear additional gear in the form of special chest and shoulder protectors.

Before going off road, you should know the land you are riding on and the capabilities of your machine. Stay away from terrain that is beyond your riding abilities, like hazardous slopes or deep mud. You should be able to identify various conditions that are likely to be present and adjust your speed and riding style accordingly.

Responsible riders stay out of trouble not only by handling their machines well, but also by being smart enough to stay out of risky situations in the first place. Often the terrain will dictate how you ride. Learn how to read it as you ride and apply SEE principles discussed earlier in this book—these strategies are applicable off-road too.

When climbing hills you should shift your weight forward by sliding up on the seat. You may have to stand on the footrests if the hill is steep.

Proper posture, reading the trail, and good throttle control are keys to successful off-road riding. It's important to know how to position yourself for different riding conditions. Keep your weight centered over the motorcycle. Look in the direction you want to go. When cornering, look through the turn and shift your weight slightly forward to help give the front tire more traction. Those are some of the basics. In addition to your physical ability to control the motorcycle, you should know what actions are appropriate for a variety of different situations.

Off-road terrain is constantly changing—that's part of what makes it so fun and challenging. Rarely is the trail completely smooth or flat. The following are some typical special situations you'll likely encounter after you venture off of the paved path.

HILLS

There are separate techniques for climbing and descending hills. Remember that some hills may be too steep for your abilities, and some may very well be too steep for your motorcycle, regardless of your ability. Never ride past your limit of visibility. If you can't see what's on the other side of a hill, slow down until you have a clear view.

When approaching a hill you should:

► Keep both feet firmly on the footrests.

► Shift into a lower gear and speed up before ascending the hill.

► On small hills, shift your body weight forward by sliding forward on the seat. For steep hills, stand on the footrests and lean well over the front wheel in order to shift as much weight forward as possible.

► If the hill is steep and you must downshift to avoid stalling, shift quickly and smoothly. Also be sure to reduce the throttle while shifting to help prevent front-wheel lifting.

► If you don't have enough power to continue uphill but you have forward momentum and space to turn around safely, turn around before you lose speed, then proceed downhill.

When descending a hill you should:

► Keep both feet firmly on the footrests.

► Point the motorcycle directly downhill.

► Transfer your weight to the rear.

► Shift into a lower gear and descend with the throttle closed.

► Apply brakes to reduce speed. Be careful using the front brake. Too much on a steep hill can cause the front wheel to slide out.

EMBANKMENTS AND LEDGES

Many of the same techniques for climbing and descending hills apply to embankments and ledges. These obstacles, however, are usually shorter in length, but steeper. Only after becoming proficient at climbing and descending hills should you attempt these.

When riding down a ledge or drop-off, keep your weight to the extreme rear while standing, and gas it slightly as your front wheel rolls over the edge. If the ledge is extremely steep or more than a few feet tall, look for an alternate way around.

Climbing an embankment requires momentum, forward weighting, and careful throttle control. Stand on the footrests, keeping your chest and head forward and above the handlebars. Plan to slow the motorcycle as you crest the top of the embankment in case you have to make a quick maneuver to prepare for another obstacle.

WHOOPS

Also called "whoop-de-doos," these are closely spaced bumps usually found in heavily traveled sections of a trail. They create a roller coaster effect when riding up one bump and down the next one. You can approach them in a few ways. Whoops should be ridden while standing on the footrests.

One method of traversing whoops is to ride at a slow or moderate pace, keeping both wheels on the ground. Use your legs and arms as shock absorbers, keeping body weight directly over the center of the motorcycle. Establish an appropriate speed and rhythm over the bumps.

Another method is for more advanced riders and is performed by weighting the rear suspension. Accelerating through the whoops while standing on the footrests and keeping your body weight

Shift your weight to the back of the motorcycle when going downhill. Use caution when applying the front brake—too much pressure can cause the front wheel to slide out.

rearward allows the front wheel to skim over the bumps, smoothing out the otherwise rough ride. To avoid excessive jarring, remember to stand on the footrests, with your knees and elbows slightly bent. It also helps to squeeze the bike with your knees to keep it from "swapping" from side to side.

Depending on how far apart the whoops are spaced, experienced riders can also turn them into a series of small jumps. To do this, accelerate up the face of the first bump enough so that you will just clear the next one. You want to land on the downside of the next bump. Upon landing, use your momentum and a little throttle to repeat the process. This technique requires a good rhythm in order to be successful. If you land a bit short and your rhythm is broken, revert back to the first method until you regain full control.

PROTRUDING OBSTACLES

While trail riding, you may encounter rocks, roots, logs or stumps protruding from the ground. Such objects can also deflect your front wheel if you do not see them in time.

To avoid these problems, be sure to maintain your concentration on the trail ahead of you, scanning for obstacles protruding into your path. When riding on narrow trails, keep the balls of your feet on the footrests so your toes do not hang below the motorcycle frame. This helps prevent catching your feet on such obstacles. If your bike is suddenly deflected by an obstacle, resist the temptation to stick your leg out. This may result in knee injuries. Instead, keep your feet on the footrests and shift your body position to correct your line.

WATER AND MUD

You may find more water and slippery mud in some seasons and climates than in others. In some instances, the trail may cross directly through a stream. In cases like this, water and mud can conceal obstacles in your path. Damp leaves and pine needles can be especially slick. Ride more cautiously in these situations. Ride slowly and be prepared for what your wheels may encounter. Be aware also that you will have to apply the brakes more gradually in wet conditions to avoid the unintentional slipping and sliding of the tires on wet dirt or mud.

Your brakes may lose stopping power when wet. Dry the brakes after a deep-water crossing by applying light pressure to them while riding until they return to normal power.

► While riding in water and mud, you will most likely encounter ruts. Maintain momentum through muddy sections. Stay relaxed, and allow the wheels of the motorcycle to follow any ruts. Don't fight the front wheel or try to turn out of the rut. Look ahead to where you want to go, not down at the rut.

► Keep your weight centered and stand on the footrests.

► Maintain an even throttle setting. If you lose speed and the bike begins to bog down, do not open the throttle abruptly. This will only cause the rear wheel to dig itself deeper into the mud. Instead, apply the throttle gradually to maintain forward momentum.

At water crossings:

► Beware of hidden rocks and holes.

► Learn how to read different surfaces at water crossings. The character and action of the water can lend valuable clues about the river bottom. Areas where the stream is wide and composed of shallow ripples can be good places to cross. Areas with slow-moving water or those that appear calm are often the deeper sections of the river.

► Maintain your momentum while riding through the water, and focus on the opposite bank.

► Keep speeds relatively low to prevent water from splashing onto vital electrical components or into the airbox, and to prevent damaging the stream banks.

When you encounter water and mud, maintain momentum, stay relaxed, and allow the wheels of the motorcycle to follow any ruts. Look to where you want to go, not directly down at the mud or ruts.

Many off-roaders enjoy the challenge of sand dunes and sandy trails. Careful modulation of rider inputs—steering, throttle, and brakes—will help you maintain your intended path.

► Fast-moving streams will tend to pull the wheels downstream. Point the motorcycle slightly upstream, if possible. Keep your weight centered to provide maximum traction so the front or rear wheel doesn't wash out under the current.

BERMS

A berm is a built-up portion of dirt on the outside of a turn, sometimes called a banked turn. Heavily used turns on tracks or trails will often have berms built up from tires pushing dirt gradually into a curved wall around the turn. You can use this wall to ride around a banked turn faster than a flat turn; centrifugal force will help keep your motorcycle in the berm. Remain seated with your weight centered, and look through the turn. Be cautious about riding near the top edge of the berm; it may give way and let your tires go over the edge.

SAND

When riding in sand, maintain a relaxed posture while keeping your feet on the footrests and your head and eyes up, looking ahead. The motorcycle will waver in its path slightly; this is normal. Keep the throttle on and shift to a higher gear, enabling the motorcycle to gain enough speed to rise (or plane) on top of the sand. Rolling off the throttle will effectively provide a braking action; the motorcycle begins to plow back into the sand as speed decreases.

When turning in sand, it's easy for the front wheel to knife into the sand and practically stop you in your tracks. To prevent this, shift your weight to the rear as much as possible and apply the throttle to help keep the front end light through the turn.

A rule of thumb for riding in sand is to accelerate sooner and brake later than you would on surfaces having greater traction. Because of the nature of

171

When riding on narrow trails, search ahead for branches or rocks protruding from the ground. Keep your feet on the footrests and use your body weight to help maintain balance.

sand, the motorcycle takes longer to get going and slows down much faster than on a hard surface. Therefore, you must adjust your use of throttle and brakes accordingly.

If you are riding in large areas of bare sand (on dunes, for example), be careful of hills or drop-offs that may be camouflaged by the absence of shadows. When the sun is high in the sky, sandy hills, holes, and cliffs can appear all the same color, drastically affecting your depth perception or sense of perspective.

ROCKS

Soft surfaces like dirt, sand, and grass are somewhat forgiving if you make a mistake. Rocks are not forgiving at all. If the rocks are numerous and small, the motorcycle will handle much as it does in sandy conditions. If the rocks are large, you will have to carefully select a path around or over each

one. Again, momentum is very important, especially if the rocks are loose. Smooth throttle control is critical when riding through rocks. Watch for rocks with sharp edges that could damage a tire, engine case, or foot pointed down. Maintain a higher tire pressure in rocky conditions and make sure your motorcycle has a heavy-duty skid plate to help protect the engine.

RIDING DURING DIFFERENT SEASONS

Ideal riding conditions are usually found in spring and fall, though many motorcyclists ride off-road year-round. In summer, when temperatures are higher, be especially conscious of the effect of heat on engine and body. Be sure all motorcycle oil, coolant, and lubrication levels are sufficient. Carry drinking water along on trail rides, and protect yourself from dehydration.

In winter, when temperatures are low, be prepared in case you are stranded. You should wear layers of warm, protective clothing and carry waterproof matches and a flashlight. If riding in snow, be careful of hidden obstacles. Do not ride on groomed snowmobile trails. Motorcycles are single-track vehicles and will spoil such trails for wide-track and flotation-tired vehicles.

Remember, never ride alone in any season. A buddy will be able to help you or go for assistance if needed. Plus, the riding experience is more enjoyable when shared with friends.

NAVIGATION

Carry a detailed U.S. Forest Service (USFS) or Bureau of Land Management (BLM) off-road area map or topographic map with you at all times. A compass will help you determine your direction of travel. If you think you may have trouble finding your way back, stack stones beside the trail in a recognizable shape known to your riding party. Use the stones to mark directions through intersections on the trail.

In wide-open areas, make mental notes of surrounding landmarks. Determine by compass your direction of travel before you leave your base camp. Take an occasional look behind you on the way out so you know what the ride will look like when you return. If someone is staying in camp while you go riding, let that person know where you intend to travel.

KNOW THE LAWS

The laws and regulations that control how and where you use your off-road motorcycle are important. They help to keep you out of trouble; they keep the sport healthy by controlling less-responsible riders; they help protect the land you ride on and the people who own it. Always obey posted signs. Motorcycle dealers and off-road motorcycle clubs can often provide you with a summary of local laws or direct you to park rangers, game wardens, or others who will be glad to help you.

YOU AND THE REST OF THE WORLD

There's one fundamental factor that controls your riding access to land—riding responsibly. Developing and maintaining riding opportunities means getting along with the private landowners, public land managers, and other recreationists you meet on trails. The better you get along with all these people, the easier it will be to find and keep good riding areas.

Many organizations seek to preserve off-road recreational opportunities. One such organization, Americans for Responsible Recreational Access (ARRA; www.arra-access.com), was formed to ensure that Americans are not arbitrarily denied the right to experience and enjoy the public lands that belong to all citizens. ARRA's members include horseback riders, personal watercraft users, off-road vehicle and snowmobile riders, and vacationing families. These constituents have banded together to provide input to

policymakers on decisions regarding land use designations, recreation opportunities, and conservation. Legislators are encouraged to base their decisions regarding the suitability of diverse recreational activities on sound environmental principles. ARRA strongly advocates that all land and water users respect the environment, so that recreational opportunities on public lands will be available for future generations.

YOU AND NATURE

Riding behavior that harms the land is self-defeating and irresponsible. Learn to protect and preserve your riding areas—in other words, be environmentally friendly!

► Obtain a travel map whenever possible, and check which trails are open or closed. Learn the rules and follow them.

► Keep your motorcycle quiet. Don't make your exhaust system noisier—there is nothing other land users dislike more than a loud off-highway vehicle. Keep your spark arrester in place as well.

► Avoid running over young trees, shrubs, and grasses, damaging or killing them.

► Stay off soft, wet roads and trails readily torn up by vehicles (particularly during hunting seasons). Repairing the damage is expensive.

- Travel around meadows, steep hillsides, or stream banks and lakeshores that are easily scarred by churning wheels.

- Resist the urge to pioneer a new road or trail, or to cut across a switchback.

- Use courtesy when you meet others on the trail. Pull off and give right of way to horseback riders or hikers. It is best to shut off the engine whenever near horses—a panicked horse is a danger to you and its rider.

- Never chase animals or otherwise subject them to stress. Stress can sap their scarce energy reserves.

- Obey gate closures and regulatory signs. Vandalism costs tax dollars.

- Stay out of wilderness areas. They're closed to all vehicles. Know where the boundaries are.

- Get permission to travel across private land. Respect landowner rights.

Serious off-road riders go beyond the basic array of riding gear and add chest and shoulder protection.

FINDING A PLACE TO RIDE

Some sources for finding places to ride are:

- Your motorcycle dealer
- Off-road motorcycle clubs or associations
- State maps (features and topographical)
- U.S. Forest Service
- Bureau of Land Management
- State agencies such as Parks & Recreation, Fish & Game, or Forestry
- Organized riding events. Enduros, hare scrambles, and poker runs can be a great way to ride and explore new trails. Clubs often get access for specific events to trails and areas that are closed the rest of the time.

REGISTRATION

In many states the law requires that you register your motorcycle as part of the state's off-road vehicle-registration program. Fines for riding unregistered vehicles can get expensive, to say nothing of the risk of having your off-road motorcycle impounded. Besides, most states use the registration fees to develop riding trails and facilities. So by registering your motorcycle, you and your friends may be helping to buy or maintain places to ride. Remember that, except for dual-purpose machines, off-road motorcycles are not designed for use on pavement. Registered or not, they should never be ridden on the highway or any public roadways.

MOTORCYCLING EXCELLENCE MEANS:

- You learn the skills of off-road riding before venturing off the pavement.

- You appreciate the value of off-road riding skills in helping become a better street rider.

- You complete an off-road riding course, like the MSF *DirtBike School*, before riding in the dirt.

- You practice your off-road riding skills and use safety strategies similar to those of street riding to ensure safety and fun.

- You supervise your children under the age of 16 when they ride dirt bikes and make sure they wear proper protective gear.

RIDER TRAINING AND THE CONCEPT OF SAFETY RENEWAL

The best way to get your start in the world of motorcycling is to attend a hands-on rider training course that uses a curriculum developed by the Motorcycle Safety Foundation (MSF). MSF *RiderCourses* are taught by MSF-certified Rider-Coaches, all of whom are experienced motorcyclists and are qualified to help you develop the mental and physical skills required to safely operate a motorcycle. Instruction takes place in a controlled, off-street environment—typically a parking lot at a high school, college, civic center, or other approved, controlled location.

Most states waive the riding or knowledge test portion of your motorcycle license test if you've completed a Basic *RiderCourse*. Many insurance companies offer discounts to students who have passed an MSF *RiderCourse*.

Course fees vary from state to state and from location to location; some are free to the student or are offered at a minimal cost, thanks to special fees collected through licensing and motorcycle registration. Some motorcycle distributors and brand-sponsored clubs will reimburse all or part of your tuition. With more than 1,500 *RiderCourse* sites throughout the United States, there's probably one near you. All will offer the Basic *RiderCourse*; the availability of the other courses noted below varies by location. To find a course near you, call MSF at 800.446.9227 or visit www.msf-usa.org.

Even after you've attended a Basic *RiderCourse*, don't assume that your education has ended. Research indicates that the effects of safety training do not last a lifetime—skills tend to diminish over the years. Safety renewal refers to the need for riders to refresh and renew their perceptual techniques and riding skills. This is best accomplished by practicing and improving in a formal course of instruction with the guiding help of an MSF-certified RiderCoach. The MSF Rider Education and Training System (RETS) provides multiple opportunities to renew one's skills, through a comprehensive array of *RiderCourses,* stand-alone modules, and other training opportunities. Taking advantage of these opportunities helps a rider renew fundamental riding techniques as well as more advanced skills, such as braking and traction management and collision avoidance maneuvers.

MSF BASIC *RIDERCOURSE*

The **Basic *RiderCourse* (BRC)** is typically a two-day course and is aimed at beginning riders. A minimum of five hours classroom instruction and at least 10 hours of practical riding exercises are provided. Motorcycles and helmets are included in your course fee. In this course, you'll learn how to operate a motorcycle safely, with emphasis on the special skills and mental attitude necessary for dealing with traffic.

RiderCoaches will start you off with learning clutch/throttle control, straight-line riding, turning, shifting, and stopping. You'll gradually progress to cornering, swerving, and emergency braking. In the classroom you'll learn about the different types of motorcycles, their controls, and how they operate. The RiderCoaches will advise you on what to wear for comfort, protection, and conspicuity.

You'll find out how alcohol and other drugs affect your ability to ride safely. A key segment of the course will show you how to develop a strategy for riding in traffic and dealing with critical situations. The course concludes with a knowledge test and skills evaluation.

MSF EXPERIENCED *RIDERCOURSES*

The **Experienced *RiderCourse* (ERC) Suite** is a major component of the Motorcycle Safety Foundation Rider Education and Training System, and provides riders with a seamless opportunity to progressively continue developing their riding and safety awareness skills. The ERC Suite is a set of three distinct MSF *RiderCourses*, all guided by MSF-certified Rider-Coaches. Each Experienced *RiderCourse* lasts about five hours and includes nine riding exercises and pertinent group discussions.

The Skills Practice *RiderCourse* is for motorcyclists who have successfully completed the BRC or who possess basic operational skills but wish to further develop their riding skills and strategies. The course focuses on managing traction, stopping quickly, and swerving techniques. Riders may use a training motorcycle or their own safe, street-ready motorcycle; no passengers are permitted. Riders can take this course as soon as they've completed the BRC.

The License Waiver *RiderCourse* is for motorcyclists who have been riding with a permit but have not yet obtained their state motorcycle license endorsement. A state may use this as a license waiver course for experienced riders with permits. Riders may use a training motorcycle or their own safe, street-ready motorcycle; no passengers are permitted.

The Skills Plus *RiderCourse* is for motorcyclists who are already licensed and frequently ride, and who are looking for extra skills training or perhaps a skills refresher after a long winter's break from riding. Students are encouraged to repeat the course periodically—especially whenever they buy a new motorcycle—to keep their skills sharp. A rider must bring his or her own safe, street-ready motorcycle. Passengers may participate.

MSF ADVANCED BRAKING AND TRACTION MANAGEMENT *RIDERCOURSE* (AVAILABLE IN 2006)

This half-day *RiderCourse* is designed to add skill, finesse and smoothness to a rider's cornering and braking maneuvers. Consists of a brief classroom session that lays the groundwork for controlled, on-cycle exercises in which riders practice to improve their techniques to effectively manage traction when braking and cornering. Participants use their own street-legal motorcycles. Requires experience and proficiency in basic riding skills.

MSF ON-ROAD *RIDERCOURSE* (AVAILABLE IN 2006)

The **On-Road *RiderCourse*** is a half-day course for motorcyclists who desire to learn more about street riding strategies by experiencing a multitude of riding situations on the street. Class size is limited to six riders and is facilitated by two MSF certified RiderCoaches. Classes are made up of entry-level riders who have completed a Basic *RiderCourse*, or experienced riders who desire to further improve their street strategies. A qualifying skills assessment is required prior to the on-street lessons.

MSF *SCOOTERSCHOOL*

ScooterSchool I (SS1) is an entry-level, learn-to-ride scooter training course. It is designed to help new scooterists acquire the basic skills to ride skillfully and safely. The half-day course consists of 10 riding exercises in an outdoor setting. Instruction is provided by MSF-certified ScooterCoaches. Participants may use their own scooters, and some training sites may provide loan scooters. The course is designed for scooters with engine sizes up to 200cc. Participants who enroll must be able to ride and balance a bicycle. Participants receive the helpful booklet *You and Your Scooter: Riding Tips.* No license test waiver is provided.

MSF *DIRTBIKE SCHOOL*

The MSF also offers an entry-level **DirtBike School** for those interested in riding off-road. This fun, one-day, hands-on training session for those at least six years old offers a no-pressure, controlled environment in which students are taught basic riding skills and responsible off-road riding practices, including risk management and environmental awareness. For more information and to find the location of a *DirtBike School* near you, call 877.288.7093 or visit www.dirtbikeschool.com.

HOST YOUR OWN SAFETY EVENT

MSF offers several safety programs that can be conducted by anyone—especially motorcycle enthusiasts

As part of an effort to encourage motorists to share the road safely with motorcyclists and other vulnerable roadway users, MSF developed the Common Road kit for use in high school driver education classes and other community events.

or others who are concerned with traffic safety. Whether you're a riding club leader, a schoolteacher, or just someone who enjoys the sport of motorcycling, you'll find it rewarding to present MSF curricula to your peers, your students, or your community. The following kits are available from the MSF website on the Host An Event page.

The **Riding Straight Module** is a stand-alone kit that can be used by those who have an interest in conducting seminars or events related to the hazards of impaired riding. It contains a Facilitator's Guide, "Riding Straight" video and interactive Fatal Vision® Simulator Goggles. The goggle activities can also be used by anyone willing to be a facilitator for special events, riding club meetings and rallies, and community outreach programs to deliver a

message without the formality of a classroom environment.

The **Cars, Motorcycles and a Common Road** kit includes an eight-minute video directed at motorists and provides a driver's eye view of the special needs of motorcyclists. It also comes with Leader's Guide and 10 Student Handbooks. Drivers will learn why a safe motorcyclist will ride in various lane positions, the "two-second" rule for following a motorcyclist, and how to avoid the most common scenarios in which motorists and motorcyclists collide.

The **MSF Guide to Group Riding** kit is essentially a group ride training event in a box, with a video and enough materials for a class of 10 students. You'll learn about ride preparation,

standards for organizing the ride, hand signals, and proper formations in complex traffic situations.

The **Seasoned Rider Module** is a stand-alone kit that can be used for conducting seminars or events related to the effects of aging on a motorcyclist. The content addresses the need to identify and compensate for factors such as diminished vision, reflexes, and strength in order to manage risk. It contains a Facilitator's Guide, Seasoned Rider video, a core lesson plan, and several optional learning activities.

A RESOURCE FOR USEFUL REFERENCE MATERIALS

Refer to the **Library/Safety Tips** page and the **State Laws and Reports** page on the MSF website (www.msf-usa.org) for useful information including:

► General motorcycle safety tips

► Sample MSF Basic *RiderCourse* Rider Handbook

► Operator licensing procedures and standards, by state

► Motorcycle equipment requirements, by state

► Public Service Announcements for print and television

► Motorcycling statistics

ABOUT THE MOTORCYCLE SAFETY FOUNDATION

Since March 1973, the Motorcycle Safety Foundation® (MSF) has set internationally recognized standards of excellence in motorcycle rider education and training. The MSF works with the National Highway Traffic Safety Administration (NHTSA), state governments, the military, and other organizations (such as the American Association of Motor Vehicle Administrators, the International Association of Chiefs of Police, and the National Association of State Motorcycle Safety Administrators) to improve motorcyclist education, training, and operator licensing.

In addition, the MSF Government Relations office, based near Washington, D.C., is the Foundation's advocate for motorcycle safety before the United States Congress and federal regulatory agencies as well as at state legislatures and state regulatory agencies. The Government Relations office also serves as a clearinghouse for information on federal and state legislation and regulation relating to motorcycle safety, rider education, and licensing issues. MSF-developed model *Motorcycle Safety Education Program* legislation has helped state legislatures craft rider education program laws that have enabled millions of riders to participate in motorcycle safety courses.

The MSF is a national, not-for-profit organization sponsored by the U.S. manufacturers and distributors of BMW, Ducati, Harley-Davidson, Honda, Kawasaki, KTM, Piaggio/Vespa, Suzuki, Victory, and Yamaha motorcycles.

T-CLOCS ITEM	WHAT TO CHECK	WHAT TO LOOK FOR	CHECK-OFF	
T-TIRES & WHEELS				
Tires	Condition	Tread depth, wear, weathering, evenly seated, bulges, embedded objects.	Front	Rear
	Air Pressure	Check when cold, adjust to load.	Front	Rear
Wheels	Spokes	Bent, broken, missing, tension, check at top of wheel "ring" = OK — "thud" = loose spoke.	Front	Rear
	Cast	Cracks, dents.	Front	Rear
	Rims	Out of round/true = 5mm. Spin wheel, index against stationary pointer.	Front	Rear
	Bearings	Grab top and bottom of tire and flex: No freeplay (click) between hub and axle, no growl when spinning.	Front	Rear
	Seals	Cracked, cut or torn, excessive grease on outside, reddish-brown around outside.	Front	Rear
C-CONTROLS				
Levers and Pedal	Condition	Broken, bent, cracked, mounts tight, ball ends on handlebar levers, proper adjustment.		
	Pivots	Lubricated.		
Cables	Condition	Fraying, kinks, lubrication: ends and interior.		
	Routing	No interference or pulling at steering head, suspension, no sharp angles, wire supports in place.		
Hoses	Condition	Cuts, cracks, leaks, bulges, chafing, deterioration.		
	Routing	No interference or pulling at steering head, suspension, no sharp angles, hose supports in place.		
Throttle	Operation	Moves freely, snaps closed, no revving when handlebars are turned.		
L-LIGHTS				
Battery	Condition	Terminals; clean and tight, electrolyte level, held down securely.		
	Vent Tube	Not kinked, routed properly, not plugged.		
Lenses	Condition	Cracked, broken, securely mounted, excessive condensation.		
Reflectors	Condition	Cracked, broken, securely mounted.		
Wiring	Condition	Fraying, chafing, insulation.		
	Routing	Pinched, no interference or pulling at steering head or suspension, wire looms and ties in place, connectors tight, clean.		
Headlamp	Condition	Cracks, reflector, mounting and adjustment system.		
	Aim	Height and right/left.		
	Operation	Hi beam/low beam operation.		
Tail lamp/brake lamp	Condition	Cracks, clean and tight		
	Operation	Activates upon front brake/rear brake application		
Turn signals	Operation	Flashes correctly	Front left	Front right
			Rear left	Rear right

O-OIL

T-CLOCS ITEM	WHAT TO CHECK	WHAT TO LOOK FOR	CHECK-OFF	
Levels	Engine Oil	Check warm on center stand, dipstick, sight glass.		
	Hypoid Gear Oil, Shaft Drive	Transmission, rear drive, shaft.		
	Hydraulic Fluid	Brakes, clutch, reservoir or sight glass.		
	Coolant	Reservoir and/or coolant recovery tank — check only when cool.		
	Fuel	Tank or gauge.		
Leaks	Engine Oil	Gaskets, housings, seals.		
	Hypoid Gear Oil	Gaskets, seals, breathers.		
	Hydraulic Fluid	Hoses, master cylinders, calipers.		
	Coolant	Radiator, hoses, tanks, fittings, pipes.		
	Fuel	Lines, fuel valve, carbs.		

C-CHASSIS

T-CLOCS ITEM	WHAT TO CHECK	WHAT TO LOOK FOR	CHECK-OFF	
Frame	Condition	Cracks at gussets, accessory mounts, look for paint lifting.		
	Steering-Head Bearings	No detent or tight spots through full travel, raise front wheel, check for play by pulling/pushing forks.		
	Swingarm Bushings/Bearings	Raise rear wheel, check for play by pushing/pulling swingarm.		
Suspension	Front Forks	Smooth travel, equal air pressure/damping anti-dive settings.	Left	Right
	Rear Shock(s)	Smooth travel, equal pre-load/air pressure/damping settings, linkage moves freely and is lubricated.	Left	Right
Chain or Belt	Tension	Check at tightest point.		
	Lubrication	Side plates when hot. *Note:* do not lubricate belts.		
	Sprockets	Teeth not hooked, securely mounted.		
Fasteners	Threaded	Tight, missing bolts, nuts.		
	Clips	Broken, missing.		
	Cotter Pins	Broken, missing.		

S-STANDS

T-CLOCS ITEM	WHAT TO CHECK	WHAT TO LOOK FOR	CHECK-OFF	
Center stand	Condition	Cracks, bent.		
	Retention	Springs in place, tension to hold position.		
Side stand	Condition	Cracks, bent (safety cut-out switch or pad if equipped).		
	Retention	Springs in place, tension to hold position.		

A T-CLOCS inspection before each ride will let you spot problems early and help ensure a trouble-free outing.

ALCOHOL Specifically ethyl alcohol, a depressant drug consumed as a beverage such as beer, wine or liquor; affects vision, judgment and coordination.

ANTI-LOCK BRAKES; ANTI-LOCK BRAKING SYSTEM (ABS) Type of system that that automatically releases brake pressure prior to wheel lockup. The system senses when a wheel first begins to lockup and automatically releases pressure to allow the wheel to begin to roll again. Helps prevent skidding and loss of directional control. Most helpful on slippery surfaces.

APEX The location in a curve where a motorcyclist comes closest to the inside edge of the road.

APPROACH SPEED The safe and legal speed a motorcyclist is traveling when a curve is identified (see Entry Speed and Exit Speed).

AUXILIARY LIGHTS Lights added to a motorcycle to better illuminate the road at night or to make the motorcycle more visible.

BAC An abbreviation for Blood-Alcohol Concentration. BAC expresses the amount of alcohol in the body as a percentage of the body's total fluid.

BANKED CURVE A curve where the roadway is tilted either to the left or right, rather than being flat. Properly designed roadways are typically banked in the same direction as the curve (e.g., a left-hand curve is banked to the left) and is sometimes referred to as an "on-camber" or "positive-camber" turn.

BLIND CORNER A turn in the road that is hidden from view so the rider cannot see the path of travel or what may be in the path of travel.

BLIND SPOT An area behind or beside a vehicle that cannot be seen with rear view mirrors or is blocked from view by an object. Relates to the No-Zone (see No-Zone).

BLIP A short, quick throttle input between downshifts to bring the engine rpm up to match road speed.

BLOOD ALCOHOL CONCENTRATION See BAC.

BODY ARMOR Padding, hard-shelled material or other impact-absorbing material fitted to a motorcyclist's apparel to help protect the rider in a crash.

BODY PROTECTION Typically refers to the protective equipment worn by a motorcyclist and sometimes referred to as body armor.

BRAKING DISTANCE Space traveled between brake application and completed stop. The distance required to bring a motorcycle to a complete stop once the brakes are applied.

BRAKING TIME The total time from when the brakes are first applied until the motorcycle is completely stopped.

CAMBER Sideways angle or slant of the road surface; the angle of the roadway in relation to the direction of travel. A flat roadway surface has a zero camber; a roadway surface tilted in the direction of a curve (to the left for a curve to the left; to the right for a curve to the right) is referred to as an on-camber roadway; a roadway surface tilted in the opposite direction of a curve is referred to as an off-camber surface.

CARBURETOR A device that mixes fuel and air in the correct proportions for combustion, and passes this mixture into the combustion chamber(s) of the engine. Carburetors have been replaced by fuel injection systems on many newer motorcycles (see Fuel Injection).

CARGO NET Sheathed bungee cord net or webbing with multiple hooks useful for securing odd-shaped loads to a motorcycle.

CENTER OF GRAVITY (CG) The point in an object where the force of gravity appears to act. The point around which the mass of an object is evenly distributed. If an object is suspended at any point on the vertical line passing through its center of gravity it will remain balanced.

CENTER STAND A mechanical device for supporting a motorcycle while at rest. Standard on some motorcycles, this stand lifts the rear wheel off the ground slightly, which is helpful for some maintenance and repair procedures.

CENTRAL VISION The sharpest part of the visual field; the core vision used to identify what is seen versus peripheral vision, which picks up quick movements in the visual field; consists of only a three-degree cone.

CENTRIFUGAL FORCE An apparent force that is evidenced by an increasing side load on motorcycle tires when cornering. The higher the speed while cornering, the higher the side loads on the tires; experienced as the force that tends to pull a vehicle toward the outside of a turn.

CHASSIS The frame of the motorcycle to which the suspension, drive train (engine/transmission, tires/wheels/brakes, rear wheel drive), steering system and other vehicle components are mounted.

CHOKE A mechanical device for enriching (more fuel, less air) the fuel/air mixture in a motor vehicle for a "cold" engine start.

COEFFICIENT OF FRICTION (C_F) The ratio of potential friction between two surfaces to the force pressing them together. A measure of the amount of friction or grip between a vehicle's tires and the roadway surface.

COMBINATION BRAKING The act of simultaneously applying both front and rear brakes on a motorcycle. This type of braking will typically result in the best braking performance.

COMPLEX REACTION TIME Interval between when a rider *perceives* a new situation and takes action. Normally around 0.75 seconds. (Also see Simple Reaction Time.)

CONSPICUOUS To be easily seen by others; to be highly visible

CONSPICUITY Refers to how visible a motorcycle or motorcyclist is to others. Enhanced by bright upper torso clothing, a light-colored helmet, and daytime high-beam headlight use. Improved at night with reflective clothing.

CONSTANT RADIUS TURN A turn that has been designed and constructed with the same radius throughout the turn.

CONTACT PATCH Portion of a tire that touches the road surface.

CONTROLLED BRAKING The condition of applying the brakes of a motor vehicle in a controlled manner (see Maximum and Threshold Braking).

CONVEX MIRROR A mirror with an outward-curved surface. This type of mirror shows more area than a flat mirror, but objects are closer than they appear.

CORDURA A highly durable trademarked fabric from INVISTA. It is resistant to abrasions, tears, and scuffs and is used in a wide range of products from luggage and backpacks to boots, military wear and performance apparel, such as motorcycle riding gear.

COUNTERBALANCING Adjusting body position and weight to balance a motorcycle at very low speeds. Requires weight shift which is counter, or opposite, to the lean of the motorcycle.

COUNTERSTEER A momentary steering deflection away from the intended direction of travel caused by pressing on the handgrip in the direction of the turn; used to produce/initiate a lean in the desired direction; press right, lean right, go right; press left, lean left, go left (see Gyroscopic Precession).

COUNTERWEIGHTING Same as counterbalancing.

CROSSWALK The painted roadway lines that show the path for pedestrians to cross the roadway.

CROWNED ROAD Road surface that is higher in the middle to allow for water runoff.

DECREASING-RADIUS TURN A turn that becomes progressively tighter (smaller radius).

DEPTH PERCEPTION The ability to determine how far away an object is through sight alone.

DIMMER SWITCH A mechanical or electrical device used to switch headlight(s) between low beam and high beam.

DISC BRAKES A braking system consisting of a thin disc rotor fixed to the rotating wheel and a set of one or more fixed brake pads, which rub against the disc when the brake lever or pedal is applied.

DRY CLUTCH Clutch setup that requires no fluid between clutch and pressure plates and is less tolerant of using the friction zone with high rpm and low speeds (see Wet Clutch).

D-RING A metal ring in the shape of the capital letter "D" commonly used to fasten the chinstrap on a motorcycle safety helmet. The retention system may have a single D-ring with a sliding friction bar to hold the chinstrap from moving or double D-rings where the chinstrap is threaded between the two rings to prevent loosening.

DUAL-PURPOSE A motorcycle equipped for riding on streets as well as off-road. Characterized by full on-road lighting plus high fenders and aggressive tire tread patterns to allow for off-road excursions. Sometimes called dual-sport.

ENGINE BRAKING Braking force created by the engine in a moving motorcycle when the throttle is rolled off. Internal engine friction and combustion chamber pressure will cause the engine and motorcycle to slow down.

ENGINE STOP SWITCH A switch that cuts electrical power to the engine ignition system. Sometimes referred to as the Engine-Cutoff Switch or Emergency Stop Switch.

ENTRY SPEED In turning and cornering, it is the motorcycle's speed at the point where the steering input to lean into the turn occurs. The maximum desired entry speed is one that allows for some roll-on of the throttle to maintain speed and stability while cornering, one that assures no deceleration in a turn will be required, and one that provides time and space to "straighten and brake" if necessary (see Approach Speed and Exit Speed).

EXIT SPEED The safe and legal speed a motorcyclist is traveling at the exit of a curve (see Approach Speed and Entry Speed).

EYE CONTACT Looking at another person's eyes in an attempt to ensure they notice and react to your presence (see Inattentional Blindness and Visual Perception).

EYE PROTECTION A device that protects the vehicle operator's eyes from airborne debris or wind; e.g., safety glasses, goggles, helmet face shield, handlebar-mounted windshield, fairing-mounted windshield, etc.

FIELD OF VISION The width or angle a person can see to the sides while focusing straight ahead. This angle normally is 180 degrees.

FIXATE To focus one's eyes or attention on (see Target Fixation).

FLIP-FACE HELMET See Modular Helmet.

FLOODED ENGINE A condition where the engine's combustion chamber contains an excessive amount of fuel preventing it from starting up and running.

FOG LIGHTS Lights designed to provide some measure of visibility during fog conditions.

FOLLOWING DISTANCE Distance measured in terms of the time it takes a "following" vehicle to pass a point in the road that a "leading" vehicle has already passed. The minimum following distance in clear, dry conditions is two seconds.

FOUR-STROKE (FOUR-CYCLE) An internal-combustion engine design in which four strokes of the piston within the cylinder complete the power cycle of the engine (equivalent to two complete revolutions of the crankshaft). The four strokes consist of intake, compression, power, and exhaust (see Two-Stroke).

FRICTION The force that resists the relative motion between two objects in contact.

FRICTION ZONE Area of clutch lever movement that begins where the clutch starts to transmit power to the rear wheel and ends just prior to full clutch engagement.

FUEL INJECTION A method or system where fuel in a motor vehicle engine is reduced to a fine spray and injected directly into the combustion chamber(s) of the engine. This system has largely replaced carburetor/intake manifold systems on many motorcycles (see Carburetor).

FUEL SUPPLY VALVE Valve, usually on the left side of the engine, that controls the flow of gasoline. Typical positions are ON, OFF, RESERVE, and PRIME.

FULL LOCK STEERING The point at which the handlebars cannot be turned further.

GAUNTLETS Protective gloves that extend past the wrist and/or forearm of the rider; useful for cold weather riding where air may move through gap between the wrist of the glove and the arm of the jacket.

GLARE RECOVERY Refers to the time required for a rider to recover from the effects of glare; a rider's ability to distinguish objects is greatly diminished during this period.

GROOVED PAVEMENT Pavement with channels cut into it to aid in draining rainwater or in preparation for resurfacing.

GYROSCOPIC PRECESSION Refers to counter steering. The tendency of a gyroscope (e.g., a rotating wheel) to lean in the direction of a force applied to the axis of the gyroscope (see Countersteering).

HEAD CHECK Refers to a rider's head turn to either the left or right to check the blind spot [i.e., the area behind/beside that cannot be seen in the rear view mirror(s)]. Also can refer to checking for gaps in traffic while waiting to cross an intersection.

HEADLIGHT MODULATOR Electronic device that pulses the headlight, ideally to make the motorcycle more visible during the day (see Modulating Headlight).

HIGH-CROWNED ROAD Usually found on a rural roadway. Road surface arcs with high center and low sides. Permits road drainage. Can cause clearance problems when cornering.

HIGH-SIDE CRASH When a motorcycle is leaning, the side closest to the road surface is called the "low-side"; the other side is the "high-side." A high-side crash is one in which the rider goes over the motorcycle's high side.

HIGHWAY FURNITURE General term used to describe objects in or along the roadway including signs, signals, and obstacles.

HYDROPLANING Water buildup under the tires resulting in loss of traction; the condition where a motor vehicle's tires are actually riding on a thin layer of water and not in actual contact with the roadway surface.

HYPOTHERMIA Subnormal body temperature due to the cooling effects of cold air and wind on exposed skin. Hypothermia can cause loss of concentration, slowed reactions, and loss of smooth, precise muscle control/movement.

IMPENDING SKID Used to describe a wheel at traction limit prior to loss of traction. Usually used in discussing maximum braking.

IMPLIED CONSENT Refers to a state law that mandates if a person is stopped for a possible DUI/DWI, they have implied that they have given their consent to take a test for BAC determination (a test of blood, breath or urine); refusal may lead to automatic loss of license.

INATTENTIONAL BLINDNESS Inattentional blindness is a failure to see an object because mental attention is too narrowly focused (see Eye Contact, Visual Perception).

INCREASING-RADIUS TURN A curve in the roadway where the radius of the turn increases (i.e., gets less severe) as you progress through the curve.

INDICATOR LIGHTS Small lights on the motorcycle (usually on the instrument panel) that show when a function or system is operational (e.g., turn signal indicator, neutral indicator, high beam indicator, side stand down warning indicator, etc.).

INTEGRATED BRAKING SYSTEM System that also applies partial front braking when the rear brake is applied.

LADDER OF RISK A metaphor (figure of speech) used in the Motorcycle Safety Foundation *RiderCourses* to describe/discuss the concept of risk; that different individuals are willing to accept different levels of risk.

LANE POSITION Refers to the motorcycle position within a lane. A motorcyclist has more than one option.

LEAN ANGLE Degree that the motorcycle is leaned during a turn. Turning occurs as a result of the lean angle.

LEAN IN The process of the motorcyclist leaning farther to the inside of the curve than the motorcycle is leaning. A common technique on the racetrack where speeds are higher and the amount of ground clearance for the motorcycle is limited (see Lean Out, Lean With).

LEAN OUT The process of the motorcyclist leaning less than the motorcycle, or in the opposite direction of the motorcycle. Typically used at extremely low speeds such as in parking lots, this technique allows the motorcyclist to actually balance the motorcycle during a tight, low-speed turn. This technique is also referred to as counterweighting or counterbalancing (see Lean In, Lean With).

LEAN WITH The process of the motorcyclist (or passenger) leaning in the same direction and at the same angle as the motorcycle. This is a proper and effective technique for normal cornering (see Lean In, Lean Out).

LEGAL LIMIT A blood alcohol content (BAC) limit that a state sets as the level of presumed intoxication. In 2005, the legal limit for adults in all 50 states was 0.08%.

LINE (CORNERING LINE) A motorcyclist's chosen path of travel through a curve. Multiple cornering lines are possible.

LINKED BRAKES (LINKED BRAKING) A motorcycle braking system that applies brake pressure to both brakes when either brake is applied.

LOAD TRIANGLE The imaginary triangle formed by the lines from the rider's head to the front and rear axles, and the line between the two axles. When loading a motorcycle, heavier items should be placed within or as close to this triangle as possible.

LOCK-UP A condition in which the wheel(s) stop turning, causing a skid; results from too much brake pressure (see Locked Wheel).

LOCKED WHEEL Braking to the point where the tire is no longer rotating, and is skidding on the pavement.

LOW-SIDE CRASH Crash in which the rider falls to the motorcycle's low side (see High-Side Crash).

LUGGING Rough or jerking engine operation due to selecting a gear that is too high for road speed. The condition where a motor vehicle's engine speed decreases to the point where the engine does not have enough power to run and drive the vehicle forward efficiently.

MAXIMUM BRAKING Application of both brakes simultaneously to the point just short of skidding (see Controlled Braking and Threshold Braking).

MAXIMUM LOAD CAPACITY Difference between the empty weight and the maximum allowable weight of the motorcycle and all of its load, including the rider and passenger. Specified by the manufacturer. The total weight of the motorcycle and maximum load is called GVWR (gross vehicle weight rating).

MEDIAN The dividing area, either paved or landscaped, between opposing lanes of traffic on some highways.

MESH CLOTHING Highly perforated riding gear designed to maximize the wind's cooling effects in hot weather.

MODULAR HELMET DOT-approved full-coverage helmet whose chin bar can be swung up to ease taking the helmet on/off, taking the glasses on/off, and ease the ability to talk/eat/drink with the helmet still on, and is designed to have the chin bar down and locked when riding. Sometimes called a flip-face helmet.

MODULATING HEADLIGHT A headlight that rhythmically cycles from high intensity to low intensity. It is used to improve conspicuity to the front of a motorcycle (see Headlight Modulator).

NIGHT BLINDNESS A condition of the eyes in which vision is normal in daylight or other strong light but is abnormally weak or completely lost at night or in dim light.

NOVELTY HELMETS Helmets that are sold for appearance or fun only; not designed to meet Department of Transportation standards.

NO-ZONE The area around a truck or other vehicle that is a blind spot; the blind spots behind, next to, and directly in front of a tractor-trailer rig in which the operator cannot see other vehicles (see Blind Spot).

OFF-CAMBER TURN Corner in which the road surface slopes downward toward the outside of the turn.

OVERRIDING THE HEADLIGHTS Riding at a speed for which the total stopping distance exceeds sight distance available from headlight illumination at night.

OVER-REVVING The condition where a motor vehicle's engine speed is excessively high for the road speed of the vehicle. The engine is being over-revved when the engine speed (revolutions per minute or rpm) is at or over the "red line."

OWNER'S MANUAL A publication distributed by the motor vehicle manufacturer that contains useful information about the operation and general maintenance of the specific vehicle to which it applies.

PATH OF TRAVEL Where the motorcycle will go.

PERCEPTION Accurate recognition and interpretation of sensory stimuli; e.g., the point where a motor vehicle operator sees an object or condition.

PERCEPTION DISTANCE Space traveled between when factors are developing until there is a recognized problem that requires a response.

PERCEPTION TIME The time it takes for a rider to recognize that a hazard or problem has developed.

PERIPHERAL VISION The area to the sides that can be seen while looking straight ahead. Perceived or perceiving near the outer edges of the retina; i.e., how far to the side a person can see objects without turning his/her head. It is typically around 180-190 degrees; less than 140 degrees is considered tunnel vision.

PETCOCK Another term for fuel supply valve.

PILLION (PILLION PAD) Synonym for passenger. A small seat mounted on the rear fender for a passenger.

PRESUMPTION LEVEL A level of intoxication (BAC) that authorities use as a threshold in determining if a motor vehicle operator is in violation of the law.

PUSH START The process of starting a motorcycle engine by pushing the motorcycle or rolling it downhill (with the engine pre-start routine completed) with the transmission in gear and the clutch lever squeezed in. Once sufficient momentum is attained, the rider releases the clutch lever. This causes sufficient engine rotation to create combustion in the cylinders. This technique is commonly used when the vehicle battery is too weak to start the engine.

PUSH STEERING (SEE COUNTERSTEERING)

RAIN GROOVES The thin grooves, approximately one quarter inch deep by one quarter inch wide, that are cut into the pavement to promote water runoff between a vehicle's tires and the pavement. Designed to minimize hydroplaning.

RAKE The angle of the steering head from vertical. Sports bikes usually have a steep rake (little angle) making them quick to steer as compared to cruisers which typically have more rake—the steering head and therefore the forks are at a greater angle from vertical.

RANGE A term used to describe the practice riding facility. Typically a large, paved parking area where riding skill exercises are conducted.

REACTION DISTANCE The space traveled between perceiving a situation and taking action; the time between when an object/hazard is seen until a rider begins to brake or otherwise react to the object/hazard.

REAR WHEEL SKID See Locked Wheel.

RED LINE The line on a tachometer that indicates maximum engine speed or engine revolutions per minute (rpm).

REFLECTIVE Ability of a surface to reflect light (see Retroreflective).

RETROREFLECTIVE A specific type of reflective material where the surface is designed to reflect a major portion of received light back to the light source, rather than in all directions equally (see Reflective).

RIDERCOURSE Rider-training class developed by the Motorcycle Safety Foundation. There are two versions, the Basic *RiderCourse* (aimed at beginning riders) and the Experienced *RiderCourse* (which helps veteran riders fine-tune their skills).

ROLLING MOMENT A technical term used to describe the inertial forces that operate about the axis of rotation while a motorcycle is leaning or "rolling."

ROLL-OFF Refers to the process of decelerating a motorcycle by rolling the right (throttle control) hand/wrist forward (away from the body) (see Roll-on).

ROLL-ON Refers to the process of accelerating a motorcycle by rolling the right (throttle control) hand/wrist toward the body (see Roll-off).

RUMBLE STRIPS The intentionally constructed rough edge of a roadway designed to generate noise and a rough ride when traveled over to alert the driver or rider that he/she has left the main traveled portion of the roadway.

SAFETY MARGIN Time and space that a rider chooses to create to allow for errors by her/himself or others; considers rider capabilities and limitations, motorcycle capabilities and limitations, and roadway/traffic conditions (see Space Cushion).

SCANNING A method of looking in multiple directions to visually identify potential hazards.

SEE Mental process used to make judgments and take action in traffic. Stands for Search, Evaluate, Execute.

SHIFT PATTERN The sequence of the transmission gears on a motorcycle and the corresponding operation of the gearshift lever to access these gears.

SIMPLE REACTION TIME Interval between when a rider *decides* what to do and when he actually begins doing it. Normally around 0.44 seconds (also see Complex Reaction Time).

SINGLE-TRACK VEHICLE An engineering term used to describe motorcycles, bicycles, and other two-wheelers with one wheel in front of the other. Single-track vehicles must lean to turn.

SKID (Also called slide.) Movement that occurs when a tire loses its grip on the road and slides, either along or across the surface (see Locked Wheel).

SLIPPING THE CLUTCH See Friction Zone.

SNELL Refers to the Snell Memorial Foundation, an organization that has established testing standards and procedures for motorcycle safety helmets (and other types of helmets).

SPACE CUSHION Area you create and maintain between yourself and other vehicles. Having a margin of safety; the gap, or space, that the wise motorcyclist maintains between his/her vehicle and potential hazards on or near the roadway (e.g., other vehicles, roadway debris, animals, pedestrians, etc.). Allows time for reacting to changing situations and leaves an alternative path of travel (see Safety Margin).

SPEED BUMP An intentionally constructed bump (hump) in the roadway designed to slow the speed of traffic.

SQUARE THE BARS (HANDLEBARS) Refers to centering the steering with the motorcycle upright and moving in a straight line; putting the handlebars in a straight-ahead position. The condition where a motorcycle's handlebars are straight with the front wheel pointed directly in front of the motorcycle.

STAGGERED FORMATION Group riding formation where motorcyclists ride in alternating portions of a lane. In a staggered formation, the leader rides in the left third of the lane, while the next rider stays at least one second behind in the right third of the lane, with the rest of the group following the same pattern behind. If the formation is correct, the third rider is two seconds behind the leader, but only one second behind the second rider.

STALE GREEN LIGHT A traffic signal that has been green for a time period and is likely to change at any moment.

STANDING ON THE PEGS Refers to the technique of a motorcycle rider shifting his/her body weight from the seat to the footrests by standing up slightly before riding over an obstacle.

STOPPIE An extreme braking maneuver (stunt) in which the rear tire leaves the ground.

T-CLOCS Simple acronym used to remember motorcycle components that should be examined during a pre-ride inspection. The components are: Tires and wheels; Controls, such as levers, cables, and throttle; Lights and electrics; Oils and other fluids; Chassis and chain; and Stands (side or center).

TAILGATE Following at a distance of less than two seconds; the condition where a following motorist is too close to the vehicle in front to be able to react appropriately if, a) the front vehicle stops suddenly, or b) the front vehicle swerves aside, revealing roadway debris.

TANK SLAPPER Situation of wobble that increases in intensity to the point where the handlebars appear to slap the gas tank.

TARGET FIXATION Staring at an area or object to such an extent that it draws you to it. To stare at an object that you are trying to avoid; the condition where a motorist is visually and mentally focused on one object to the exclusion of everything else (see Fixate).

THRESHOLD BRAKING To apply brake pressure to a point just short of lock-up; the act of fully applying the brakes as much as possible without causing the wheel(s) to stop rotating and skid. Sometimes referred to as braking to the "point of impending skid" (see Controlled Braking, Maximum Braking).

TIE-DOWN A strap and locking device designed to secure a motorcycle on a trailer or other platform.

TOTAL STOPPING DISTANCE The total distance required to stop a motor vehicle; the sum of the perception distance, the reaction distance, and the braking distance (see corresponding definitions above).

TOTAL STOPPING TIME The total time required to stop a motor vehicle; the sum of the perception time, the reaction time, and the braking time (see corresponding definitions above).

TRACTION Adhesive friction, as of a tire on a road; the grip between the tire and the road. Traction is affected by tire and road conditions. The Motorcycle Safety Foundation Experienced *RiderCourses* identify three forces to describe the dynamics of traction: side force, braking force, and driving force.

TRAIL The distance along the ground from the steering axis to the center of the contact patch, generally used in connection with "rake" to describe a bike's frame/steering geometry.

TRAIL BRAKING This term refers to using the brake(s) while entering a corner as opposed to completing all of the braking prior to the corner. Many riders who use this technique use the rear brake only. Trail braking is not the same as braking once you are already in a curve, which can create an unstable situation.

TRAFFIC-ACTUATED SIGNAL A traffic light that senses a vehicle's presence; activated by the vehicle's weight or magnetic properties.

TRAFFIC CONTROL DEVICES Signs, signals and pavement markings designed to control traffic and make highway user actions predictable.

TREAD The grooved face of a tire that makes contact with the road.

TRIALS A specialized class of motorcycles characterized by spartan appearance, no seat, light weight and acrobatic ability to tackle very challenging obstacles.

TUBELESS TIRES Tires that, like those on most modern street motorcycles, run cooler because tire tube friction is eliminated and heat-retaining mass is reduced. Unsprung weight is also reduced.

TWO-STROKE (TWO-CYCLE) An internal-combustion engine design in which two strokes of the piston within the cylinder complete the power cycle of the engine (equivalent to one complete revolution of the crankshaft). The two strokes consist of a combination intake/compression stroke and a combination power/exhaust stroke (see Four-Stroke).

VACUUM FUEL SUPPLY VALVE A device that uses the vacuum created by a running engine to open a diaphragm-controlled fuel supply valve. Automatically shuts off fuel supply when engine stops. Vacuum-operated fuel supply valves are most easily identified by the lack of an "off" position and the designation of a "pri" (prime) position on the petcock (see Fuel Supply Valve).

VISUAL ACUITY Sharpness or clearness of vision as tested with a Snellen eye chart that uses small letters. Normal visual acuity is expressed as 20/20, meaning a person sees at 20 feet what a person with average visual acuity sees at 20 feet. A person with 20/40 vision sees at 20 feet what a person with 20/20 vision can see at 40 feet.

VISUAL PERCEPTION The act or faculty of apprehending (perceiving) by the sense of sight; the mind must understand what the eyes see (see Inattentional Blindness).

WEAR BAR A motor vehicle tire wear indicator; a raised portion of rubber extending across the width of the tire tread and below the surface of the unworn tread blocks. The wear bar is exposed when the tire tread is worn down to an unusable level.

WEAVE A relatively slow oscillation of the rear of the motorcycle; this condition may be caused by a flat rear tire, suspension problem or other mechanical malfunction.

WEIGHT TRANSFER Refers to the shift of a vehicle's mass forward under braking, and rearward under acceleration.

WET CLUTCH Clutch setup that has fluid between clutch and pressure plates and is more tolerant of using the friction zone with high rpm at low road speeds (see Dry Clutch).

WHEEL LOCK-UP Condition where brakes cause a wheel to stop turning, even though the machine is still moving. It occurs when the braking effort is greater than the available friction between tire and road surface. The tire slides instead of gripping the surface.

WIND BLAST Refers to the sudden change in wind direction or magnitude produced by passing another motor vehicle (in either direction, but usually more unsettling when passing a vehicle traveling in the opposite direction) or when the roadway conditions change (e.g., between hills, over bridges/overpasses, through mountain passes into open plains, etc.).

WIND BUFFETING Refers to the effect caused by air turbulence when riding alongside or passing a vehicle.

WIND CHILL FACTOR The temperature of air on exposed human skin given the combination of wind speed and air temperature; the lower the air temperature and/or the higher the wind speed, the lower the chill factor.

WOBBLE A rapid oscillation of the front wheel and steering components due to a mechanical problem or chassis instability.